March 17, 2023

My copy.

First published in the UK by Foxy Media Ltd 2023

Paperback ISBN 978-1-7393563-1-6

The Collected Rants of Fleet Street Fox

CONTENTS

FOREWARNED

The Fleet Street Fox columns have appeared, mostly online and some in print, in different places since 2012. Mostly they have surfaced in the Daily Mirror, which for the benefit of non-readers is best described as a newspaper that sells to people who count their pennies as well as their chickens.

Mirror readers work hard, care hard, and vote for whoever isn't the worst dipshit they've ever seen strut across their telly. The Mirror runs frequent campaigns for things like organ donations, free school meals, and survivors of Britain's nuclear tests, and to lighten the mood it sometimes sends a reporter in a giant chicken suit to chase the Prime Minister around.

Foxy's columns are a combination of satire, fact bombs, and finely-tuned fury. Or pisstakes mixed with rage by a hack who won't wind her neck in - depends.

They are taglined "often sarcastic, occasionally right". This is a collection of all those missives from her keyboard that have yet to be proved wrong.

There are no giant chickens. No editor has dared.

You amaze me

September 10, 2012

ONE day soon, mankind will achieve the most amazing feat of all time, and you won't even notice. You'll be asleep, or on the toilet, or standing in a queue impatiently waiting for a poncey kind of coffee. The amazing thing will happen, and you will carry on doing whatever you were doing before.

It's not just the most amazing thing mankind has done. It's the most amazing thing, so far as we know, that has ever happened. Better than a Mayor on a zipwire, better than a Queen parachuting into the Olympics, better even than a man with no legs climbing a flagpole. We're leaving the solar system.

Go on, shrug. So what? We've been tinkering around in space for ages. Except without you noticing it we've gone 11.2 billion miles from home using computers not very different to a ZX Spectrum. That's the same as travelling the 93 million miles between the Earth and the Sun 121 times, relying on the power of something less advanced than a modern digital watch.

There are two unmanned Voyager probes flying through space at 35,000mph, operating at temperatures so low they're 1/10,000th of those on Earth and surviving radiation doses 1,000 times worse than that needed to kill you or I instantly.

They were launched in 1977 - confusingly Voyager 2 set off first - to have a peek at our nearest planets, which just happened to be lined up in a row so that it would take a minimum of power to use the gravitational pull of each to ping from one to the other. They were intended only to last for five years but have worked seven times as long. They were going to look at just two planets, but NASA got some extra cash and the probes - by this point millions and millions of miles from Earth - were reprogrammed remotely via radio wave to go and look at the rest of the solar system as well.

(Think about that, the next time the gonk from IT says it can't be fixed. He'll probably tell you deep space doesn't spill orange juice on the keyboard, but it's worth a try.)

The total cost of design, build, launch and 35 years of operation is £540million. It cost us 17 times more than that to put on the Olympics.

And what did we learn? Well, the big red splodge in the middle of Jupiter is a giant storm so huge Earth could fit inside it three times over. It has three moons we didn't know about, and one, called Europa, has a crust of water ice on its surface floating above an ocean 30 miles deep. Jupiter also has a magnetic field which, when it passes over Io, strips it of heavy ions that create beautiful auroras more amazing than our own Northern Lights, and which generate 3 million amperes of electricity - enough to boil 333,000 or so kettles with every pass.

One of Saturn's moons, Titan, has ethane oceans and loads of organic matter with an atmosphere just like Earth before life evolved. Uranus has a corkscrew-shaped magnetic field because it's on the yang after being knocked on its side somehow, and Neptune should have been named after Michael Fish rather than a god of the sea as it's the windiest place in the solar system, with gusts of 1,200mph.

The probes run on electricity produced by plutonium, and although it's about one-quarter the power needed to run the average American house, over time more of their equipment has been switched off to conserve it and keep the important bits going. Heaters, cameras and scientific instruments have been powered down and about all that's left is a gyro, an ultra-violet light meter and the digital tape recorder used to store data. Yes, a tape recorder. Google it, kids.

This information is transmitted back to Earth in radio waves which take 17 hours to get here, and the signal is about 20 billion times less powerful than your wristwatch. One of the last pictures Voyager took is of Earth, from 4 billion miles away - the famous 'pale blue dot' image where our planet is a pinprick of light in the darkness. The probe is more than twice as far away now, at the edge of our system where the solar winds have dropped to nothing, and any day it will leave the protective bubble of charged particles called the heliosphere which covers our sun and all the planets which orbit it. We don't know quite when it will happen, because we haven't sent anything through this frontier before.

When the two Voyager probes pass out of the heliosphere they will be in the gap between stars - the interstellar medium. It is as different to our system as the Atlantic Ocean is to a paddling pool, filled with gas from the Big Bang, dust from smashed planets, stars dying and being reborn, and loads of stuff that is either spooky, scary or entirely unknown.

If ET finds them he's going to have a lot to wonder about, because on board is a gold record - we should be grateful it's not a TDK 60 I suppose, but do aliens prefer vinyl? - explaining a little about human life.

There are pictures of a foetus, a page from Newton, music by Bach and Beethoven. There are photographs of scientists and traffic jams, a handy map of the solar system and whereabouts in it we are, and people saying 'hello' in 55 languages, including those now extinct.

There are beeps and clicks from human brain waves recorded while a lady read some philosophy aloud and thought about the man she was in love with, and handy instructions etched on the outside of how to use a stylus to play the record and what speed to do it at.

Once it passes into the turbulent unknown, Voyager has enough power for another eight years or so. Then the plutonium will be used up, and it will drift in the interstellar winds. Scientists reckon it will take about 40,000 years for it to reach the nearest planet, which of course might be inhabited by nothing but methane, bacteria, or creatures who have evolved beyond CD players.

But there are two even more amazing things about all of this.

The first is that humans decided to do it at all - to see what is out there, for the hell of it, because it would be interesting, to wave at whoever might see, and just because. It's a lot more inspiring than going to Mars because it has minerals, or closing down bits of the space programme because it's all got too expensive.

We are leaving our own solar system with the technological equivalent of a piece of paper flicked by a rubber band, and whether it quietly disintegrates, sends us new things to amaze, or is sucked into a black hole and made sentient by a race of robot beings so it tries to return home and destroy us all, it will always have been the most enlightening thing mankind ever did.

The second thing is that on that record are a series of grooves which, when played correctly by an alien who figures out how to do it and has recently found a hi-fi in some space junk and didn't know what it was for, will boom out Chuck Berry's Johnny B. Goode at full volume.

When summer's over, and you wave goodbye to the heroes of the Olympics and Paralympics while wondering what's left to feel good about, think about little green men bopping around to a 1958 twelve-bar blues riff in 'B' and know that you can be proud of yourselves for at least another 40,000 years or so.

Well done, humanity.[1]

---

[1] Voyager 1 entered interstellar space on August 25, 2012. Voyager 2 entered interstellar space on November 5, 2018. Both are travelling at more than 30,000mph, and are more than 12 billion miles from Earth. They are still amazing, still unnoticed by most humans, and so far untouched by Klingons

What's space exploration ever done for us? All of THIS

17 Dec 2015

If there's one thing that gets up my nose it's idiocy. Not just idiots – there's plenty of them on the planet – but the actual quality of idiocy, of being as idiotic as possible and spreading it around and trying to multiply it.

First, we've enough already. And second, every moment of human evolution has been about trying to be cleverer. Anyone trying to reverse that trend needs to be disavowed by the human race, ASAP. I am talking, in this instance, about Simon Jenkins of The Guardian.

I don't hold with columnists going at one another. It's boring, and how awful would the world be if we all thought the same? I don't know anything about Simon. He may be a fine and lovely man. But the words he's written today are so ignorant I can't help but spit out my dummy, instruct toys to exit pram one at a time and hurl some fury in his direction. Because Simon says there's no point going to space.

Simon says Tim Peake's six-month stay on the International Space Station is "sheer political vanity". He complains about the cost to the taxpayer, while at the same time describing it as "a measly £16million". It's just 0.002% of the UK's spending.

He bemoans the "national rejoicing". He criticises the "chauvinist glory" of the ISS. He says robots should go to Mars, not people, without mentioning many of the robots we've sent so far land on their arse, malfunction, get lost or run out of battery.

Jenkins makes scathing mention of spin-off inventions such as memory foam and "cures for arthritis", so presumably he doesn't like to recline in a soft bed and has a written guarantee he won't develop a crippling degenerative bone disease. He compares the ISS to high speed rail links only the Tories want, and says such spending is taking money away from other things. There are lots of people who think the same. And all of them ought to try living in a tree with the rest of the apes, send a robot down to walk on the savannah for them and see just how far they get.

There are many things people think space gave us but it didn't. It didn't give us Teflon, Nylon, Velcro, cordless power tools, barcodes or a space pen. But it did do a lot of other stuff.

NASA research has produced 1,800 spin-off technologies, including infrared ear thermometers to take babies' temperatures, a heart pump for people waiting for a transplant, imaging used by the Hubble space telescope in MRI scanners and handheld LEDs to treat cancerous tumours. Perhaps Simon would like to tell paediatric nurses, people who need a new heart, and cancer patients they can all get stuffed? Pah. Who needs mammograms?

NASA also helped to produce artificial limbs with robotic sensors and custom-mouldable materials which means everyone from war veterans to family pets can have prostheses that move properly, look real and don't blister their stumps. Perhaps Simon would like to tell landmine victims, children who've survived meningitis and Vincent, the cat born with no back legs, that they'll just have to hop.

The 40,000 people who run the London Marathon raising a total of £771million so far for charity afterwards get wrapped in NASA-designed foil thermal blankets designed to reduce heat loss. The same blankets are used to wrap up people plucked from mountains by search and rescue teams in bad weather; perhaps Jenkins thinks hypothermia is preferable.

Goodyear developed a tyre with material five times stronger than steel for NASA to use on its Viking Mars lander. You can now buy radial tyres made of the stuff and put them on your car, if you'd like to not die horribly. The glasses I am glaring through have scratch-resistant lenses, first developed by NASA to protect the visors of spacemen's helmets.

Amazed at the quality of nighttime CCTV on Crimewatch? Thank NASA. See the need for fire-retardant paint and foams? Funded by NASA. Think firefighters shouldn't get burned to a crisp? They wear materials developed by NASA to protect astronauts on re-entry.

You might think it's poncey that Heston Blumenthal has designed a curry for Tim Peake to eat in space, but space food means we now have enriched baby foods and formula.

Water purification, solar power, cleaning up oil spills in the ocean, food safety protocols – all down to space, and all stuff which, I am sure, any intelligent human being who doesn't want to live in a swamp and de-evolve back to an amoeba would find welcome.

And as for Tim Peake – what's he going to add to the sum of human knowledge? Jenkins might argue that, seeing as he wants a Speak'n'Spell to go to Mars for us, there's no point to Peake's testing human physiology and food needs to make a manned mission more possible.

But I can see the point of Peake testing how to operate robots on the planet below while in orbit, how lichen are surviving on the outside of the ISS and why you'd want to take plant seeds to space and send them back to see if they germinate. Even a Guardian columnist would surely see that seeing as we need 1.82 million new engineers before 2022, inspiring a few schoolchildren to do STEM subjects might be a good idea.

This stuff is useful to men and women alike, space geeks or otherwise. It's not chauvinistic, it's not political vanity, it's not spendthrift Tories forcing us into a jingoistic weep-in as though Lady Di's just snuffed it.

One of the experiments Peake is doing is to grow protein crystals in freefall. Proteins make up the viruses which cause disease and to replicate them in a laboratory is difficult. Contamination makes them do different things, so it's harder to suss them out. On the ISS, they grow properly, and scientists can assess their form to make the right vaccine which needs to physically fit onto that protein and switch off whatever it's doing.

Tim's efforts might save not just our lives but those of countless generations yet to be born. Unless Simon Jenkins or anyone else has some kind of cast-iron promise from a particularly benign Almighty that we'll be immune to all disease forever, that sounds like a f***ing useful way to spend £16million to me.

Of course there are other things to spend money on. Of course government gets it wrong. But not here – not this time.

If you don't like it, just give back or turn down every bit of space-originating technology in your life and see what happens.

Personally, I'll stick with the science.

Let's hope the other babies born yesterday keep their lucky royal penny, because they're going to need it

July 23, 2013

A boy was born yesterday[2].

Well, more than one. Around 2,200 babies were born in the UK, another 370,000 in the rest of the world, and roughly half of them were boys. The boy we're talking about was luckyish because he was born in Britain rather than North Korea where he'd be four times more likely to die before he was five.

He's also lucky he wasn't a girl, because globally there are 100 million missing females who should have been born at normal rates but simply don't exist. Those girls were aborted, abused, murdered, denied healthcare and otherwise mistreated just for being girls. So being a boy is a lucky break for most people on the planet.

And this one was born in 2013, rather than any other point in history with less science and maternity care and more in the way of childbed fever, dirt, or surgical procedures that involved a sharpened stone. But what world is he going to grow up in? What will his life be like? What chances will the average baby boy have?

Well, his parents probably aren't married. It's no longer seen as necessary, and increasing social improvements have made it more likely people can afford, and want, to get divorced.

Unfortunately the laws of the land haven't quite caught up with those facts, which means every child born to unmarried parents in the UK is a second-class citizen. They are not called bastards any more, and illegitimacy is no longer a shame. But if your parents aren't married the law will not recognise you in the same way it does others. The father is not presumed to be the father. He has no parental responsibility, unless he chooses to accept it. If his mother has given up work to look after their son, the father

[2] On the same day as Prince George Alexander Louis, son of William and Katherine, and then 3rd in line to the throne

has no duty to feed and house her. If it's not a marital home, the couple do not have an equal right to live in it.

His parents' average wage is £26,500. His mother is likely to earn less, and work part-time. If she's a single parent she's going to find it hard, and even with a partner she has to fend for herself.

With a shortage of affordable homes and an average first-time buyer's mortgage of £239,000 it's quite likely the family will have to rent somewhere to live. But the average rent is £736 a month - perhaps as much as half the family's take-home pay - so they might need to claim housing benefit to top up the rent demanded of them.

If the place they live in is owned by a council or housing association, and if the children are not able to sleep two to a room or a member of the family is not quite disabled enough to be exempted, they'll have to pay the bedroom tax.

When his mum goes back to work (the chances are she can't afford not to) the government will help pay for childcare. But the costs are rising faster than inflation, so by the time he goes to school it could have cost anything up to £50,000. Let's hope he has grandparents near enough to babysit.

Let's hope too he is not one of the 28,200 children taken into the care system every year - a system beset by widespread sex abuse, neglect and cutbacks and which is not the subject of any inquiries to fix it.

It's difficult to know what schools will be like five years from now, but if current trends continue a cynic might think by the time this boy attends one, pupils will be force-fed salad leaves, have compulsory psychiatry sessions and face daily exams in Latin grammar.

It's more likely that a fortunate few will go to schools their parents pay through the nose for, while many millions will pass through a state education system in which teachers are harassed and criticised, politicians constantly tinker, and pupils learn only what they feel like while corporations are invited to make a buck out of school meals, books, buildings, security and teaching agencies. When our boy smashes his head in the playground he'll be taken to a hospital where the Accident & Emergency unit has been replaced by an Urgent Care Centre run by Richard Branson, who by then will probably be living in orbit.

After he's been assessed by Virgin staff he'll get punted on to the only remaining proper A&E within 50 miles and a state-trained junior doctor who's filling time before entering a reality show. If he gets admitted to hospital overnight, he'll be expected to pay to watch the television, use the phone, and eat food which cost a quarter of what is spent on prisoners' food. His parents will have to pay to park and visit him, and it's likely as not that private business will be making a bomb out of supplying the bandages, drugs, agency staff and just about anything else they can get their hands on.

When our boy grows up he probably won't go to university. If he's white, he's less likely to apply than boys who are black or Asian. And girls will probably do better than him in all his exams.

Perhaps he'll fall in love and perhaps he won't. Perhaps he'll have children of his own. Perhaps he'll be gay, and able to get married, and no-one will think any differently of him for it. Perhaps he'll beat the odds, win the lottery, find a cure for cancer, or be one of the astronauts who takes part in a manned mission to Mars.

But he's probably going to be fatter than his parents. We already email family members rather than speak to them - perhaps our boy will lose his voice altogether. He's probably going to suffer extremes of weather like floods and heatwaves on a regular basis. If he gets a garden he'll probably buy cacti rather than a hosepipe.

Our boy will more than likely have to care for his parents as they get older, has double our chance of suffering from dementia, and probably won't be able to retire before he dies at the age of about 79. By then there will be 21 million people aged 65 or older, and almost 10 million over 80.

Maybe he will live long enough to see, in 2065 or thereabouts, a baby born on the same day as him, in the same country, be crowned King of England.

That baby was born with the help of the best doctors in the land, will live in a house recently given a £1million makeover, with parents who are millionaires, and a great-grandmother around for most of his childhood. He'll go to the best schools, might join Richard Branson in orbit one day, and his only involvement with Virgin staff will be of the first class kind

He won't be called on to care for anyone, his exams won't matter, he'll get to eat and drink the best of everything and from the day of his birth everyone will notice him - for better or worse - and care about him, even if they have never met him and are never likely to. The most difficult thing he will probably have to do is think of 20 different ways to say 'Hello, have you come far?'

Of course people are different. Of course some babies are more fortunate than others. But it's a little medieval to be so happy for the arrival of a single child of privilege while doing nothing to help the thousands of others born yesterday whose lives are going to be significantly less pleasant than those of our generation.

Our baby - the other boy, whose birth is not special in any way unless you know him - may very well be proud of the lucky silver penny he will be given for sharing the future king's birthday. But wouldn't it be great if he got the same chances too?

What's Queen Elizabeth II ever done for us?

September 9, 2015

Roll out the bunting, tug the forelock and bend the knee. For it's time to be glad we're not living with King Charles Three!

Today the Queen has been forced to mark passing the record of her predecessor Victoria as Britain's longest-reigning monarch. Fair enough, perhaps – 63 years and seven months is longer than the rest of us would ever want to be doing one thing for[3].

But her namesake Elizabeth I ran the country, began the British Empire, sponsored scientists, spoke seven languages and turned international diplomacy into an art form, before giving her name to the age.

Elizabeth II hasn't managed any of that. Under her, the country has run itself and the empire crumbled.

She can speak two languages, both French and Posh, can't be said to have sponsored any great discoveries and has possibly turned the word 'Elizabethan' into something that means 'sort of boring'. So, since 1952, what has she actually achieved?

1. Four children, only two of whom are any use

Well done and thank you Brenda for the Olympian, the selfless charity work, the Prince's Trust and the jolly lovely biscuits. But she could have stopped after that, because Andrew and Edward have turned out to be little more than the Royal equivalent of the bystanders in Albert Square, and half as useful.

2. Coronation chicken

This dish was invented to mark her accession to the throne and involves a mix of meat, mayonnaise, spices and raisins, of all things, most commonly used as a cold sandwich

[3] She managed to do 70, in the end

filling. Thanks, Betty. It's just what we always wanted.

3. She has never denied being a lizard controlled from the far side of the moon
Which, if nothing else, gives us something to ponder even if it is only how lizards built and launched satellites to transmit the signals without us noticing.

4. 256 official overseas visits to 129 countries

Now, a cynic would say this was the greatest free holiday blag of all time, while a monarchist would point out the pomp and waving has knitted the Commonwealth into a cohesive community. A realist, however, would say the Commonwealth doesn't mean much to most people, that Royal visits are damned expensive, and the sight of people nationalist enough to throw off the yoke of empire bending the knee to their former Empress is, well, just daft.

You know what else? She didn't have to go through passport control ONCE.

5. Pioneered the walkabout

The very first royal walkabout took place on a trip to Australia and New Zealand in 1970, as a way of meeting "real" people and not just dignitaries. Seeing as it took 18 years to pioneer it, we might presume that it was a PR move but it's proved to be a wildly popular one. It's what's expected of Royals at every appearance – even when Prince Harry, then 12, and Prince William, then 15, appeared after the death of their mother to see the flower tributes left for her outside Kensington Palace.The walkabout means they're ours to see – even when staring is just about the worse thing we could do.

Yay.

6. Twice asked for, and received, a pay rise during recession

First in the 1970s and again most recently, Her Majesty has waited until the nation is in its worst financial straits for decades before asking it for more cash. I mean, fair play to her – who wouldn't want a pay rise? – but she could pick her moments better.

7. She might have been running things all along

Officially, Brenda's job is to advise and support each of the 12 Prime Ministers of her reign. In reality, she's put up with people she can't stand, listened to all kinds of bonkers policy ideas, and done as she's told when it comes to inviting Martin McGuinness over for tea. She might have persuaded each of those 12 PMs to do her bidding – but we'll never know. Any papers revealing what power she's wielded won't be released until long after anyone who gives a toss has snuffed it.

8. Sat through 35 Royal Variety Performances

Could you take that much Des O'Connor? I couldn't.

9. Helped raised £1.4billion for charity

She's patron of more than 600 charities, 400 or so of them since the 1950s, and her presence on the letterheads guarantees them funding, photos, openings and coverage. Could you do that?

10. Is the nation's most prolific joyrider

She's never had a driving licence, which must surely mean she's not insured, and while she can easily afford a driver she persistently takes the wheel herself on both private and public roads despite the fact she's now 89. Anyone else would be subject to regular medical checks, never mind arrest. Woman's a menace.

11. Has bent to the public will

She is possibly the first British monarch ever to pretty much always do as she's told – she's paid tax, she's given up her yacht, she lowered the flag and bowed to Diana's coffin, she's had terrorists and dictators to dinner. Had she not been so flexible and compliant the monarchy could well have not survived past 1997 – or at least, not in one piece. Had it not, it would have been Tony Blair who designed the replacement. And nobody would want that, so even if she is the most expensive white elephant in the world she is at least better than the alternative.

Besides, no president would flash their knickers while jumping out of a helicopter.

12. Watched her family become national pets

In 1952, the Royal Family were treated with deference and consideration. In 2015, they're treated like a cross between a soap opera and Celebrity Big Brother. And you can't just blame the media – it's the public who snap Harry on cameraphones while playing strip billiards, dissect Kate's wardrobe and ruminate on Camilla's complexion. Whereas she was born into a family of immense wealth, privilege and personal freedom she now presides over a family of immense wealth, conditional privilege and all the freedom of Auntie Ethel's favourite budgie.

13. Made royalty irrelevant

This woman is 89 years old, today's record depends entirely on the fact her father died young and means her son will likely die unfulfilled, and she let it be known quite clearly she didn't want to mark it. Yet she's nevertheless been forced out of Balmoral to open a train line. What's the point of being Queen if no-one listens to you?

14. The biggest thing she's done is nothing at all

People talk about her personal sacrifices – there haven't been many – her grace and dignity – not difficult when you're forced to be silent – and 63 years of duty and hard work – not that she was exactly down the pit. But the trickiest thing she's done is nothing. She's not upset anyone, she's not cocked up, she hasn't been involved in any scandals involving mobile phones, tampons or toe sucking.

I don't know about you, but I can't go five minutes without saying or doing something that pisses off somebody, somewhere, yet this woman – presumably with opinions, insights and ideas of her own – has managed it for more than half a century.

In so doing, she's guaranteed her family's continued strange existence, saved the nation from gruesome political alternatives and entertained the world with the sort of pomp we all secretly love. It's cost us squillions, but no-one's been offended or hurt by it and we have at least got a sandwich filling out of it, which is more than most of our monarchs managed.

The trouble is that after her comes Charles Three – a man with such a knack for scandal and gullibility that he could very well ruin everything.

Give thanks today that, thanks to Queen Elizabeth II, her genes and her excellent medical care, we're not there yet.

Après elle, le déluge.

Why can't Meghan Markle choose her own doctor for the birth of a royal baby?

April 8, 2019

Brexit is DOA, Donald Trump is still a thing and they're about to turn the internet off. Let us adjourn, then, to the 12th century.

In this happy enclave of the Dark Ages, sword fights have yet to evolve into Sunday morning politics shows. Men can grab any passing genitals they choose, so long as they're not male genitals which will result in a red hot poker up the bottom. And women are a form of property categorised as either maiden, mother or crone. Witches and princesses alike wear pointy hats, but they have very different lifestyle outcomes.

Witches are clever, but any female who expresses an opinion about children who steal sweets, girls who let princes into their tower or don't keep promises made to frogs will more than likely wind up being done to a crisp in her own oven. Princesses are stupid, and therefore don't wonder why no-one ever hears about them after they get married. It's because most of them die in childbirth.

Prolapsed wombs, cervical weakness, incontinence, sepsis, PTSD and dead babies have been left out of the fairytales. Which is silly, really, because the whole point of them is to threaten dark consequences for a lack of morality.

The Greeks got it right - treat a woman badly, and the Furies would turn up to extract a blood vengeance. The Brothers Grimm concentrated on naughty little boys and perfect princesses, and our world is the worse for having forgotten the more natural morality of our forefathers. It's because of this attitude, you see, that Meghan Markle is being accused of "snubbing" the Royal Family's team of gynaecologists. The upstart foreigner has chosen her OWN doctor for the birth of upcoming ginger baby Sussex. Clutch your pearls, dears, the Americans are revolting.

Those who call this a snub need to check their dictionary, which will inform them it means "to spurn disdainfully". Think how a foolish king in a kingdom full of spindles was rude to a bad fairy over a christening invitation: now that's a snub. In fairytales, such scorn has consequences.

In real life, the scorn of kings causes the deaths of their wives, daughters and daughters-in-law. Midwives and herbalists were rejected for the advice of male doctors who believed in leeches and Scripture. Princesses who gave birth were locked in rooms with the windows nailed shut for months. 'Doctors' examined their patients without touching them or looking under their skirts, and during labour shouted advice from the other side of a door.

Henry VIII lost his mother and a wife that way; his 6th wife died in childbirth, too. Mrs Beeton, Neville Chamberlain's mum, Abraham Lincoln's sister, Teddy Roosevelt's wife, and the youngest daughter of Captain von Trapp all died in childbirth, along with millions of nameless others.

Princesses were worse off than peasant women. Peasants had access to the village wise woman - or witch, if you were a man - while princesses were told their child was so important the men had to take charge of it. All were subject to the same medical ignorance, but the witches at least had the benefit of experience. Royal physicians usually specialised in narcissism, insanity and latent homosexuality. Ladybits were a mystery. That's why you didn't use to hear about princesses after they married. All too often, they ceased to exist.

Today we live in a world where princesses are celebrities, capable of selling a million pounds' worth of products with one change of clothes or car. We look up to them, and they have power. Meghan's great strength is that she was a celebrity before she became a princess. She had wealth, status and experience, and wanted to use them to help those who had none. She's the greatest piece of luck that's ever landed in the Royal Family's lap - an adornment that's actually useful.

She hasn't "snubbed" the "men in suits" who delivered the Duchess of Cambridge's babies. She's snubbed the lethally-ancient attitude that princesses have doctors foisted upon them, their children are public property, and their vaginas belong to the Crown. It's no wonder that Prince William can hardly bear to look at her when they're in public. She makes him look bad.

Here we are in a world where a princess can choose the perfectly-capable, world-leading and experienced gynaecologists who attend to the female Head of State, or she can choose her own doctors, who won't be any worse.

She can have her first child at 37 and probably not die. She can write on bananas, practice yoga, fly her mum over from the US, annoy a future king and not at any point be burned as a witch, which would have been the punishment for all those things in years gone by. This princess is allowed to be clever, and free, and marry for love. And because we still look up to the beautiful, famous and royal, a billion girls around the world see what she's doing and want some of that, too.

If the Royal Family's got one problem, it's that some of its members and courtiers think continuity depends on being the same for centuries. It doesn't. It depends on evolution, which has been the way of things for 4 billion years so far.

The fact that there's a new member with new ideas is only a threat to the established order if that order is weak, pointless and silly. Healthy traditions last; stupid ones die.

Long live Princess Meghan - and woe betide all those who don't see what her fairytale is teaching them[4].

[4] No wonder she left

Here are my 15 examples of where the Royal Family was racist as hell

March 12, 2021

If you dive into anyone's family - black or white - you'll find someone to accuse of racism.

Grandad will say something daft, a teenager something thoughtless, and if you start going through the ancestors there'll be a good chunk of them for whom skin colour was a handy way of deciding who to beat, marry or kill.

It's a powerful and damaging word to hurl around these days, and people should remember that humans have been crappy to each other for about 2 million years now, and we're going to have to let most of that go.

Centuries ago we elevated those humans who were good at war, and today their descendants still rule over us although we now handle the battles ourselves. And if they want to stay on that blood-stained pedestal, they need to deserve it.

So when the Duke and Duchess of Sussex said a member of the Royal Family inquired after their son's skin colour, during debates about whether to give him a title or security, we wondered if these higher-than-thous were pretty low. When Buckingham Palace didn't comment for 56 hours, we became restless.

And when a stiff-backed Prince William declared "we are very much not a racist family" yesterday, there was relief he had deigned to mention it, although, to be fair, he didn't really sell it. Which family was he talking about? His closest living relatives, the Windsors in general, or everyone going back to William the Conqueror, whose DNA is probably, by this point, distributed equally around the British Isles?

The trouble with William's claim is that, whichever family he's talking about, there is racism. Quite a lot of it, in fact. And it's not out-of-context, reasonable-for-the-time racism. It's eye-poppingly-bad-even-then-racism.

Here are just a few examples.

1. The time someone senior in William's immediate family repeatedly asked what colour his nephew's skin would be while discussing his security needs, and which he has yet to deny.

2. The time Prince William allegedly went to a party dressed as a gorilla[5], but couldn't be clearly identified behind the mask, so pictures of Harry at the same party dressed as a Nazi caused a scandal instead.

3. The time his uncle Andrew left then-Home Secretary Jacqui Smith "slack-jawed" at a dinner for the Saudi royals by making "racist comments about Arabs that were unbelievable... it involved a comment about camels".

4. The time that same uncle referred to "the n***** in the woodpile" to one of David Cameron's advisers, who was of Sri Lankan descent.

5. The time his granny's uncle[6] said Adolf Hitler was "not a bad chap" and taught three princesses to throw a Nazi salute, in the same year the Reichstag burned down, Hitler had seized power, the Gestapo was created, Dachau was built, and thousands of Britons protested against rabid anti-Semitism and persecution of Jews.

6. The time that same granny's uncle ignored government advice to visit Nazi Germany, dined with Goering, Goebbels and Hess, take tea with Hitler, and gave a speech saying that what he had seen "is a miracle; one can only begin to understand it when one realises that behind it all is one man and one will".

7 - 9. The time the Queen Mother told a diarist during a drunken lunch "beware the Blackamoors", the time she told a journalist she "had some reservations about Jews," and the time she told a lady-in-waiting that "the Africans just don't know how to govern themselves…what a pity we're not still looking after them".

10. The time Princess Michael of Kent wore priceless jewellery depicting an African slave kept as a domestic pet to the wider family's first meeting with Meghan Markle.

11. The time the same princess told black New Yorkers to "go back to the colonies" and named two black sheep on her farm Venus and Serena.

12. The time Queen Victoria became close friends with an Indian Muslim, and her son Edward VII sacked him within hours of her funeral, had him deported, then ordered every record of their relationship to be destroyed.

13. The time the Royal Family set up the Royal African Company, of which Edward Colston was merely a shareholder and employee, and shipped more African slaves across the Atlantic than anyone else.

[5] Or a lion - there's only rumour, but he doesn't seem keen to say which

[6] *cough* Edward VIII *cough*

14. The time that wealthy slave-owner, banker and MP George Smith became enormously wealthy, his granddaughter married the Earl of Strathmore, and her granddaughter Elizabeth Bowes-Lyon married a prince, became Queen, and on her death left most of her £70 million estate and fine art to the Royal Family.

15. The time she also left about £7million each to Princes William and Harry, who have, presumably, happily lived off the profits of slavery ever since.

Some of these have roots deep in the mists of time. Others are bang-up-to-date. And it's worth pointing out that Britain ended the slave trade, too, and freed those brought to its shores by Americans who held on to the nasty habit for decades longer.

In 2018 Prince Charles condemned "the atrocity" of slavery. Prince William has spoken about the horrors of racism in football. Princess Michael of Kent, Prince Harry, even Prince Philip, have apologised for what have become known as "gaffes".

And at the end of last year, the Historic Royal Palaces announced a review of their buildings' and contents' links to slavery, which will probably see a lot of heavy annotation in souvenir handbooks rather than having to lose, er, pretty much every palace and private home.

If you go through history, everyone's got a link to slavery. Most of our ancestors, black or white, were slaves at some point. But there are few families we could point to as having consistently been the enslavers, the profiteers, and the beneficiaries of deep and unreasonable nastiness. You can do that with the Royal Family.

And of all the things that have been said and done, the Queen, as the current living head of it, has never acknowledged a single thing laid out above.

It would not hurt - it would, at this stage, do a lot to help - if she said what we all know: this is not a private family matter. It's an issue of constitutional significance, in the UK and for the 2.4 billion mostly-brown people in the Commonwealth, and it's about time the Royals elevated themselves in our eyes.

Princess Diana's explosive BBC interview: 5 things that they're not telling you

May 21, 2021

Martin Bashir and the BBC have done the world a great service. They have proven, beyond all doubt, that lying doesn't work.

In 1995, after meeting Bashir for the first time, Prince William reportedly told Princess Diana: "He's a sly creep, Mummy." A quarter of a century later, that opinion is shared by any who glance at the fallout of the BBC inquiry into its failures around the explosive *Panorama* interview that year.

The fact Bashir faked documents, lied about her in-laws, played on the fears of a vulnerable woman, and groomed her brother to help him get access, is foul journalism. Not only was it unethical, and potentially criminal, they could be so easily refuted that they could only ever destroy the trust of the princess and undermine the credibility, not only of the reporter, but the organisation he worked for. Every journalist in the world will, now, have to overcome what he did when seeking an interview with almost anyone.

The Press are enjoying kicking the BBC, which kicked them so hard over phone-hacking. Politicians are relishing the chance to haul Auntie over her own coals, for once. And there are two princes who find it easy to criticise media coverage, and harder to talk about the wearing of seatbelts. As a result, there are a lot of things in Lord Dyson's report into the affair not getting the attention they should - and quite a lot that's been forgotten entirely.

1. Princess Diana was desperate to do an interview

Diana officially separated from Prince Charles in December 1992, following a shocking biography by Andrew Morton which detailed her bulimia, personal misery, and her husband's affair with Camilla Parker-Bowles. In March the following year, Dyson found that she rejected the offer of a BBC interview with Sue Lawley. Then in June 1994, her husband gave an ITV interview to Jonathan Dimbleby in which he admitted adultery. It was shattering and humiliating for Diana, and, the report found, she "would probably have agreed to be interviewed by any experienced and reputable reporter in whom she had confidence, even without the intervention of Mr Bashir".

In August 1995 her friend Baroness Jay approached the BBC on her behalf. The suggestion was for a *Panorama* interview with then-diplomatic correspondent Nicholas Witchell, focusing on her charity work and future role in public life. Dyson writes that: "It is clear that Princess Diana was now very keen to talk to the BBC." Later that month, Diana's staff were organising a meeting with Witchell and she wrote a memo saying "I am v keen to be in this meeting" and asking what time it would be.

Panorama bosses switched Witchell for Bashir. Lord Dyson does not say why, nor whether it derailed the project, or made no difference. He also does not explain why, when the princess was already negotiating with *Panorama* , Bashir approached her brother to gain access. But it's clear that, if she didn't talk to Bashir, she'd have talked to someone else.

2. The Panorama interview did not cause Diana's divorce

In his statement yesterday, Prince William said: "The interview was a major contribution to making my parents' relationship worse." By the time the interview aired, his parents had each conducted multiple affairs; his mother had attempted suicide; she had co-operated extensively with Morton on his book, revealing her bulimia and naming Camilla Parker-Bowles; she and her husband had both fed stories to favoured journalists; secret tapes of her being called 'Squidgy', and her husband fantasising about being Camilla's tampon, had been leaked to the Press and aired on premium-rate phone lines; and the Prime Minister had announced the Wales' official separation three years earlier. And of course, her husband had allowed Jonathan Dimbleby more than a year of access for a documentary in which he admitted cheating, trashed his parents, and was seen chatting to his geraniums. It is hard to see how the *Panorama* interview could possibly have made that marriage any worse. It would always have led to divorce, but perhaps one that was slightly less embarrassing to the young prince.

3. Princess Diana was paranoid long before she met Bashir

Prince William said the interview with Diana "contributed significantly to her fear, paranoia, and isolation". The Dyson report is clear that Bashir met her for the first time on September 19, 1995, and found that he had shown her brother fake bank statements to convince him that household staff were selling information to the Press and the security services. There were claims, too, that some royal reporters were taking bribes, that cars, phones, and watches were bugged, and a lie that Royal nanny Tiggy Legge-Bourke had an abortion. Yet by the time of the interview, Diana had been under the influence of crackpot clairvoyants for years. They subsequently were sources of hundreds of newspaper articles, wrote books, and even now claim to be speaking to Diana in the afterlife. Dyson found that two years earlier, in 1993, Diana had written to her butler Paul Burrell that Charles was "in love" with Tiggy.

He also found that, in his meetings with Bashir, Charles Spencer had revealed that he had taken out an injunction against a former staff member over fears he was selling stories about his family. And on October 31, 1995, Diana had a meeting with her personal lawyer Lord Mishcon in which she made a series of paranoid claims. Dyson reveals a note made at the time, which says: "Efforts would be made if not to get rid of her (be it by some accident in her car, such as pre-prepared brake failure or whatever), now and then, then at least to see that she was so injured or damaged as to be declared unbalanced. She was convinced that there was a conspiracy." Dyson concludes: "I am satisfied that, by the time of the meeting, Princess Diana had paranoid fears about various things including that she was being spied on and was in danger of her life." Bashir undeniably played on her fears, perhaps made them worse - but they were pretty bad before he showed up.

4. The interview did not lead to her death in a Paris car crash

The fallout from the interview was so bad that the Queen urged Charles and Diana to divorce. During talks, the princess offered to give up the title of Her Royal Highness, reportedly in return for more personal freedom. She also dropped her Royal protection, which she had come to distrust as her paranoia grew. But with her brother injuncting his own staff, and Royal households notoriously leaky, she would probably always have suspected her bodyguards. Journalists have frequent, unofficial contact with police officers for all sorts of reasons - with Royalty, it's usually so the police know who's a genuine reporter and who's a nutter. A paranoid Diana could easily have misconstrued that as a betrayal.

Her brother said he draws a line between the interview and her death. "When she died two years later, she was without any form of real protection," he said. Former editor Andrew Neil writes today that, had the BBC admitted what had happened in its first investigation in 1996, "she might have realised that the 'Establishment' was not out to get her and that there was no need to cut herself off entirely from it". But if you remove Bashir and his lies, you still have years of misery, mistrust, and fury at the Royals who left her to tumble down the stairs, cut her wrists, and struggle with the effects of extreme anxiety and massive media attention.

And had she divorced Charles but kept her taxpayer-funded protection, as she travelled to UN conferences and African minefields, used Mediterranean yachts and pop stars' mansions, dated heart surgeons and playboys, there would have been outrage in the media, in Parliament, and among the public that an ex-Royal was still costing millions. She would have been under huge pressure to drop it and fund it herself as soon as she stepped back from Royal duties, because that's exactly what happened to Harry last year. The chances of her retaining that security when she died in August 1997, a full year after the divorce was complete, is next to non-existent.

5. Nothing has changed or looks likely to

Prince Harry said: "Our mother lost her life because of this, and nothing has changed." Well, yes and no. Diana was vulnerable from childhood, treated horrifically by many of those that she loved, and betrayed by many of those she trusted. She was a global icon of womanhood, and as such was repeatedly exploited and mistreated by men. Her chances of a happy old age were as slim as those of Marilyn Monroe, or Anne Boleyn. We are unable to say it, because a young girl marrying a prince is supposed to be the answer to everything, but Diana was a tragedy waiting to happen.

But he's right in that nothing has changed. Journalists have always been excellent at sniffing out things that smell bad, like foxes who've had a whiff of raw chicken. They had Bashir and his lies early on, and 25 years later they have persisted to get the BBC and its cover-up, too.

That cover-up was conducted by idiots, who had the journalistic nose of Lord Voldemort. Knowing that Bashir had lied to them 3 times, they did not smell a rat and instead called him a man of integrity. Lord Dyson found him to be "incredible, unreliable, and, in some cases, dishonest" - a summing up that will be in his obituary. It seems that the more useless a person is, the higher in any organisation they are promoted. In this case Bashir's boss Tony Hall made it all the way to Director-General. Royals are still determined to give interviews. Diana managed two in her entire life, but her youngest son has given so many people have perhaps not noticed that in his latest he's accused the Royal Family of "total neglect", the same as his mother did quarter of a century ago, and with significantly less impact.

Yet the Royals are still rewriting history as it suits, finding it easier to attack the media that they are desperate to speak to, for saying things they don't want to hear. Harry and William have every right to criticise Bashir and the BBC, and to be furious over the loss of their mother and her unhappiness. But her death was due to a thousand things that went wrong over decades. The last two to which she fell victim were a drugged and drunk driver, and not wearing a seatbelt, something which in 2018 cost 261 lives in the UK. Her sons have yet to find the time to campaign on either of these things.

Nothing has changed. A "sly creep" committed a foul act with absolutely no reason to do so, an organisation run by prats protected itself in the short-term at the expense of its reputation in the long-term, and a complicated woman exploited all her life has been exploited, yet again. The same things will happen today, and tomorrow, in any given group of humans. Judging from the fact it has 7 separate inquiries underway into unethical behaviour, lies and institutional failures, it's happening right now in Downing Street.

While bashing Bashir, we ignore the fundamental issue which is the utterly toxic way Royal women are treated, an issue raised by Boudicca, Empress Matilda, and every single queen and princess since. Lying about that won't make it go away.

And it is proof of what every journalist knows is true: whatever they don't tell you is the story.

More pictures like this, please

August 18, 2011

Another A-level results day, another slew of pictures of photogenic young girls in not many summer clothes, jumping around looking happy.

You don't see the ones who didn't get the grades they wanted. Tearful teens are in newspapers only when there's a school killing spree, generally. You also don't see the fat girls, the speccy ones, or the plain ones, who may be celebrating just as much but a picture of whom won't sell a single newspaper.

You don't see teenage boys either. Spotty oiks don't take much of a picture, and anyway girls get better exam results. They also express emotion in photographs and boys, with the best will in the world, just don't.

It all adds up to a lot of well-intentioned people grumbling about sexist and slightly-pervy newspapers - tabloid and snoresheet - photographing barely-legal young women.

How dreadful of us. How appalling that millions of extra people will look at our websites today and buy the papers tomorrow to see those same pictures, keeping our struggling businesses afloat while telling themselves how bad it is that they are being forced to look at pretty girls in tiny shorts and my, what long hair they have!

But to be frank, it doesn't matter a damn.

Firstly because A-levels are like popularity - important when you're 18, and for the rest of your life you couldn't care less. And secondly because the sight of a happy teenage girl with a whole life of possibilities in front of her is one of the most magical things you'll ever see.

There aren't many countries where that happens. Europe, North America, Australasia, Japan. Those girls you'll see in the pictures are smiling because they can be anything they want to be. The right exam result means you can get into the right university, get the right degree, land a dream job.

In India, if you're a girl, you're lucky to survive to 18. In most of Africa, school is an expensive luxury that comes a long way down a parent's list. In China, a girl will probably be aborted if her parents can afford it, and dumped after she is born if they can't. In fact, while we're busy bewailing pictures of successful young kids in the newspapers covering our tiny, self-important part of the planet, there are 100 million women in the rest of the world who have simply disappeared.

Let me say that again, because you skimmed over it a little quickly. One hundred million. The equivalent, if you're into comparisons, of the Holocaust sixteen times over. Or 66,000 Titanics sinking. Remember the Norway massacre a few weeks ago? Sixty-nine young people slaughtered. Well, imagine that happening every day for 3,835 years. Yeah. That many.

Boys outnumber girls, very slightly, when they're born. If they get a good diet and are lucky enough to live in a wealthy country like yours and mine - you're among the 30 per cent of the world with the internet, so you're ahead of the game - women will outlive men, for simple biological reasons. They are more resistant to disease, deal better with the sniffles, and are generally nails.

Except there are many parts of the world where males significantly outnumber women. These are in the parts where diet and disease would, naturally, mean things should be the other way around. But in Asia, the Middle East, Africa, girls who should have been born are missing. In these places they are more likely to die at every stage of their lives; they are more likely to be aborted, abandoned, to be denied medical care, to be abused, neglected, beaten and murdered.

In China alone, there are 50 million women who should be there, but aren't.

Even if they survive, in most of the world girls are seen as less deserving of education, first aid, gynaecology, property, a driving licence, or the protection of the law. And before you stop and think how glad you are your country isn't like that, here in the UK and in most of the developed world women are less likely to earn the same as men for the same job, to be elected to Parliament or to become CEO of a company. If one of us is raped, a jury will be asked to consider whether we were "asking for it". In Britain there are 1.05 million women on the dole, the highest for 25 years, because the recession is hitting them harder than men - women are more likely to work in the public sector which is being cut, more likely to work part-time, and are generally seen as more expendable by bosses.

It's not quite as bad as the Congo, of course, but all our science and technology hasn't moved us quite as far as it could. And imagine what we could do in the Congo, if only it had oil.

So, do you know what? Shake your head ruefully at the exam results photos, at the fact those kids don't realise this is the thinnest and most carefree they'll ever be, that they feel so positive and thrilled about a life which is going to kick them in the chops every chance it gets. But don't get het up about pictures of young girls who are happy, who by and large and with a following wind will be able to have long and fulfilled lives in which they can do (almost) whatever they want.

Just be angry there aren't more of them.

To those of you who think a 12-year-old girl from Rochdale in a short skirt can't be raped - you're very wrong

May 11, 2012

NINE Asian men went to jail this week for sexually abusing young white girls. The girls were poor, from care homes and extremely troubled - so of course, it was their own fault.

On Question Time last night Tory writer Peter Oborne said the victims had "accepted the advances" of their attackers and blamed modern social decline. He added: "What does it tell us about what's happened to our society that we have 12 year old girls, 13 year old girls, who are happy to give up their affection and their beauty to men in exchange for a packet of crisps?"

I don't think any of them were happy about it, Peter. And I'm pretty certain child abuse isn't a recent thing.

Then a man of the cloth in the front row piped up that young girls in Rochdale, where the abuse happened, "go out dressed as if they are looking for that sort of issue to take place".

Oh fine. The clergy never abuse children of course - unless they dress like they want it. Those choirboys can be very provocative!

The ringleader of the gang, when jailed for 19 years, accused the judge and jury of racism rather than defend or admit his actions.

The views of all three men are equally abhorrent. And similar opinions are being expressed on Twitter, in pubs and offices up and down the country because of the belief that the only kind of rape which counts is when a man in a mask jumps out, armed with a knife, and a woman screams and fights while he has sex with her.

I've sat through an awful lot of rape court cases and interviewed dozens of victims, I've had friends who've been attacked, and I can tell you the reality is very different. When that stereotypical rape happens sometimes a woman is so desperate to get away she will pretend she's enjoying it so he doesn't kill her. It doesn't mean that she is - she's just trying to survive, and it's still rape.

In about two thirds of cases a woman is raped by someone she knows - a boyfriend, a husband, a mate. It happens in her own bed. And more often than not, once the protests aren't listened to and they realise they can't get away, the victims stop fighting because they don't want to make things worse. To get through it, to get away, to minimise their injuries. It's still rape.

In the vast majority of stories I've dealt with the woman is too drunk to uncross her eyes, never mind her legs. A man protests she was fine with it, and juries split over whether he was merely unchivalrous. He feels hard done-by, she feels abused, and it's still rape.

Training children to not fight you off doesn't make it consensual. It's grooming, and it's rape. Over a period of time these girls were plied with alcohol, money and drugs, bullied, and made to feel reliant on their abusers. They were extremely vulnerable, with damaged childhoods that made them glad of any attention no matter how vicious and wrong it was. Because the abuse was being spread among friends it was normalised, but nothing detracts from the fact the men who carried out those acts are rapists.

It doesn't matter what colour they are, or how they went about it, how long it took or how much money they spent on drugs and booze, or whether crisps were offered. Rape is rape.

I've long thought the best way of making women safer would be to make the punishment include having the word 'RAPIST' tattooed on a guilty man's forehead. They'd all be a lot more chivalrous then, and maybe the guys with the knives would think twice too.

In the absence of being able to stop bad men being bad, the main issue now is how those girls were victimised while they were in our care. The abuse was first reported by the girls a decade ago, but nothing was done. When one teen was lured away from her care home repeatedly and bullied into sleeping with up to 25 men in one night, the social workers looking after her just sent her a text message asking when she was coming back. They didn't try to find out what was going on, get her to trust them enough to reveal the abuse, or show any of the care they were being paid to even though she disappeared for up to two weeks at a time. She ended up having to write them a letter about it before they took any notice at all.

Another girl was sent to visit the men by her own father, a heroin addict who used the money she brought back afterwards to buy his drugs. One of the victims, Victoria Agoglia, ran away from her care home 21 times in two months, was found by the police five times, and on the same night she was picked up from the care home by a gang of men in a car she died from a heroin overdose. She was 15 years old.

There are suggestions another four of those girls have died since. And what are we doing about it?

OFSTED has launched an investigation[7]. And that's it.There are 65,000 children in care in the UK today - how many of them are perfectly safe?

These 'homes' are anything but. They're either run on a shoestring by a local authority or a private business, neither of whom want to devote cash or attention to troubled children who need both. The people who work in them aren't able to enforce curfews or take a degree of parental responsibility. And they are being run in our name, with our money, and are failing our children.

It's a national scandal of appalling proportions which demands an inquiry. There won't be one, because people who need our help the most are left to fend for themselves while politicians badger for inquiries into their pet projects.

The nasty truth is that too many people of wealth and privilege believe that a 12-year-old girl from Rochdale in a short skirt simply cannot be raped.

And they damn well can.

[7] Ofsted reported back in December 2012 that Rochdale council's child protection services were 'inadequate'. The government issued instructions to improve, but in August 2022, Ofsted found one Rochdale children's home was still failing to protect young people at risk of sexual exploitation, or effectively monitor them

Emily Davison, 100 years on

June 4, 2013

A hundred years ago this week, a 40-year-old woman breathed her last.

It wasn't all that an unusual thing; in 1913 you weren't guaranteed to reach adulthood, and if a woman made it through the hell of childbirth and flu epidemics she'd probably die at around 50 anyway. This 40-year-old was different though.

Not only did she die after falling under the King's horse at the world-famous Epsom Derby, but because she was, by any standard, stone cold barking mad.

Emily Wilding Davison, were she to pop round for tea at just about any time in history, would strike you as someone who was obsessed, crazed, blinkered and probably best avoided.

A nice middle-class upbringing hit a brick wall when she was 21. Her father died and she had to drop out of university for lack of cash, and she was forced to do the only thing well-brought up impoverished ladies could do, and become a governess - a servant who once used to have servants of their own. She was a determined lass though, and saved up enough to get her degree. She won first class honours at Oxford, but because they refused to admit women wasn't allowed to graduate.

After a stint teaching she went back to university full-time, and in 1906 joined the Women's Social and Political Union - the Suffragettes. Thing is, the WSPU was the militant end of the suffrage movement. The Pankhurst family which led it felt that 50 years of asking nicely had got women no nearer the vote, and vowed to step things up a gear.

They leafleted the 1908 FA Cup Final. They trained their members in hand-to-hand combat and ju-jitsu. They started chaining themselves to railings, disrupting men-only political meetings, firebombing post boxes, smashing shop windows, cutting newly-installed telephone wires. They burned down rich men's empty stately homes, dug up golf courses, and even tried to blow up the Coronation Chair in Westminster Abbey. In

1909, one woman tried to horsewhip Winston Churchill, who was Home Secretary at the time.

As they got more mischievous the authorities cracked down harder. In 1910 a new law which would have granted the vote was talked out of Parliament, and 300 women marched on Westminster to protest. Churchill ordered the police to go in hard; there were accusations of mass sexual assault, groping, and breaking of limbs. Two hundred women were arrested, and two died. If such brutality had been practiced today there would be uproar.

In the midst of all these things was Emily, getting angrier and more cussed by the day. In 1909 she served two prison sentences for obstruction and two for stone throwing. A year later it was smashing windows at the House of Commons, and a year after that she hid in the crypt so that she would appear on the 1911 census as a resident.

In 1912 she served six months for setting fire to post boxes, followed by 10 days for attacking a vicar she'd mistaken for a cabinet minister. She went on hunger strike in jail so they force-fed her 49 times, holding her down and forcing a rubber tube down her throat or nose while she struggled and screamed.

When she barricaded her door to keep them out they flooded the cell with freezing water. Emily was prepared to drown, but they broke down the door. Out of her cell, she took the opportunity to throw herself off a set of stairs. She told a prison officer 'a tragedy was wanted'. She lived, but with severe spinal injuries.

By the time 1913 rolled around, Emily was regarded as a loose cannon even by the militant feminists of the WSPU. She'd had seven solid years of extreme violence visited upon her, and the fierce intellect and determination which had driven her as a young woman had calcified into a kind of insanity. She was beyond the point of seeing that violence begets violence, and that the angrier she got the harder she was hit. She was punch-drunk, and however good the cause she was never going to win it.

At the Epsom Derby with a friend selling Suffragette newspapers in the crowds, she took a Votes for Women silk sash from her pocket, stepped onto the track, and tried to pin the colours to the King's horse.

Let me explain that more simply - a 40-year-old woman with barely-healed spinal injuries tried to pin a bit of silk on half a ton of muscle thundering past her at 35mph. Those are not the actions of a sane person.

She may not have intended to kill herself - suicide was illegal in 1913, and deeply disgraceful - but she didn't care if she died. She had been brutalised to the point where she thought there might be more point to that than staying alive.

As she lay dying in hospital the ward was deluged with hate mail. Queen Mary, who being queen had no reason to complain about being ignored, called her 'that horrid woman'. At her funeral she was lionised by the suffrage movement which hadn't much liked her when she was alive, and today she is praised as a martyr to her cause.

Except her cause was not what we think. The WSPU didn't want votes for women, but votes only for women of wealth, just like men. And despite their agitating, despite their logic and the basic rightness of their case, the suffragettes never won the vote on their own merits.

Women got the vote because of the First World War and no other reason - because of women who went into the armament factories and worked until the men came home, and more often didn't come home at all. Practicalities proved their case, not exploding letter boxes or a horse's hooves.

And how far have we come since Emily died - a clever, inspired woman who could have achieved so many things had she lived and not been corrupted by the unfairness she fought against?

Well, I'm probably going to live to over 80. If I have children, it probably won't kill me. I have a thousand different choices Emily never did: I have the Pill, breast and cervical cancer screening, the right to a safe abortion, and I can pick my own university. I'll still do better if I'm middle-class than if I'm poor, and a lot depends on my level of education so things ain't that fair.

I've been lucky to have a job where being female is a bonus, and to have worked in places where if someone is sexist you can tell them where to shove it without getting fired. Most women don't get the same chances, and all of us are likely to be told that sexual abuse is our fault, that domestic abuse is our fault, that sexism is just banter and we need to get a sense of humour.

But we live in a country where the most powerful woman isn't allowed an opinion. The Queen's been on the throne 60 years today, and aside from the fact she likes horses and corgis and isn't too fond of Fergie, we don't know a lot else about her. Kate, as lovely as her hair might be, is not allowed to be anything more.

Women have the right to vote, but no right to be imperfect. Whether we lose our hair, remove our breasts, fall in love with the wrong people, drink the wrong amount or want to get married to each other we're not allowed to do it without a man somewhere saying we're ugly, fake, stupid, boring, or smashing society to pieces.

When a group of very wealthy and successful women appeared at a charity concert campaigning for women's rights in the developing world, they did it in spike heels and knickers.

J-Lo and Beyonce are millionaire businesswomen capable of many things, but they still don't want to appear in public without looking sexy. When did being sexy make anyone happy? Ask Marilyn Monroe.

Even Madonna, one of the strongest and most determined women of her generation, who propelled herself from struggling New York dancer to someone capable of setting up a charity with the aim of raising an entire African nation out of poverty, is not only judged by others on her looks but is so insecure she farts around with her face to the point it looks like a collapsed souffle.

Women today are little more than vessels whose worth is valued by who they sleep with and how they look, and it is a poison which seeps into our brains so early that by the age of 10 there are girls with eating disorders and a desperate craving to do whatever Harry Styles wants them to.

And when they grow up, they don't vote. They don't think 'I must find a way to educate myself if someone else will not pay'. They do not think 'how do I change the world?' I do not know what Emily would think if she knew what our world had become, but I bet you she'd wonder why she bothered.

Emily was a brilliant woman who died for a cause which brutalised and twisted her for years. We should remember her not as a martyr but as a woman abused and mistreated and whose experiences our daughters may well repeat if we do not demand better of the world we live in.

Our daughters will not be force-fed, but they'll make themselves vomit in order to fit into someone else's idea of what's attractive. Our daughters will be dismissed as hysterical whenever they get angry. Our daughters learn, every day, that success happens when people want to have sex with you, and not when you invent, build, solve, cure, teach or change anything.

The one beautiful, pure thing about feminism and suffrage is that we have a choice: we can choose to pity Kate, despair of Tulisa, and see Emily as an example of what not to do. Just because women have been victimised by others is no reason for us to continue doing it to ourselves.

Emily would think we were mad. And she'd have a point.

It's a man's, man's, man's world - and wouldn't it be good if it wasn't?

June 7, 2013

Men were told today to just calm down.

The women who run the world say the males of the species need to stop getting their knickers in such a twist over every little thing and have more of a sense of humour.

A request to the Ministry of Justice to ban websites glorifying sexual violence against men was turned down when the female-led government pointed out there was no scientific link between rape porn and actual rape.

However, male victim groups quoted a series of recent court cases in which women were known to have viewed explicit porn sites before abusing and murdering boys.

In the City, the female who runs High Street giant Marks & Spencer has pocketed a bonus 25 per cent bigger than last year, even though the firm's profits are plummeting. A spokesman said it was "entirely appropriate".

As a series of female TV stars from the 1970s face a string of historic sex abuse charges, Justin Bieber and Jay-Z were criticised for launching a new charity campaigning for men's rights in the developing world while wearing spike heels and fishnet stockings. "They looked sexy," said one concert-goer. "No-one would listen to them if they didn't dress like that."

In Germany, Chancellor Angela Merkel made a rare appearance with her husband to admit in a live TV interview she has had enough of him. It is believed she intends to set up home with a 30-year-old male Olympic gymnast she has been linked to for several years.

Actor Brad Pitt has made his first red carpet appearance after bravely revealing he had his testicles removed to avoid cancer, and earned praise for the way his trouser package seemed to look no different after reconstructive surgery after everyone had a jolly good stare. "I don't feel any less of a man," he said, adding he was extremely lucky to be going out with Angelina Jolie and would never consider plastic surgery on his increasingly craggy face.

Meanwhile a Hollywood starlet was forced to put out a statement 'clarifying' an interview she gave earlier this week in which she boasted of contracting a sexually-transmitted infection from a dirty old man. The actress said she had not intended to claim her amazing bedroom skills were the cause of her recent cancer scare, or to spout a load of rubbish that made no scientific sense. She refused to comment on her long smoking habit and the slightly-more scientific link between that and cancer.

And Rod Stewart was criticised by campaigners for traditional families when he announced he was pregnant with his umpteenth baby with his umpteenth wife. "That Rod Stewart is such a slag," Kate Winslet was overheard telling Ulrika Jonsson over a coffee.

Rod should be careful though, as doctors have revealed a long list of things expectant fathers should be wary of if they want a healthy baby. They have been warned to avoid non-stick frying pans, new cars, paint fumes, air, caffeine, alcohol and TV remote controls. Lifting toilet seats is said to cause unnecessary stress. The Royal College of Testicologists advised fathers-to-be to put their feet up, take it easy and only do light housework as having babies is extremely risky and dangerous and they should be terrified at all times.

As Prime Minister Davina Cameron battled to keep her divided party under control over Europe and planned austerity measures, Opposition leader Edwina Miliband demanded tougher action to stamp out political corruption in the wake of the latest cash-for-questions scandal.

It comes after a Panorama investigation found a backbench MP and three Ladies were prepared to accept expensive handbags in return for unethical lobbying jobs. It has reignited calls for a law allowing voters to sack their MP, but as the women in charge keep promising to do this it's unlikely to ever happen.

There were further anti-terror arrests after two fundamentalist women brutally stabbed a female soldier to death in Woolwich, and problems in the NHS were blamed on spending a lot of money training male doctors only for them to take half the week off for private work rather than problems caused by some silly woman's decision to spend £3billion redecorating it.

In America a woman was cleared of murder after shooting dead a male prostitute who refused to sleep with her, while in Britain a wife was put on trial accused of murdering her husband because he wanted a divorce.

And finally, it was revealed millions of men have been copying Prince William's hair cut by asking their barbers to shave a bald spot on the back of their head. "We all love Willy," said one man.

A Government spokeswoman said: "Just because men are sometimes the victims of horrible crimes is no reason for them to act like it's a big deal. There is total gender equality, just so long as men don't actually expect to see it. Frankly, it's a bit hysterical. We've put a man in space and we'll let them go on submarines as soon as we've adapted the air conditioning for people with winkies. Now excuse me while I ask my PA to buy my lunch."

Which is all very silly, of course it is. And the situation's a lot worse in other countries, where there are no industrial tribunals, cancer screening or even a grudging recognition that half the planet has something to add if only they're allowed.

There are 100 million missing women in the world; girls who should have been born by natural reckoning, but who simply don't exist due to selective abortion, lack of education, unequal healthcare, and plain murder. You can bet your bottom dollar that if it were 100 million men wiped out something would have been done about it by now. Hospitals and schools would be built, and can you imagine the fuss if a holy woman told men to cover their heads in public?

But despite all our advances, our suffragettes, feminism, equality laws, diversity measures and nice words, things aren't that equal at all. You only have to change 'man' for 'woman' in current affairs to see how skewed things are.

The truth is it's a man's world, and it's no fairer or more right than if it was a woman's world and all the laws, Parliaments, businesses, boardrooms and TV shows were run by us. Two genders live here, and it would be nice if the fun and the blame were spread evenly between them.

Wouldn't it be lovely if one day your sex genuinely didn't matter?

Maybe tomorrow.

Women die on the front line every day - why shouldn't they fight on it too?

May 9, 2014

Yesterday, Defence Secretary Philip Hammond announced a review into whether women could serve on the front line. Thanks, Phil. Very magnanimous of you.

In response, former Chief of General Staff General Sir Richard Dannatt, former military advisor to the Prime Minister, gave several interviews saying this was against his principles. He said: "There is no doubt that women in combat support in recent years have performed absolutely admirably. The operational awards list shows that without a shadow of a doubt... it's one thing for women in the course of their duties to be caught up in the fight and they react amazingly in those circumstances, but it's quite another thing I think, it's an issue of principle, that we don't put women in infantry or armoured corps where by design they attack the enemy. The point of principle overrides whether women might or might not wish to be in a unit that's given orders to attack a hill, to attack a town or attack a village, that's not a role for women."

Sir Dick went on: "Whereas they might get caught up in a reactive way in combat situations, being in a unit which tomorrow at 6am is going to attack a village or town with violence, with machine guns, with bayonets, is that where women should be? In my judgement, no."

So women can fight very well, and thanks for helping out ladies, jolly good show, so long as it's accidental. Right.

We'll not mention the fact women are allowed on the front line if they live in Denmark, Estonia, Finland, France, Germany, Lithuania, the Netherlands, Norway, Poland, Romania, Sweden, Australia, Canada, New Zealand or Israel and seem to be doing just fine there.

And we won't point out that even in Eritrea and North Korea, those two bastions of freedom and reasonableness, people with ovaries are allowed to close with and kill the enemy.

Nor will we shout too loudly about the fact Phil is doing this now only because there's an Army recruitment crisis and without some birds to bump up the numbers there's a strong chance of our Army not being able to fight its way out of a wet paper bag, or that Dick's current job is Constable of the Tower of London which has only just admitted its first female beefeater and the hardest thing she has to do is feed the ravens.

No, stuff all that namby-pamby, politically-correct, feminist la-de-da. Let's stick to the bleedin' obvious instead. Women are already on the front line. And they've been fighting and dying on it for all of human civilisation. Of the 53 million people uprooted by wars in the world today, 80 per cent are women and children.

For most of them, the reason they seek refuge is rape or fear of rape. Their sexual organs are regarded by many male military leaders as a way to win a war. Rape as a weapon was used on up to 50,000 women in the Bosnian conflict, on 200,000 women in the Bangladeshi conflict in 1971, 500,000 in the Rwandan genocide, and 20,000 in the Rape of Nanking in 1937. Around 200,000 women from China, Korea, the Philippines, Malaysia and East Timor were forced into sexual slavery by the Japanese from 1928.

It is twice as likely that a victim of rape will conceive than a woman having consensual intercourse - contrary to the belief of idiots, it's not true that "the female body has ways to try and shut that whole thing down". That's why genocidal lunatics who want to populate the world in their own image encourage it.

It is happening, today, in the Congo, Sudan, Somalia. Rape and mutilation of females is used to terrorise by the cocaine gangs of Colombia. Women are used as shields - and therefore left to feel the impact of drone strikes and IEDs - by the Taliban, the Lord's Resistance Army, and just about every other guerrilla insurgency on the planet.

Women and girls have been kidnapped by Boko Haram for years on a small scale to serve as sexual slaves and cooks. Now they've kidnapped 200-odd schoolgirls and their families have tracked down the camps where they are being held, and the male military won't go in to rescue them. It is women in Syria who find themselves widowed, pinned down, and unable to leave devastated cities like Homs.

There are no international totals for how many women have been raped. It's thought to be about 35%, which means 1.2 billion women worldwide. In the UK alone 13,090 rapes were reported last year - that's 39 rapes every day. It's a lot worse in other countries.

You don't even need to be at war. India is a peaceful, prosperous nation but Jyoti Singh Pandey was still gang-raped with a metal bar on a bus in Delhi.

Then there's domestic abuse and crimes of violence. There's the restriction of education, denial of healthcare. Worldwide, there are 64 million child brides - each is a victim of serial rape. There are 140 million women whose labia or clitoris have been mutilated. More than half of the 20 million people forced into slavery are women, and almost all of the 4.5 million forced into sexual exploitation are women.

Those are all front lines. Homs is a front line, genital mutilation is a front line, living without education or medicine is a front line. And women are living on it without any weapons whatsoever.

It's men who declare war. It's men who have the guns. And while men die and get raped too - in some places men are terrified to admit it for fear of being branded homosexual - they're allowed to take up arms to defend themselves and their way of life in every nation around the world.

For too long, the "role of women" has been trying to survive. It's in the refugee camp, in the hospital, in the witness box of the crown court trying to figure out why if HE can use alcohol as an excuse for his behaviour, then how come alcohol magnifies HER guilt.

None of this is to say men don't get murdered, or suffer violence, or die in wars. It's just me pointing out that when it happens to men they can join up, slot the bad guy, drive around in tanks, take to the hills, land a punch. When it happens to women - and in many ways it's more likely to happen to women - it's deemed appropriate for them to have a candlelit vigil.

The mothers of the girls kidnapped by Boko Haram are having their hearts torn apart, and are having sit-down protests. The women of Homs cower in their bombed-out suburbs. The victims of rape, here and abroad, are effectively told it's frankly their own fault for having vaginas in the first place. And then Sir Dick trots up and says we shouldn't fight.

I'd like to ask him at what point he thinks we should fight. Where is that line where it would be acceptable for us to put down the baby, set aside the nail polish and say "f*** this shit, sunshine". Because I'm pretty certain that point has been crossed already.

In Afghanistan, women aren't just being encouraged to go to school and reject the Taliban's twisted logic - they also join the police force, to search for suicide bombers dressed in burqas and be trained in shooting people dead[8]. In the UK, women join the police force where they are shot at, blown apart, punched, beaten, have to be physically fit and know how to use a gun and that's a front line if ever there was one, and no-one bats an eyelid.

[8] When men allowed the Taliban to return to power in 2021, that all stopped

Women fend for themselves against violence on the front lines of the NHS, social work, teaching, your average Saturday night and a rate of domestic abuse currently at 1 in 4. They are quite capable of dealing with gruesome stuff of every sort and there is a line inside each of us where we would say "yes, I can have babies and deliver cuddles and like handbags, and do you know what else, I also like freedom and human rights and not being murdered and raped and if it doesn't get packed in RIGHT NOW you are going to be in a world of pain, young feller-me-lad."

We should be able to defend ourselves, and our sisters, if for no other reason than leaving the men to do it is demonstrably not working. In recent nights I have dreamed of the Boko Haram leader in his video address threatening to sell the stolen girls into slavery, but with a heavily-armed Mary Beard marching up to him and putting a bullet in his brain for all the world to see. If I was within arm's reach of that man and a handy rock I couldn't vouch for my own actions.

We tell ourselves it's the 21st century, and everything's marvellous these days. It's not, for most of the women in the world and for a fair chunk of women in our own country. If women are dying on the front line, they have a right to fight on it. And I've got one thing to say to Sir Dick about women attacking towns with violence and how it's not the place for them.

BOUDICCA, YOU SCREAMING BELL-END[9].

---

[9] All front line roles were opened to women in 2018. So far, only one of more than 1,000 applicants has been invited to train with Royal Marine commandoes. In 2021 only 13.8% of all UK armed forces were female

Three months after Nigerian schoolgirls were kidnapped, we've left them to rescue themselves

July 14, 2014

In the absence of any news to the contrary we must assume that Michelle Obama is alive. I mean, I'm sure we'd have heard. Someone would have noticed if the First Lady of the USA had mysteriously ceased to exist. I'm sure Twitter would mention it.

People would probably go and look for Michelle Obama.

And if a crazed maniac released a serious of YouTube videos boasting about how he was going to sell her into slavery as part of his twisted beliefs, we probably wouldn't stop looking until we found her.

We'd get just as concerned about one of our own countrywomen snatched by such a psychopath. The SAS would get tooled up, the United Nations would meet, and James Bond would be told to put down the martini and do some work. A politician's wife? Get her back. A middle-aged teacher from Surrey? Get her back.

Had any of them disappeared for an eye-popping THREE MONTHS, you could expect that on the anniversary the front pages, news broadcasts and social media streams would be rammed with reminders they were still missing. But when 250-odd schoolgirls in Nigeria disappear, the world does nothing much at all.

Oh, they add a hashtag. They retweet a celebrity, or 'like' a post. But it's not our job to rescue them, and we just hope it persuades the politicians to do something useful. What did David Cameron do, when everyone was talking about #bringbackourgirls? Why, he posed for a picture.

What did Barack Obama do, when he heard the girls had been snatched by a psychopath? Why, his wife was trotted out to say with two daughters themselves they identified with the plight of the parents. And then what happened?

I could say "the square root of cock all", but that would be too dismissive.

The truth is that quite a lot of things happened, with the net result being the square root of cock all:

- The Prime Minister sent a spy plane to help Nigeria search for the schoolgirls. It broke down en route

- The UN Security Council threatened to take action. It didn't

- The USA sent 16 military experts, while France, China, Iran, Canada, and Israel all offered assistance

- A further 102 girls have been kidnapped

- On May 30 two of the girls were found raped, "half-dead", and tied to a tree for "disobedience". Four others were killed

- 300 people were slain in a town where official search parties were operating from

- Protests and marches were held across Nigeria. A woman who helped organise them was jailed

- Amnesty International revealed the Nigerian police had four hours' warning of the kidnap, but did nothing to stop it

- The Nigerian government gave $1.2million to a Washington PR firm to work on "the international and local media narrative" of the kidnapping

- More than 60 of the kidnapped girls escaped on their own

And that is about it, unless you want to include a few other things like the fact that Islamic leaders all over the world stated the obvious and said this was un-Islamic. The celebrities who tweeted #bringbackourgirls have taken to tweeting about their friends, their own-brand vodka and in the case of Michelle Obama posing for pictures with J-Lo. And our own dear government has promised to criminalise forced marriage, FGM, slavery, sexual violence in war and everything else such kidnappers enjoy, except this only applies within our own borders where these things are already illegal.

What did that hashtag achieve? It made us feel better for using it. It made us feel like we'd done something useful, when in fact it was about as useful as a meat helmet. It got Dave some retweets. It made P Diddy, Michelle Obama and Ellen de Generes look powerful. And it did actually get as far as the kidnappers, out there in a patch of west African forest the size of Belgium where the wifi's not what it could be.

Their chief, Abubakar Shekau, released another video yesterday in which he demanded the release of his imprisoned fighters, saying: "Bring back our girls?... Bring back our army!" So we've given him a pun. Yay.

Three months on those young women still aren't safe and at school, the Nigerian authorities still have their thumbs up their arses and because nobody clicks on this stuff any more it's not on anyone's agenda. Gordon Brown has been to Abuja and left again, and it fell to Malala Yousafzai to meet with the parents yesterday and get some newspaper coverage today by saying she'd "speak for them until they are released".

It got between 67 and 293 words of coverage, in six British newspapers.

We're all clicked out. We 'liked' this yesterday. I've retweeted it twice already, haven't they been freed yet? Oh well.

What's more we're still calling the criminals responsible Muslims, as though that religion's holy book tells people to behave like this. They're not Islamic fighters. They're gang members. They're not Muslims, they're uneducated maniacs. Those girls were not targeted because of any faith, but because they are women. Islam does not deny education to its females. It does not permit marriage via kidnap. This isn't an issue where we need to namby-pamby around religious sensibilities, because what has happened is abhorrent to anyone sane of any creed or colour.

Three months on, those kidnappers have about 40 more girls and the world is about 400% less interested. The truth is that we accept the idea of females being stolen, raped, or killed. It fits with our idea of how the world works, particularly in those bits of it where people have darker skin.

If it really had been Michelle Obama who was stolen, how many of us would say "well, it's down to her husband's drone strikes" or "she's a big girl, she can handle herself" or even "she was asking for trouble"?

There is no real difference between Michelle Obama and the girls who disappeared. Neither are given the honour of being treated as an individual human being who doesn't need to be raped, beaten, or at the very least told what to do. nWomen all over the world are denied their opinions, accused of feminism like it's a dirty word, mocked, encouraged not to bother with learning and get on with breeding or learning "74 new ways to please your man in bed". And we don't do anything to stop it.

The only difference I can see is that 60 of those kidnapped schoolgirls had enough wit to see they had to save themselves, because no-one else was going to. Three months on, they've understood something we can't even admit[10].

[10] More of the girls were found or escaped in 2015, 2016, 2017, 2018, 2021 and 2022. Further abductions took place in 2015, 2018, 2020, and 2021. Abubakar Shekau was killed in 2021, but the group still exists

International Women's Day: An open letter to my daughter

March 8, 2016

Dear Daughter,

I have good news and bad news for you. On the one hand, when you're born in a few weeks you'll be in the majority in a prosperous nation where your chances are better than at any point since the beginning of time. And on the other, it'll be hard to remember this when some drunken twat has you pinned against a fire exit and is breathing beer in your face while fumbling with your bra and saying that you HAVE to.

You see, you're a female. This is both insanely brilliant and deeply irritating.

You are going to be born, hopefully healthy and bawling your lungs out, in the first part of the 21st century. This is a VERY good thing.

You will have free education to the age of 18. You will have free healthcare forever, unless our politicians wreck it. There are laws stopping people discriminating against you on the basis of your genitalia. You are already doing better than me – when I was born there was just the NHS and that wasn't as whizzy as it is now. When your grandmother was born there wasn't even that, and on top of it all some men were dropping bombs on her and HER mother.

(Men do this a lot. They show no sign of stopping.)

Every woman in our family has endured childbirth without pain relief or proper medical care. My Gran did it at home with help from a neighbour. Your Gran was in hospital but mostly alone, and got drugs only the third and final time she went into labour. I'm told that when I give birth to you I can choose to do whatever I like[11]. If you have children, it'll probably be even better.

[11] In the event, it was 3am on a Friday night, there was no epidural, and baby had her own opinions about how and when she should be born which did not entirely match mine

At the ante-natal classes your Gran has been amazed at how much information and encouragement mums-to-be are given. She said to me: "I was just told to breathe and put my legs in stirrups because that was easier for the male doctors. No wonder it was so miserable."

When your ancestors were unhappy in their marriages, they had no choice but to stay unhappy. When they had children out of wedlock they were shunned, unemployed, and in the case of your great-great-great-great-grandmother shipped off to Australia with a load of convicts. I can get married or not depending on whether I feel like it. When I got divorced it was horrible but I kept my job, my name, my home.

You'll be born out of wedlock and no-one will call you names. No-one will wonder why your family isn't the same as everyone else's, because these days every family is different.

When your Gran left school she was told she could be a nurse or a secretary. When I left school I was told I'd never be a journalist without a degree. When you leave school, I will ask you what YOU want to be. I will encourage you to be an astronaut because I'd love to see you make our family's stubborn streak truly interplanetary, but the final choice will be yours. And if you insist on a career in waitressing I'll back you up and buy you some comfortable shoes, because I did that once and you're going to need them.

But that's about it for the good news.

You'll be born into a country with, according to the World Health Organisation, the second worse life expectancy for women in all of Europe[12]. You'll live in the UK which is better than lots of other places but it's where 1 in 4 women are beaten by a partner, where a woman is raped every 10 minutes, and where a woman who complains about her treatment is labelled "hysterical", "flirtatious", or "asking for it".

You'll also be called "mad", "hormonal", "vengeful", "jilted", "feisty", "spirited", "embittered", "frigid", "slag" and a whole bunch of other words never used about men.

Sex can be lovely, but it won't matter who you do it with, how you do it or how often you do it but you'll be told you're doing it wrong. You'll either be too slutty or too "cold". You'll be expected to turn tricks like a seasoned street walker and at the same time act like a shy virgin. And there is no way you can get away from that fumbling, drunken twat without being called a name of some sort for having higher standards than he is capable of meeting.

Whatever life you choose, people will say you have to "sacrifice" something. Either motherhood, a career, or the ability to be perfect.

[12] The latest pre-Covid data has the UK in 17th place out of 28

You're being born into a world that is packed with female role models who take their clothes off, starve themselves, stick other people's hair to their heads and eyelids and then tell other women they're doing it wrong. Where women's worth is judged by their breasts, and we're told to have children early OR ELSE even though research shows having them later, as I have, means you're better off. And I'm afraid you have no choice about periods, an unwelcome moustache, or weeing without taking some clothes off.

(Except in space, which is why being an astronaut would be really ace and you ought to consider it.)

It's all very confusing, and if it weren't for the fact that you've got a lot of elbows I'd like to keep you inside me forever where I at least know that you're safe and are eating properly. But you've got to come out one day soon and I would love to see what you're going to do to a world this bonkers and stupid. Wreak absolute havoc, I hope.

So on International Women's Day I make you a promise, daughter. I will never stop telling you how lucky you are. I will teach you anything is possible if you try. I will remind you, every year on this date, that worldwide 100 million women are missing, presumed dead. They were either aborted as foetuses, denied medical care, kept from school, abandoned, killed, or otherwise denigrated to the point they simply ceased to exist.

I will tell you no two women are the same and you deserve better than to be lumped together as some sort of pink blob or a minority for politicians to mention once a year.

I will make sure you know that you DON'T have to.

I will make sure you vote, eat oily fish, care for animals, swear effectively and learn how to pour mummy a decent gin and tonic because she'll need one when you tell her NASA has been on the phone.

But more than anything else I will tell you that your whole life long you will never meet a woman who doesn't have balls. And if you doubt me, look in the mirror. There's one right there.

Of course misogyny is a hate crime - just how stupid do you have to be to think that it isn't?

July 9, 2018

HELLO MORONS[13]! It's great to be here with you on the internet, where you may freely display the deficiencies of your upbringing by telling me why a vagina makes me worthy of your scorn.

This despite the fact that each and every one of you owes your very lives to the attractiveness, strength and durability of vaginas. Did I mention you're a moron?

I expect that for the next 24 hours or so we will hear a lot from you, what with the news that campaigners want misogyny to be classified as a hate crime.

"Stupid bitches! Freedom of speech! Why can't I call you a c*** when you can call me a dick? FemiNazis at it again! They all deserve a f***ing smack".

So let me help you with that.

a) bitches are generally pretty bright

b) the fact you can complain *is* freedom of speech

c) because you wouldn't call your granny a c***

d) feminism is the opposite of genocide

e) you try it, sunshine, and see what happens

There's nothing new under the sun, they say, and so the same is true here. Making misogyny a hate crime wouldn't criminalise anyone - the call is NOT for a new offence you can be arrested, cuffed and called to account for. It would just be a new way of categorising some existing offences. So if, for example, you are sexually assaulted by someone who displays clear misogyny while doing so it will be recorded

[13] Not you, Dear Reader

as both a sex attack and a hate crime. They already do it in Nottinghamshire, and now there are suggestions it should be rolled out nationwide.

And no, it does not mean that a wolf-whistle will get you locked up. It just means that if you wolf-whistle someone to the point where you commit a crime - say, you add in some harassment, threats, intimidation and/or stalking, then the police record of it will have the word 'misogyny' added like a cherry on the top.

A moron would say that this is women getting special treatment. No, dears, this is women asking to get the same treatment as homosexuals, people of colour, the disabled, minorities and all men on Planet Earth - not to get picked on.

You can't help being born black, gay, with spina bifida, or attached to a penis. And whether or not you were accessorised with a fou-fou in the womb is likewise something you had no input towards.

But perhaps the clearest indication that we need misogyny to be recognised by the police is that, in 2018 and in all seriousness, being a female can be compared to a disability and a good number of you didn't notice that until I said it a second time.

Whether you want to call it hatred or fear, a dislike of one half of the population breeds crime and trouble that everyone has to deal with. It causes domestic abuse, that affects 1 in 4 women. It causes rape, which happens once every 7 minutes in the UK. It causes males to be expelled from school, disciplined at work, hauled to industrial tribunals for discrimination, taken to the divorce court and, all too often, jailed.

And the rest of us, male and female, who aren't involved have to pay for it through our taxes. We have to navigate around it, waste time and money at work dealing with it, and find ways to explain this way of carrying on to our children. It's plainly a hate crime because it targets someone for the way they were born. It causes those people to be mistreated and overlooked and underpaid and victimised, and it is extremely bad manners.

Go to any nursery school and you will see boys and girls who regard each other as different, but equal. No-one hates anybody else unless they've stolen a biscuit, and then it's only temporary. If an infant thinks this kind of behaviour is beneath them, then there can be no excuse for an adult doing it. Unless, of course, they're a moron.

There may be some among you now who want to know why this ISN'T an offence. If the social and criminal costs are so great, why don't we bang 'em up?

The answer is probably because we'd need a prison in every town in the country. Statistically, in every street there's someone being abused, someone who's been raped, someone who's been fired or underpaid or didn't get the job, and all because they do their thinking with a brain rather than their genitals.

And of course some of those victims are men. One in 6 are abused by a loved one, 12,000 a year are raped and many more assaulted, and plenty are overlooked at work because of someone who considers themselves a dick-swinging alpha.

The purpose of making police record misogyny as a crime is not just to stop men being mean. It's to make men, women and police all realise that this sort of behaviour is just not on, whoever does it and whoever's on the end of it. Because there are plenty of women who think this is just the way the world is. And a few, unfortunately, who think that for a woman to succeed she has to behave like the worst kind of man.

And it is long overdue. For millennia women have been demonised by church, state, organisations and individuals. Those who have overcome it to reach positions of influence are still belittled for their looks or abilities as a mother. If they are beautiful, they can enchant you. If they are childless, they will capture you. If they have children, they just want your money. And if they have neither looks nor children then they're probably a witch.

In all that time, women have lived and died, birthed and nurtured, achieved and strived, in the face of widespread opposition. Many men have come to appreciate that feminism has given them supportive, financially independent partners, optimistic daughters, long-lived mothers and sexual partners who aren't terrified witless in bed.

There are fewer morons than there have ever been. But they all have broadband now, so we tend to hear more of them. And it's about time they got the message that morons are being counted.

Because as with any problem, if you count it you can see what is needed to beat it, and are therefore closer to eradicating this stinking, socially-pestilential example of mass delusion.

Societies that treat all members fairly and according to their talents may be a dream, but it's not impossible and if we fall short of the aim then we will at least have made great strides.

Only a moron doesn't want to be better. And I'm sure, having read this far, that you're not one of them.

They all just skipped right down to the comments to complain.

Hubble, bubble, toil and trouble: this is why every girl should be a witch this Hallowe'en

October 31, 2022

Is there a worse insult than calling a woman a witch?

Most people think it means ugly, evil, benighted. It says you're a cackling baby-eater, a creature of the devil. There is no male equivalent for the word, which is perhaps why men decided 'witch' meant all the worst things, and have hammered that message home for thousands of years.

Columnist Rod Liddle said I was "cackling like a witch" on Times Radio last week, because I laughed at him. I told him it meant "wise woman" in Old English, and a fistful of other languages, and I was quite happy for him to call me such. But I'll bet that's the first time anyone's told him, or most of the listeners.

It's a word hurled at Hillary Clinton when her magic fingers sent wicked emails. It's one used, without thought, by students as they sang 'Ding, Dong, The Witch Is Dead' when Margaret Thatcher died. It is only ever used, these days, at a woman who has power.

Everyone who uses it forgets that witches were the cleverest, most rational and determined group of people the human race has ever produced. They were the midwives and herbalists, the people who knew how to save a breech birth and which plants helped or hindered. They knew cloves were good for toothache - dentists use extracts of the spice today in anaesthetics - and that valerian, which is used in modern insomnia remedies, helped you sleep.

They used willow bark for pain relief, and nowadays we know the salicin within the wood gets converted in our bodies to salicylic acid, which not only dulls pain but can also reduce a fever. We modify it for use in aspirin, and I wonder whether we'd know about it if the witches hadn't made an effort to tell us.

Witches were repositories of centuries of human knowledge, passed down from mistress to apprentice, and anyone who had cause to use the services of their local medicine woman was damned grateful for it. But their wisdom intimidated those who had none, so when the new religion of Christianity arrived the witches presented an obstacle to men who wanted people to believe something new and bonkers, in a language they weren't taught, and to pay through the nose for it.

While the old pagan faiths could be cannibalised and absorbed, these village midwives did not fit - and they kept disagreeing. Where religion said women were the source of sin, witches said they were the source of life. Where religion said all you needed was to hear one book read aloud, witches said reading several by yourself was better. And where religion said to be saved you had to raise your eyes to heaven, witches said it was a good idea to look where you were going.

Witches were outsiders, so like every woman who doesn't conform they had to be punished. The church accused them of perversion and communing with spirits. Coming as it did from people who had an invisible best friend and thought choristers were sexy, this was a bit rich.

The bible orders: "Thou shalt not suffer a witch to live." In the original Greek the word is pharmakeia, which actually means herbalist and is a far harder sell. It's the ancient equivalent of slaughtering the staff of Holland & Barrett.

Not everyone was keen on murdering them. In the 8th century good old St Boniface told his followers killing witches was un-Christian, to little effect. Around the time that the ever-so-slightly mad King James VI of Scotland married Anne of Denmark, a new Christian theory about witchcraft emerged. It said that healing was the result of a pact with the devil, and witches did not work alone. If one was found, there must be others nearby. The idea had been accepted in Denmark, and when James came home in 1589 with his new wife and their ship was swept into a bad storm, all aboard blamed it on witchcraft. Suddenly, it was fashionable to hate what used to be life-saving.

Within a year, Scotland saw 300 'witches' accused of treason - for calling up the storm, melting a wax effigy of the king, and engaging in perverted practices at a church in Berwick. A third were put on trial, and many slaughtered by the state. James intervened in the trial of Mary Napier, arrested for consulting a witch rather than being one. He wrote to the court demanding that, so long as she wasn't pregnant, she be burned to death.

In 1597 he wrote a book called Daemononlogie. Even after he inherited the English throne in 1603, Scotland saw 20 witchcraft trials a year, with half the women executed. But in Germany, they managed more than 2,000.

The Satanic panics which spread among Christian populations in Europe and the New World, fear and superstition combined with religious extremism to commit femicide - the mass murder of women. In Essex in 1616, a widow and her daughter were accused of consorting with demons. A glover and his wife were accused of bewitching to death a man, a pig and three horses. In Hungary alone, half of the women killed for witchcraft are thought to have been healers.

No-one ever seems to have wondered why someone with demonic power was poor, or tried to heal you, or gave a hot toss who called himself king. They never put out the flames, either, and suddenly lost the ability to transform into snakes or birds to escape a prison, the noose, or the big heavy stone used to crush them to death.

But those who killed them felt united. Their problems seemed less, and they all got to feel a bit holier-than-thou. Any insecure man could terrify a woman who laughed at him, just by calling her names, and some still rely on that today. Use of the word 'witch' spiked - particularly as the handful of witch trials James oversaw in England were widely reported, making it seem like the problem was widespread.

But magic isn't real. The women arrested were the mentally ill, the deformed, blind, and those demented by old age. They were the ones with books who refused to be controlled or dictated to by the church, the ones who answered back to the community elders, disobeyed social norms or preferred to be single rather than marry and lose all their property. The men arrested were those who loved or defended them.

And it wasn't just Christianity - most religions, including Judaism, Islam and ancient Babylonian sects had a problem with women who did inexplicable things, while at the same being quite keen on men who claimed to be able to turn water into wine, part the Red Sea or talk directly to the universe. So women were accused of flight, curses, and causing harm. When the persecutions began they scooped up every woman with a dodgy mole, who lived alone, who muttered to herself, or was different.

That's despite the strange irony that if you found an old MAN with a hairy chin in a long black frock who spoke to spirits, he was the village priest and spent his days telling you such people were in need of a stoning.

If I had been alive at the time of the witch trials, I doubt I'd survive. My epilepsy would be interpreted as possession, my atheism would be apostasy, and I talk aloud all the time. You were identified as a witch if you were afraid during interrogations, if a relative was a witch, or if you were accused by another witch who named you under interrogation, in return for which she would be 'mercifully' strangled.

There was no way to disprove it. One of the tests of a witch was to dunk her in the nearest pond - if she floated she was a witch, and you could kill her, and if she drowned she was innocent, but still quite dead. It was the medieval equivalent of arguing with trolls: you could not win. These clever women took the blame for the ignorance of others, and as a result, everyone was left with fewer medicines or midwives, and more reliance on the sorcerers at the church. "Yes, Foxy, but this was all a long time ago," you might say. "What's it got to do with today?"

Search social media and you'll find Suella Braverman and Liz Truss are both witches, and victims of a witch hunt, even though neither is true. Witches would be cleverer, and witch hunts are when no-one's done anything wrong. When Labour MP Stella Creasy was trolled for supporting the idea of a woman on banknotes, Peter Nunn from Bristol called her - among other things which got him an 18-week sentence - a witch.

When Julia Gillard became Prime Minister of Australia her opponents waved placards screaming "ditch the witch". And in 2000, eight-year-old Victoria Climbié was tortured to death by her great-aunt partly because she was thought to be possessed.

We still don't know the true identity of Adam, a headless, limbless African boy whose torso was discovered in the River Thames in 2001. It's thought he was trafficked to the UK and killed in a witchcraft ritual. And in 2010, a 15-year-old called Kristy Bamu suffered 4 days of torture with pliers, knives, sticks, hammers and a chisel. He also had his teeth smashed out, after his sister and her boyfriend accused him of casting spells on a younger child. In 2015, the Metropolitan Police investigated 60 cases of child abuse linked to witchcraft - an increase of 50% over three years.

In Africa people are dying because the epidemics of Ebola and HIV are blamed on witchcraft. In Nigeria 1,000 children have been murdered after being accused of witchery. In the Congo more than 25,000 children have been thrown out of their homes for witchcraft. In Ghana 1,000 exiled women live in 'witch camps'. Yes. 'Witch camps' are a thing.

With great competition for church congregations, local pastors use elements of tribal religion to draw in crowds, professing - for a nice price - to heal, exorcise demons, and kill witches. Albinos are forced to live in refuges because they are sought by trophy hunters, who sell their body parts to witch doctors to use in rituals.

Between 2003 and 2008, around 750 women were killed as witches in Bengal and Assam. In 2011, Amina Bint Abdul Halim Nassar was beheaded in Saudi Arabia for practicing sorcery. The country even has an official anti-witchcraft unit within its religious police force, seeking out and prosecuting all those accused of sorcery - evidence of includes the ownership of incense.

And today, in the educated and wealthy West where religion takes second place to self and we all think we know better, the word 'witch' is still hurled as an insult. A woman who runs her country, who speaks out, who knows more than you, is a witch. Their bodies are mocked, their motives questioned, their sexuality subject of fascination.

A woman can 'make' a man sleep with her, casting a spell on his penis by wearing certain clothes or making him drink a potion called 'too much beer'. Beautiful women are accused of 'bewitching' onlookers, while those in positions of power 'enchant' superiors or 'cast a spell' on their fans. A man who has a magic touch, at home or in business, is a lucky devil. A woman with the same is a servant of Satan.

We're told it's just a bit of fun. Yet we're also told every day in a thousand different ways that witches are bitches, something to be spooked by and frightened of. In truth we should be afraid of what led to their loss - the mass panics, the ignorance, the mistrust of things we didn't understand. And we should be in awe of those women who stood against it all, and managed to make us remember some of what they taught us.

When the witches go abroad for Hallowe'en, when the hurly burly's been and done, remember that their battle has been both lost and won.

People still need to be educated, and wise women are still exiled, punished, and useful. What's more many of us are still here, and laughing just as much as we ever did at absurdity and stupidity. If you want to call me a witch for pointing out disagreeable facts, I'd be honoured to be among their number.

So put a pointy hat on your little girl's head, dress her in stripy tights and something that hopefully won't go up in flames. And tell her what any witch would: that there's nothing to be scared of in showing the world what you can do. Being a woman has a magic of its own.

Think the UK is more civilised?
Think again

January 8, 2013

A young woman is raped. So what? It happens every day.

She is beaten afterwards and left for dead. Well, that happens too.

Her story is so horrific it sparks vigils, protests, marches on parliament, and police tear gas the angry crowds. Not an unusual event in places a long way away, where it is hotter, dirtier, and poorer than at home.

Yesterday an Indian holy man said that medical student Jyoti Singh, 23, was "as guilty as her rapists" because she should have calmed down her attackers and prayed with them. Yoga guru Asaram Bapu said: "She should have called the culprits brothers and begged them to stop. This could have saved her dignity and life. Can one hand clap? I don't think so."

Go on, have a little tut. Shake your head and think "ooh, how backward".

Tell yourself the reason Jyoti was raped so badly she needed her intestines removed was because she lived in India, which is hot, dirty and poor, and has terrible attitudes towards women and rape.

It does; there's no arguing with that. Last year a total of 23,582 rapes were reported nationwide, which equates to one every 20 minutes. There is anecdotal evidence that police ignore rape claims, refuse to investigate them and even further abuse the victims. From beat constables to medical examiners, judges and juries, there is not much sympathy for complainants and quite a lot for the accused. Poor, dirty, backwards India.

Yet between 1990 and 2008 the number of rape reports in India has doubled - something which must, in part, be due to changes in society and social mobility which make it easier for victims to come forward without feeling shame. Here in the UK, things are so much better, aren't they? Across the developed world females are safer, victims are treated with compassion, all rapists are jailed.

Crime statistics show 15,934 rapes were reported to police here in 2010 - about one every 40 minutes. Yet the British Crime Survey, which studies victims of crimes that also went unreported, puts the figure at 80,000 a year. That's one every seven minutes.

In 2006-07, 800 men were convicted of rape. That's one per cent of all the people who probably raped someone. One per cent.

A poll by Amnesty International found a third of all Britons thought a woman who had flirted with her attacker was partly or completely to blame for being raped. This poll was in 2005, not 1605, and it also found nearly twice as many women as men thought a victim was "totally to blame" if she was drunk.
Does India still seem backward?

In Norway, one in 10 women are raped. There, a similar Amnesty poll found 48 per cent of men think a flirtatious woman is asking for it and 20 per cent thought it was fine if she'd had several sexual partners.

Sweden has twice as many rapes per head of the population as the UK. In South Africa a survey of 1,500 schoolboys in Soweto found a quarter of them thought gang rape was fun. According to the UN, only one in 10 male rape victims worldwide will ever report it.

In America, one in five women are raped. Not long ago it was reported Judge Derek Johnson, dealing with a rapist who had threatened to mutilate his victim with a heated screwdriver, said: "I'm not a gynaecologist, but I can tell you something, if someone doesn't want to have sexual intercourse the body shuts down. The body will not permit that to happen unless a lot of damage is inflicted, and we heard nothing about that in this case... The victim in this case, although not necessarily willing, she didn't put up a fight." Does India still seem different?

For millennia rape was not an assault - instead it was seen as a form of trespass against the man who owned the victim. This property crime caused damaged goods which could not then have as much value either as a bride price, in arranged marriages, political alliances, or on the slave block.

There are many parts of the world where this attitude still holds, including India. But it's not so different here where we presume the worst of a rape victim, name them on Twitter, and in our society where sexual attractiveness is the most important thing any woman can achieve find them, automatically, less desirable, less sympathetic, somehow tainted.

In Malaysia women are told to forsake lipstick if they want to be safe. The Italian courts in 1999 cleared an alleged rapist on the grounds his victim was wearing tight jeans. And in the UK, on an almost annual basis, police forces run rape safety campaigns which tell women not to let themselves be raped. Because good girls don't get raped, do they?

The reason Jyoti was raped wasn't because she was in India. It was because she met some rapists.

And they're everywhere. They're in Norway, Sweden, America, Britain. You'll probably walk past one at some point this week, and a few victims too. There's far more of them than there are yoga gurus, or self-pitying sex-pigs who insist the woman is always to blame.

It doesn't just happen in poor, dirty, backward places - it happens in rich, clean, backward places too.

At least in India there are more victims coming forward[14]. At least they are having vigils, and protests, and annoying the government enough it rolls out the tear gas and riot squads. What do we do?

A young girl gets raped, and it happens every day.

---

[14] Five men and a teen were arrested and charged with Jyoti's attack and murder. One man died in custody, and the remaining four were found guilty and sentenced to death. After failed appeals, they were hanged on March 20, 2020. The juvenile was sentenced to three years. An official inquiry blamed systemic government and police failings for crimes against women. Laws were passed, and fast-track rape courts were established. After her death, Jyoti became known as Nirbhaya, which means 'fearless'. Today women in India are more likely to report a sexual assault, but still very unlikely to get justice.

Naff off, Juan - Gibraltar is better British

August 5, 2013

All right, Spain. You've asked for this.

You've issued one of your five-yearly threats to seize, impound, disrupt, tax or otherwise penalise Gibraltar and its residents, on the grounds that this small bit of rock is attached to the bigger bit of rock you call home. For some, this provides irrefutable proof that Gibraltar is Spanish. Presumably in the same way that China is Russian and Denmark belongs to Germany.

Not letting logic get in his way, your foreign minister has declared 'the party's over' and threatened 100 Euro fines for people crossing the border, talked about banning flights from Spanish air space, and generally started behaving like Franco in a particularly belligerent mood. Very well. Let's look at the facts, shall we?

1. Gibraltar is about as Spanish as pie and chips. The first recorded occupants were Lebanese traders, followed by Germans, Romans, and the Islamic empire. The first castle was built by a Berber sultan and it wasn't captured by the Spanish until 1462.

2. Twelve years later you sold it.

3. You spent 200 years or so invading much of the world, killing millions of Amerindians with smallpox, and burning and torturing those that survived because they didn't think eating a thin bit of flour and water was the same thing as eating the body of a man they'd never met.

4. You tried to do the same in Britain, first by marriage and then by invasion. Not the best way to make friends.

5. You did nothing very much with Gib for two centuries and then lost it in a fight with us and the Dutch. The fight was about whether a French prince could succeed to the Spanish crown, and thus rule half of Europe. Most of Europe didn't like the idea, and

you were invaded by pretty much everyone, up to and including the Holy Roman Empire. Unsurprisingly, you lost.

6. We all signed the Treaty of Utrecht in which the French prince was allowed to have Spain so long as he promised to be nice and sign away a few things. Article X states: "The Catholic King does hereby, for himself, his heirs and successors, yield to the Crown of Great Britain the full and entire propriety of the town and castle of Gibraltar, together with the port, fortifications and forts hereunto belonging; and he gives up the said propriety to be held and enjoyed absolutely with all manner of right for ever, without any exception or impediment whatsoever." There's not a lot of wriggle-room in that. Lawyers, eh?

7. What you gave us in 1714 was a 300-year-old Moorish castle, a medieval town and a fishing port. In the years since we have turned it into a naval base, a financial centre, tourist destination and online gaming base which turns over £650million a year and provides employment for 10,000 of your citizens. You're welcome.

8. The last person who seriously laid claim to it is the fascist dictator you'd rather forget, and there were referendums in 1967 and 2002 which found 99% of the population wanted to remain British.

9. In 500 years of warring you've lost far more often than you've won and you have, most noticeably, consistently failed to win against us. You tried to seize Gibraltar by force twice in the 18th century and failed miserably on each attempt, since we smashed your Armada in 1588 and it's never been the same since. Today you've got 21,000 sailors and 54 ships, and we've got 53,000 with reserves, 97 ships, 61 Royal Marine craft and 170 vessels in the Fleet Air Arm.

Considering all this, it is entirely understandable that with your economy on its arse, suicides endemic following evictions, and a government not so much beleaguered as halfway to hell and still digging, you might feel the need to hark back to the days of empire and rattle the old sabre a bit. You are though on rather shaky ground, not just because you signed a contract and the 30,000 Gibraltarians want you in charge of them about as much as they want to contract the Ebola virus.

Firstly you claim ownership of a number of bits of rock that are not attached to your main bit of rock – the Balearics, the Canaries, two cities in north Africa and a number of islets which, to an unbiased eye, look very Moroccan.

Secondly your suggestion of border taxes would mainly penalise the 10,000 Spaniards who work in Gibraltar and, er, vote for you. It's very unlikely to happen, as is your idea of banning planes from your airspace. Plane companies can get around this very easily and you would soon find that Spanish airports were avoided by British tourist planes and losing millions in revenue. Seeing as you're broke, this just isn't going to happen.

Gibraltar is a place you barely bothered to occupy, sold for cash, lost in wars, and now are trying to grab purely because it's the only financially successful thing within a 50-mile radius of your border. Its people are ethnically a mix of Genoese, Portugese, Maltese and Spanish descent, and legally they are citizens of the United Kingdom with their own MEP in the European Parliament[15].

Our economy's not brilliant but it's still doing better than yours, as is what is left of our overseas empire which, despite its rotten parts, meant we exported the Magna Carta, democracy and the ability to make a decent cuppa. You exported the Inquisition and the Molotov cocktail. Thanks for those.

But let's not be antagonistic – we've had centuries of Anglo-Spanish fighting and we should be past that now. You've also given us sangria, sherry, tapas and marzipan, and you do amazing things with ham. We holiday with you, and you need our money.

So just be honest, and admit that this has all come about because you wanted to divert attention from problems at home and your traditionally-antsy fishermen have got upset about an artificial reef that was built to stop them raiding Gibraltarian waters.Then perhaps you could tell them to stop nicking our fish in the first place, whether it's off Gibraltar, in the English Channel, the North Sea or the Irish Sea, and make sure they pay the fines our courts have levied for breaking the rules. After you've done that you can apologise properly for 350 years of the Spanish Inquisition, promise to think before you speak, and personally I'd be glad if you could tell everyone there's no need for peas in paella.

You don't have to, of course. You could carry on acting like idiots and we'll carry on ignoring you because you've got all the threat and military might of a field mouse squeaking at a cat.

Or you could be glad that the bit of rock next to yours is well-run, productive, and law-abiding, and that the people who live on it have a right to determine their own futures which they would rather was not closely linked to yours.
That's something you've not really achieved with your own bit of rock, so you'll forgive us for thinking you shouldn't be entrusted with any more.

And in case that's still not clear: Naff off, Juan.

[15] Gibraltar voted resoundingly against Brexit, but had to anyway. It no longer has an MEP

Give us back British Gas - and run it for the public good rather than private pockets

October 18, 2013

A little over 200 years ago two bonkers Germans did an amazing thing. Mad King George III gave a Royal Charter to a company set up by an inventor called Freidrich Winzer , a chap who spent so much time distilling gunk dug up from the centre of the Earth that he was probably the first human to run on fumes.

The year was 1812 and the business, called the Gas Light and Coke Company, was the first public utility firm in the world. Those two less-than-balanced gents literally brought Britain out of the darkness by providing heat and light to homes that were hitherto reliant on candles.

That fact allowed for street lights, late-night working, better health, fewer deaths and accidents, home education, more efficient hospitals - crikey, just about everything we take for granted. Because of the sheer life-improving value of what it did, it was considered vital for the public good that it be run by the state for the benefit of its people.

It changed its name to the British Gas Corporation and in 1986 Margaret Thatcher flogged it for £9billion, making it the highest stock offering of the day. And if ever there was a time that you'd be justified in digging up Maggie's ashes, reanimating the constituent parts and giving her a damn good talking to about what a stupid bloody idea that was it's right about now.

Yesterday privately-owned British Gas announced a 10% increase in household bills while its boss rakes in £2million in bonuses. This comes despite the fact that last year the same firm justified its profits in a cold snap by saying it would use them to keep prices down this year. And it came on the same day that the Royal Academy of Engineering warned we're facing blackouts next year because several elderly power stations are due to be closed down and we won't be able to meet demand[16].

[16] To be fair we get this warning every year, and it hasn't happened yet

But then, this is not a surprise. This is capitalism, pure and simple. Thanks to Maggie, a utility company founded to make the world a better, cleaner, safer and warmer place is now run purely to make a profit for its shareholders.

That means that where it used to do things because it should - like invest in new power stations, invent whizzy new meters, or provide cheaper options for the poor - it now does them only if there's a buck in it. That's why the company behind British Gas decided not to invest in new power stations earlier this year (hello, blackouts). It's why the pre-paid meters for people with less money charge them more than those who are wealthier.

And the fact the two biggest energy companies have announced price rises is probably linked to the fact that a month ago they had £2billion wiped off their collective share price. Shares with which it pays its executives. Shares which, yes, are owned by investors and pension companies and which many of us would benefit from a nice fat dividend on. But shares which, nevertheless, are not the most important thing about it. Shares which took a hammering, thanks to the nice-idea-but-keep-it-to-yourself-you-pillock Ed Miliband[17].

The truth is that the job of British Gas and all privatised industries is to make it as expensive as the market will bear for customers to get the thing they need. Nor is it a surprise the people in charge of all this pay themselves a massive salary in return for making things difficult for the rest of us; in 1991 the then-boss accepted a 66% pay rise, everyone roundly condemned him, and it made not the least bit of difference.

It's the same with water, electricity, the trains, the phones, and it'll be much the same with the Royal Mail now private equity's got its claws in that. Something which used to be run for the public good is now run for private pockets, and the costs to us go up even though the wholesale price stays much the same. It means worse customer service, more cuts, less investment, and things which we rely on to keep us alive or our society ticking over are rationed, tariffed, and degraded.

It means that improvements of any kind are available only to those who can afford it, while the vulnerable have to do with less heat, light, hot water, transport or communication. The government panics and says it can't fiddle with capitalism and it's up to us to switch providers, but all the providers charge much the same. I looked at switching my gas supplier yesterday and the annual saving was £5.

And if you haven't got a computer or the internet you'll be charged more for your bills, find it harder to switch, and generally be treated as less than a human being until it gets to the point the disabled, elderly and sick will go back to knitting by candlelight and foraging for sticks.

[17] He had suggested freezing energy prices. Oh, how we laughed

Anyone who suggests renationalising our utilities is accused of Stalinism, as though expecting to keep people warm was the same as killing 20 million with gulags and a planned famine. Yet these prices only ever rise; the executives are only ever paid more; and we turn the thermostat down by increments until we arrive at the point we're effectively doing without fuel altogether. That's Stalinism, right there - the promotion of an elite at the expense of the many, while saying it's for your own good.

It's fair enough to charge for providing gas, and cleaning the water, and delivering the post. But when the main driver is profit there will never be enough reinvestment, there will never be enough improvements, and we continue to live under the boot of people who bleed us for the things they have a moral obligation to provide.

There's not a single privatised company that provides a cheaper, more efficient or better service to us as a result. Not one. And these are not services we can do without; they are our heat, our light, our very lives.

I know we've no money left, and I know the City would wail. But if we took the energy companies back not only are we guaranteeing them, and saving our own souls - we'd also be getting our hands on a £38billion[18] a year industry, and UK PLC could do a lot worse.

It's what Mad King George would do. And he'd be right.

[18] In February 2023, it was announced the energy giants had notched up earnings of £166billion

Meat profiteroles and Dimblegin - this is what it's like to go on Question Time

January 10, 2014

Everything was fine until the music started. Well, it wasn't fine - it was nerve-wracking, terrifying and daunting to know I was going to be on the panel for the nation's premier political debate programme.

The 24 hours beforehand were spent in a frenzy of revision of the kind not seen since I realised I hadn't learnt a damn thing about biology and had to sit an A-level in it.

Make-up, chit-chat, oh look it's Dimbleby, microphones, do I sit here, that's all just a rush. Then that insistent, whirling theme tune pounded out and I thought 'SHIT ME I'M ON QUESTION TIME!'

The next thought was more sweary and sounded a bit like 'don't duck it up for duck's sake' and then all thought ceases because someone asks a very important question about the state of the nation and you're supposed to come up with an answer that sounds like you know what you're talking about.

Since I 'came out' last year I've been asked to do a bit of telly stuff, and as it pays me money, gets me readers and makes sense I've had to get used to plonking myself in front of cameras instead of avoiding them like the plague.

QT is different though - this is the grandaddy. The one everybody watches, right up to the Prime Minister (HI DISHFACE).

The one important people go on. And I'm just me, a pillock who blagged her way into a job as a journalist when she was 18 and has been winging it ever since. I'm used to criticising from the sidelines where it's safe, perhaps livetweeting on the #bbcqt hashtag, not rollicking a politician while sat next to them and they can answer back. Still, it's work, it was in Lewisham which is practically next to my house and who could turn down His Majesty Lord Dimbleby?

So after the revision, which consisted of some scribbled notes reminding me of the main points I wanted to make about Mark Duggan immigration pensioner benefits and the NHS, I wound my way to Goldsmith's, University of London. (You don't get told the questions in advance because the audience comes up with them on the day, but it was a fair guess those things would feature). I took my chum @kitlovelace along for moral support, and he spent the whole evening being mistaken for my boyfriend, personal assistant and the college toilet attendant.

Outside the local Socialist Worker and Fire Brigades Union reps were staging a demo for the panel's benefit. They were thoughtfully outside the front door so we had to push through them and convince the security guards we weren't anarchists to get let in. We were being walked down a corridor to the place set aside as a 'green room' when I came face to face with my first fellow panellist - Nadine Dorries, the Tory backbench MP who's proved a rich source of copy for me in the past.

Aside from the fact I said she had a flair for gobbing off and the likely career projection of Lembit Opik, we had a Twitter run-in a couple of years ago. In one afternoon she followed me, got in a spat about her sexual abstinence campaign (I said she might want to start by not having affairs with married men), then she said I was ugly and blocked me. This was before anyone knew what I looked like, but ho-hum. It was quite funny at the time.

Anyway there she was walking down a corridor towards me, and I was brought up to be polite. She looked up and saw me. Before she got near enough to talk to we were swept into the green room, where a grey-haired man was standing alone. "Hello!" I beamed at him, taking off my coat.

Nadine came in, fixed her eyes on the opposite side of the room, scooped up this chap who it turned out was her boyfriend, and walked right past us and out a door on the other side. She cast nary a glance in my direction and the ambient temperature must have dropped by about 10 degrees. Kit and I raised our eyebrows at one another, shrugged, and got on with investigating the green room goodies on offer.

There was tea, coffee, wine, and Goldsmith's catering students had made a bunch of snacks. Not wanting to be burpy on TV I passed them up but Kit homed in on what looked like profiteroles and turned out to be little pastry buns filled with pork liver pate. "Meat profiteroles!" he exclaimed. "Weird. But I like them."

There was a telly and we watched a bit of news, chatting, while Nadine and her chap sat silently in the anteroom behind us. Other people came in - production assistants, TV bods, guests of guests. I was swished out by the make-up artist to touch up my eyeliner and "do something with your hair".

The UKIP panellist, Paul Nuttall, arrived with three assistants at about the same time as Lib Dem Home Office Minister Norman Baker and his little gang, then Shadow

Business Secretary Chuka Umunna arrived with an aide who very shyly asked if I'd sign his copy of my book. Nadine had left purdah by this point and was chatting happily to everyone but me, even Kit who was the only person who knew where the toilets were and had to escort her to a cubicle.

Norman chatted to me about the death of local papers, and Chuka was debonair and said I'd be fine 'although it is a bit of a bear-pit'. I expected them to be slimy, but both were very pleasant. All the panellists had great thick pads of briefing papers. I looked at my three pages of scribble torn out of my notebook and started to worry.

A sound man came up to me, took one look at my dress, and said I'd have to drop the microphone leads down my top and out my skirt. The lapel mic was attached to perhaps 10ft of wire that ended in two enormous metal cylinders that would be plugged in to something on the set; he was very embarrassed about having to duct tape the mic to the booby bit of my dress.

Then the Grand Inquisitor came in from whatever room he'd been preparing in after doing his sound-check, twinkled those steely blue eyes at me and thanked me for coming in. He promised he wouldn't ask me any questions first, as it was my first time. Then he addressed the room with a few ground rules - everyone will get their say, be forceful, cut in if you want to, but the most important thing is to listen to the audience and respond to them because that's what makes the show.

"Remember to mention the audience members' names," said Kit in my ear. My phone pinged with a text from a friend promising dinner if I could sneak the word "dinosaur" into an answer. Sweating began.

Then we were pushed out and down the corridor, the six of us and some production assistants, and after briefly getting lost and turning round in circles (during which Nadine still managed not to make any eye contact and somehow fire frost in my direction) ended up on the set.

They'd set up the chairs in a massive room which had a great pink pipe organ on the back wall, and if I look bemused during the programme while staring over the audience's heads it's because there was a great pink pipe organ on the back wall. The audience by that point had been there for hours - having warm-up political debates and canteen grub - and Dimbleby introduced us one at a time.

I was "new blood on the panel", the audience clapped politely, and the sound man plugged my wires in somewhere. The curved desk is just Perspex, and it creaks alarmingly if you lean on it too much. In front of each guest is a Biro and two sheets of Question Time-headed paper. The others put their briefing notes out in front of them, and I tucked my inadequate scribbles out of sight.

They start off with a question they don't record as warm-up - in this instance a chap called Arif asked about legalising cannabis. The whole panel were against and some of the audience were for it, and as I hadn't prepared for cannabis questions I fudged as best I could.

Then Dimbleby did his opening to camera, the music began, and we were off. And then we stopped, because his notes were stuck together, and everyone laughed nervously while we started again.

THEN we were off. Daniel asked about young people paying the bill to maintain pension age benefits, Michelle asked if it was now all right for the police to shoot an unarmed man, Nikolai asked if the racist anti-immigrant rhetoric might stop soon and a lady whose name I didn't catch asked about A&E closures. All stuff I'd revised, thank God, and it passed pretty quickly.

It's difficult to cut in because experienced panellists know not to stop for breath, and with Norman Baker between me and Dimbleby I couldn't catch his eye.

Added to which, he was being true to his word and letting me get used to it. I could have interrupted more perhaps but was inclined to watch the others and see how they operated. As each question was asked we all made notes - me of the names, question and what I wanted to say, and as far as I could see of Norman and Paul's notes they were reminding themselves of the line to take. In between answers I shivered, and tried not to jiggle my pen. TV stuff is always freezing cold because they try to compensate for the heat generated by the lighting, and I shook like a jelly.

At one point I seemed to give Nadine a death stare, but honestly I was just trying to look like I was listening.

I think I managed two solid rounds of applause - once for telling the UKIP chap his rhetoric was racist, that I was descended from migrants and the current debate is offensive and un-British, and the second time for quoting Nye Bevan on the NHS. But you've got only 30 seconds, at most a minute, to have your say and if there's too much applause you don't get to make an extra point. For example saying that before long the NHS will decide whether it's financially sustainable to resuscitate you and it's an obnoxious perversion of the principles that set it up. (That was a good one, I was bursting to say it.)

Then we were done, and we had to sit for a moment while the producers made sure they'd recorded it. Norman winked at me and said I'd done well, then whispered 'I hate going on these things as a Government minister'. All was clear, and that was that. Except it wasn't, because it was also the 20th anniversary of Dimbleby's first Question Time so there was a celebratory dinner to which everyone was invited.

I rang my mum on the way to express my great relief, ordered myself a large gin and tonic, and Kit and I sat down to a meal at one end of the table with Chuka, Norman, their aides and two producers. Nadine and her boyfriend plonked themselves at the opposite end, where Nads spent the entire evening deep in conversation with the UKIP chap. If I were into groundless speculation I'd start a rumour about her defecting, but that would be mean. There was a short film of Dimbleby's best bits, he was presented with a copy of the Daily Mail bearing a page 5 review of his first show, and he made a little speech thanking everyone who worked on the programme.

At about the same time the show was being aired, and I kept a little eye on Twitter to see how it was being received. The worst name I was called was "a Twitter drivel-smith", which I actually quite liked. Someone else said I had pixie ears, which I suppose is better than Vulcan, and Chuka guffawed when I told him someone had called him a Commie twat.

I didn't get to see Dimbleby's tattoo because he wasn't drunk enough to take his shirt off, and although I wanted to ask him for a selfie with some Dimblegin I didn't pluck up the courage. I know, I hate myself too.

Everyone said goodbye and well done to me except Nadine, and even UKIP's number two shook my hand and said "you did really well". Politicians, always cruising for a vote. But probably the best bit was that viewers seemed to like the fact someone on there was answering the damn question (even if I burbled once or twice). Not because a journo is more relevant than the other panellists, or it's nice to be approved of, but perhaps if answering the question seems to be popular a few more important people than me might do it and that is, after all, the point.

Politics can be tribal, dull, and beset with jargon. It turns people off, it makes them angry, and increasing numbers of voters don't bother. If Question Time gets us all a few more answers, then maybe a few more will vote next time around. It can't hurt to try, anyway.

"If you go on it again I'm going to start a drinking game," said Kit as we left. "Drinking a shot every time you look annoyed and then saying 'the answer to the question is NO'. You did that loads."

I think we should call it #foxytime. And next time, I'll remember to say dinosaur.

Oh, America - why ARE you so stupid?

March 30, 2016

Not for the first time, an American has been silly.

A teenaged girl went on a Twitter rant about everything that was "weird" about the British, without at any point wondering if it was more odd that an American teen didn't know how to use Google.

Because some of the answers to her questions were really very simple:

Q: What the hell is Boxing Day?
A: *It's a day when traditionally people gave boxes of gifts to the poor and now we fight over new TV*

Q: Why do yall call an elevator a lift its an elevator
A: *Because it lifts things*

Q: Why does everyone always say bloody hell w h y
A: *It's the politest way of dealing with Americans*

Q: Why do yall say maths like what's the point in making it plural its math
A: *'Yall' is not a word. 'Y'all' would need an apostrophe and 'yawl' is a kind of boat. Maths is a plural because it's a contraction of mathematics*

Q: Why so many telephone booths y'all got cellphones right
A: *Cellphones are RECENT*

Q: RED BUSES EVERYWHERE
A: *Red buses ONLY IN LONDON*

Q: Why is the drinking age 18 I'm still a kid at 18
A: *A kid is a baby goat, which explains why you're bleating unintelligibly*

But then again, so what? She's just a child, she's not too bright, and she's unfortunately caused such a stink on Twitter and been so inundated with irony she can't deal with that she's made her account private. It's more important to the world at large that America, as a whole, is as stupid as it is.

For example, "weird" is from a German word which means "destiny" and after Shakespeare used it in Macbeth came to mean "supernatural". If Americans actually knew anything about the language they have degraded to the point where "you all" is too much trouble to say they might realise "weird" is not an insult. I think what she really means is "inexplicable", and as far as that goes America has the edge on Britain by some distance.

For example:

1. Why are any of you voting for Donald Trump?

Aside from the hair, the general lack of policies, and the threats to the US constitution, this man has encouraged violence, criticises the looks of other people's wives, discusses dating his own daughter and has financial plans for his nation which experts from all sides agree would lead to a global trade war and multi-trillion dollar recession. I mean, you might as well vote for the cat.

2. Why do you slaughter your own children?

The total number of people killed by terrorism in Europe between 2006 and 2016 is 236. The total number of people killed by firearms in the USA in the same period is more than 280,000. Frankly, I'd be safer high-kicking down Raqqa high street in a string bikini singing Relax by Frankie Goes To Hollywood than visiting the USA. Adam Lanza killed 20 six and seven-year-olds at Sandy Hook in 2012, along with six teachers, his own mother and himself, and you STILL didn't think you needed better gun laws. You are one screwed-up place.

3. Why are you all so fat?

Size = input - output. It's that simple. I mean, well done on the crispy bacon and the hamburgers and the syrup for breakfast, very yummy, but minus a million points for doing it EVERY DAY while NOT WALKING ANYWHERE. And there's absolutely nothing wrong with a socialised healthcare system, you know. For example, NHS gastric band surgery is a lot cheaper than yours.

4. You can't call it the World Series when only America and Canada are in it

5. There's an 'H' in herbs

6. Tea needs boiling water or it's not tea

7. IT'S NOT PRONOUNCED "ROWT"

I could go on - we all could. The irritating thing about America is it's the world's superpower, tells everyone else what to do, and yet has somehow "lost" 11 nuclear warheads and celebrates Kim Kardashian even though she's never said or done a single thing of benefit to the human race. Perhaps that makes the USA the "weirdest" place of all - a nation whose destiny is to ignore all the laws of nature and common sense.

Instead it produces citizens whose brains are so clogged with doughnuts they can't think, Google or walk further than their own driveway without relying on semi-automatic weapons and a grudge against the country which gave them their language and ended the slave trade 58 years before they did.

And that's the bit I can't understand, y'all.

It's National Tea Day! Here's why tea is MUCH better than coffee

21 Apr 2017

The other week, my dad reached for the teabags and said: "You've run out! THIS IS A CRISIS."

Calmly reaching for the new pack in a cupboard and passing it to him, I asked: "If it's a crisis when you run out of teabags, what would it be if North Korea launched a nuclear missile?"

He replied: "Oh, that'll be fine so long as we can still have a cup of tea."

To someone not British this attitude might seem odd. To someone who is, it's an entirely-reasonable way of dealing with World War Three. Tea is not just the fuel with which the British Empire was built. It is not just the magic juice which propelled my grandfather and millions of others up the Normandy beaches and across Europe to set the world to rights.

It is, purely and simply, a life-saving, life-enhancing, life-lengthening piece of evolutionary brilliance which has made mankind the dominant species on Earth. And if that seems like hyperbole to you, well, let me explain.

Tea is made from the leaves of the *Camellia sinensis* plant, usually grown at altitude in tropical climates with high rainfall. For some reason, you can also find it in Scotland. All tea comes from the same plants but are processed in different ways to produce black tea, green tea, white tea and things from the twigs and roots which are, let's face it, an abomination.

The method of curing the leaves and pouring boiling water over them to produce a flavoured drink originated in south west China almost 2,000 years before the birth of Christ. And what did the Chinese achieve after that? Lacquering, silk production, jade carving, chariots, ironmaking, astronomy, fractions, magnetism, acupuncture, arithmetic, writing, the compass, weights and measures, a civil service, gunpowder, water power, sugar, porcelain and pi. Coincidence? Let's see.

Tea moved overland into central Asia, the Arabic world, and Russia. Dutch traders first shipped it out in 1607 and the first reference to it in England is in 1615. It became fashionable in Germany, France, and the Netherlands. After which period, those same bits of Europe underwent the Enlightenment, a time when religious fervour was abandoned for reason, liberty, progress, tolerance, constitutional government, and the separation of church and state. Dunking witches and burning infidels stopped when people sat down for a cup of tea and a natter. ISIS doesn't do tea, and it shows.

After tea was introduced, Britain's achievements included submarines, steam power, telephones, vaccines, lightbulbs, farm machinery, bicycles, television, the Colossus computer, fingerprint classification, the discovery of DNA, IVF, carbon fibre, text messaging, the world wide web and a space craft capable of picking a fight with Mars.

One massive change to civilisation after tea is introduced might be down to hard work. Two could be coincidence. But three? Three is uncanny.

We still have senseless wars of course, but seeing as they're mostly American it's probably coffee to blame. Coffee and tea both contain anti-oxidants, chemicals which can repair damage to human cells and reduce chances of cancer, dementia and heart disease. Tea has up to 10 TIMES the amount of polyphenols, a kind of antioxidant, than fruit and vegetables. What luck we happened upon a way of drinking clean water that was also a medicine!

Coffee has more than tea, but get this - it's safe to drink only two cups of coffee a day, because it also raises your blood pressure and heart rate. Tea can be drunk steadily all day long, so you end up getting more anti-oxidants. Researchers at the University of Western Australia found the same amount of polyphenols you get in eight cups of tea a day can significantly lower blood pressure.

And then there's the ritual - the calming business of filling a kettle, waiting for it to boil, warming the pot, doling out the loose leaf or hunting for teabags. Arranging the mugs - dad has to have the biggest one, mum insists on bone china - the stirring, the tink, tink, tink of pointlessly knocking the tea off the spoon on the side of the cup.

Tea calms. Tea is time off. Tea is thinking, chatting, socialising. You don't get that with coffee - it speeds things up, makes you jittery, gives you a high, it's a double-shot soy half-fat skinny macchitwatto, is what it is.

The leaves of *Camellia sinensis* also contain an amino acid called L-theanine which boosts alpha wave activity in our brains. That reduces stress, increases attention, and leads to a state of relaxed concentration or "quiet alertness", which counteracts the effects of caffeine in the drink. The only way you can get L-theanine in your diet is from tea.

Picture your nation's leader, their finger poised over the nuclear button. Would you rather they'd just had a cup of coffee, or a cup of tea?

Tea civilises. Tea unites. Tea makes us happier, calmer, better at thinking, and most of us can't get through the day without one. Years ago I was on a job in Ghana and all the hotel had was coffee, which I hate unless it's the Irish sort and even then I have to be drunk. On the third morning the photographer said to me: "Stuff work, I'm taking you to get some teabags. You're unbearable."

It was true - I had a thumping headache, nothing was right, and I was in a foul mood. We found a supermarket, tracked down a version of Earl Grey (my bag of choice) and in delight carried it high to the nearest kettle. "How's that?" asked the snapper, anxiously. "Better?" I looked at the pack - it was rooibos tea, made from an entirely different plant grown in South Africa. "It's wrong," I said. "It's like waiting at the airport to meet a loved one, you rush into their arms and they turn to mist. It's... empty."

The snapper sighed. "Bugger," he said. I've carried Twinings in my bag ever since. I'm not enduring that again.

I've had thick, black, espresso-style shots of super-sweet tea in north Africa. I've insisted on Earl Grey brewed in a billy can in Botswana. I've tried my best to explain things to Americans. And it seems to me the best explanation for why Britain conquered an empire was the desire to ensure that everyone, everywhere, knew how to do it PROPERLY. You don't put lemon in it. I don't care what the Queen says. You don't stick greenery in it, sod the picture on the packaging, and you don't put sugar in unless all you want to taste is sugar.

You always use fresh water, because tea needs the oxygen in it for the flavour to develop. You always boil the water, because that's how the goodness is drawn out of the leaves. You need china, because that's how you remember what tea has done. And you leave it to brew for two to five minutes depending on your preference. When pouring from a pot the milk goes in first, to prevent it scalding, and when making it in the cup with a bag the milk goes in last because we are not philistines.

YOU DO NOT SPRAY HEALTH-AND-SAFETY-CERTIFIED BATH WATER ONTO A BAG IN A PLASTIC-COATED PIECE OF CARDBOARD,SLOSH THE MILK IN IMMEDIATELY THEN CHARGE ME THREE QUID FOR THE PRIVILEGE, FOOLISH BARISTA, AND YES I WANT YOU TO DO IT AGAIN BECAUSE THIS IS AN ABOMINATION.

It doesn't matter how you make coffee. It'll always taste like hot dirt.

Yes, I can hear you say. But World War Three, really?

Tea not only makes nuclear armageddon less likely, especially if Donald Trump starts drinking it rather than Who's-A-Big-Boy-Den milkshakes, but if you survive and find yourself in a state of shock it could save your life. Shock can give you a rapid pulse, dizziness, fainting, a drop in body temperature, low blood pressure and in extreme cases cell damage and ultimately death. A warm drink with two or three sugars in it - even if you don't normally have sugar - will warm you up, sharpen your responses, up your blood sugar and give your internal organs something else to do rather than panic.

In a car crash? Have a cup of tea. Find your spouse balls-deep in your best friend? Brew a cup. Fear immediate annihilation? Pop the kettle on, why don't you.

It might not stop it, but both you and your brain will be better at dealing with it. And if you can make a cuppa then your face probably isn't melting, which is why World War Three will be fine if you can still have a proper cup of tea.

St George's Day is time to summon up the blood and cry God for curry, England and St George

April 23, 2018

Today is one of those days when nice people don't know what to do. If you mention it's St George's Day there are some who would call you jingoistic. There will be a few who'd worry you're one of those badly-spelled English Defence League morons. There'll be many who would say it's not worth bothering with.

It tends to be the shouty types who mark the date of St George's martyrdom – the ones who want to score a point about political correctness or the modern world or voting UKIP, and the borderline-deranged ones who just want a scrap and think Brighton Pavilion is a mosque.

None of these people want to know he was from Palestine, rather than Preston. That he was beheaded for refusing to abandon his faith, and never even set foot in England. He was invited to join our national story just like the Windrush migrants, and like them has been ignored and belittled by a country who think he is no longer useful.

But by disavowing the lunatics we could gain ourselves a day of national celebration for a bunch of stuff which is pretty brilliant, from Beatrix Potter to the wind-up radio by way of the Royal Society. England and her people have done amazing stuff for thousands of years, and it's time we took St George back from the haters.

If nice people started shouting about Englishness too – if we all flew the flag, and marked the day with the national dishes of chicken tikka masala and sticky toffee pudding, washed down with real ale – then maybe we could drown the racists out. We could shout about Queen Victoria and Richard the Lionheart[19], Good Queen Bess, princes the whole world wants to go for a pint with, the fact we're about to get a mixed race, imported princess and that what's more she's not the first one we've had[20].

---

[19] Richard the Lionheart not totally beloved by the people he slaughtered

[20] Princess has since emigrated

We could talk about Charles Dickens writing the wrongs of slum London, and William Makepeace Thackeray going to a hanging so he could tell the centuries how grim it was. We could invoke ska, northern soul, the Rolling Stones, David Bowie, the Beatles, buttered crumpets and Old Father Thames.

We should shout about the fact Tower Bridge has gold widdly bits on the top, that we egg politicians (but let's not tell Donald Trump before he arrives), and of all the wonderful things we can do with custard.

England can boast Winston Churchill, the Venerable Bede, Newton, Faraday, Babbage, Darwin, Turing, Wren, Hawking, Tim Berners-Lee, Trevor Baylis, and Edward Jenner whose smallpox vaccine has saved more lives than have been lost in every one of humanity's wars. We would go on about Gainsborough, Stubbs, Turner and Reynolds, Lucien Freud, Henry Moore and the genius that is Banksy.

Let's shout about world-beaters Johnson[21], Marlowe, Spenser, Shakespeare, a different Jonson, Geoffrey Chaucer, Byron, Keats, both Shelleys, Blake, Wordsworth, Auden, Tony Harrison, Orwell, Woolf, Tolkien and Blyton, not to mention Julia Donaldson and her Gruffalo and the dear, departed, Douglas Adams and Terry Pratchett.

And just think of the food! Warm scones with clotted cream and strawberry jam, brown sauce, Kendal mint cake, piccalilli, the mighty pasty, Branston pickle, gammon steak with a slice of pineapple on top, Yorkshire puddings served any one of a thousand ways BUT NEVER DEAR GOD NEVER WITH CHRISTMAS DINNER, a full English breakfast, bangers and mash, fish and chips, coleslaw, and the dish I had for dinner every single day of my childhood which was called Wait and See. Lasagne's ours too, and so are Scotch eggs.

Then there's the drink. We've actually got good wine these days, as well as champagne, warm beer, bitter, lager, mild, brown ale and stout. We invented the Sopwith Camel and the Spitfire, the cat's eye, steam engines, jet engines, tarmac, the rubber band, computers, vacuum cleaners, lawn mowers, the hovercraft, the seat belt, the atomic clock, the Spinning Jenny, the sewing machine, tin cans and the tin can telephone, the Mini (car and skirt), Christmas cards, shorthand, cinematography and even the humble pencil. Calculators, the ZX Spectrum, DNA fingerprints, the adjustable spanner, gas turbines, steel, the light switch, the pram, fire extinguishers, mousetraps and toasters – English, all.

In the great race of human endeavour, the England first team includes Isambard Kingdom Brunel, Emmeline Pankhurst, Beatrice Shilling, James Dyson, the entire Monty Python squad and the Monster Raving Loony Party, a good chunk of whose policies actually worked.

---

[21] Samuel, not Boris

On the subs' bench is the Beano, pirate radio, Hovis, St Paul's, Vera Lynn, Wembley, Big Ben, the Red Arrows and the Shepherd Neame brewery. Not only that but we invented the Beautiful Game - along with darts, bar billiards, bowls, rounders, hockey, snooker, rugby, and cricket in which, Australians might like to note, ball-tampering is strictly forbidden.

We had human rights before everyone else, thanks to the Magna Carta. And we exported them via a system of law, justice, and parliament that has been copied all over the world. We taught a third of the globe how to make a decent cup of tea, and as a result our language is the main lingua franca of the entire planet.

Our newspapers have been so successful that Fleet Street has its diaspora in almost every country. We had William Caxton and Wynkyn de Worde, and without them and the journalistic model which started in a room above a pub in Fleet Street in 1702 there'd be no check on anyone's power, anywhere.

England had the first schools on Earth and some of them are still going. It had the first railway system and most of it's still with us, and we were also the first industrialised nation with, therefore, the first rise in the standard of living for the masses. That led to the Chartists, trade unions, and the employment rights that are so universal we tend to forget blood was spilled to get them.

We beat Napoleon on land and on sea, we beat Hitler everywhere, we beat the Germans when it mattered and we're never going to let the French forget Agincourt even though we like their cheese. We've got Twiglets, Marmite, pork pies, Guy Fawkes, Betty Boothroyd[22], the Grand National, greyhound racing, Morris Men and the Morris Minor.

Unlike every other nation on Earth we know how to behave on escalators, we've got a lion on Westminster Bridge, Greenwich is the centre of the world's time, we invented Meccano and Pimm's and Wimbledon and egg mayonnaise sandwiches. In fact, all sandwiches; that was one of ours too.

We don't cast a clout until May is out, there's always a blanket in the car, and we have 100 different kinds of rain. We punt, we knit tea cosies, we shove ha'penny and we brought about the end of slavery before the Americans did.

We stopped Julius Caesar invading us twice before Claudius managed it, and then we threw Boudicca at him and she burned his capital to the ground. If you dig down deep enough, there is a black line of soot beneath London - proof of why you don't pick a fight with an Essex girl.

We've got the hoard of Sutton Hoo, the Crown Jewels which we nicked from everyone else and hid in a biscuit tin, we singed the king of Spain's beard, we beat the Armada,

[22] Betty died in February 2023

chopped off the head of a king then decided we'd have kings back so long as they did as they were told.

We've got the Cotswolds, north Cornwall, the red-brick streets of Lowry's Manchester, Stonehenge, Spaghetti Junction and the White Cliffs of Dover. Accrington Stanley, Scalextric, Dinky toys, the boat race, Colman's mustard, the suffragettes, Chumbawumba, irony, the Dulux dog, the Britain in Bloom contest, the Ski Sunday theme tune, Hob-Nobs, the V-sign, spirograph, crossword puzzles, Plasticine, linoleum, Robin Hood, King Arthur and his entire Round Table – ALL OURS.

The Blitz was supposed to soften us up but instead it toughened our resolve. History shows that, despite our current spasm of rudeness, we usually welcome immigrants. Especially if they have interesting food or are a saint with a handy myth about slaying dragons. We help people in trouble, and after 64 years[23] we still have, and love, the oldest, biggest and best national health service in the world.

We are many things, as a nation. We can be lazy and dumb and outraged at the drop of a hat, we drink too much and we don't tan well. We take all of this stuff for granted and do nothing to stop racists draping themselves in a flag which graces the shoulders of the best we can produce. We are not perfect, and there are many stains on our record. But for more than a thousand years we have left a mark upon the world and its culture that is much larger than a tiny country like ours could expect to leave, and by and large we have done good.

Many of those things we achieved we exported for free so others could benefit - printing, Victoria sponge, good manners. But England's greatest achievements are, arguably, the invention of the corkscrew and the electric kettle. Pretty much everything else would be impossible without them, so those two things alone are worth a party.

Whatever you do today, you could do worse than raise a toast to our immigrant St George in honour of everything that's great about England - and flick a V-sign in the general direction of the ignorant racists who want to steal it from you.

That's what Boudicca would do.

[23] Now 76 and, at time of writing, in need of life support

What would we make of a modern day Guy Fawkes if we bumped into him under Parliament?

November 4, 2019

Imagine you find an Afghanistan war veteran with a bomb under the Houses of Parliament. It's just you, him, and the bomb, and you chat to him so you can buy some time in which you hope someone will come along, call the police, do the decent thing.So you talk to the soldier.

There are lots of things he could be angry about with the people currently sitting above you – electoral fraud, using the NHS as a weapon, Brexiters campaigning against Brexit, Remainers who can't agree on remaining – but the thing he is livid about is the Armed Forces Covenant.

Not the idea of it, which is to ensure military personnel suffer no disadvantage due to their service, and sometimes get preferential treatment because of it. Nor the way it was enshrined in law in 2011 with much fanfare, and the then-Prime Minister promising to "treat people with the dignity they deserve".

No, he's angry about the fact that within a year of it being made law, Parliament pissed on it. He's angry that war veterans like him were made redundant just days before they qualified for a pension, while politicians facing reform to their own pensions got a higher salary to make up for it. He's angry that veterans already investigated and exonerated of war crimes face being investigated again, even when no fresh evidence has been produced, and despite official promises it would stop. And he's furious that the veterans who gave their lives and their health for Queen and country - and in some cases, that of their wives and children as well - are still being ignored.

Survivors of Cold War radiation experiments have been told evidence of their genetic damage is inconclusive; that they must prove an injury sustained 60 years ago; and that, even if they do, they might be asked to prove it a second time. He's angry that ex-forces people still face barriers in finding jobs, homes, and mental health support. A study last year showed 50,000 veterans had psychological problems, 10,000 were in prison, and another 6,000 had no permanent address.

He knows that everyone suffered in the past decade of cuts to public services. But he points out that those who are more in need of them always suffer most, and that only half of veterans who need that help ever ask for it. He's particularly angry about the current government's commitment to the covenant, and the debt of honour it represents. He remarks bitterly that they've finally signed it, 8 years on, and all that means is that the Tory party is now eligible for an employer recognition award. Oh, and they've updated the the website.

He's angry at the state of military housing, 23 years after the government said selling it off was a grand idea. He's furious at the way his family had to go on a council waiting list. At how, if they rent privately, a grasping landlord will rack up the rent for a building unfit for human habitation while their benefit is slashed. At how politicians call people who have to live in those homes "scroungers", and say they should be "put down".

He's angry at a Defence Select Committee report which said the Ministry of Defence was "immoral and incompetent", and at a minimum income requirement for immigrants which blocks Commonwealth soldiers settling in the country they shed blood for. He quotes the committee chairman, who said: "Every year we take evidence on the implementation of the Armed Forces Covenant, and every year we report similar complaints. The Government is failing in its moral obligation towards those who serve or have served in our armed forces."

He's angry about his mates killed for want of proper equipment, at a private defence industry quite literally make a killing with state-funded trips to dictatorial regimes, and he's angry at mealy mouthed letters from politicians thanking him for his service and telling him there's nothing they can do. He says politicians stand with the armed forces when it suits them, but turn their backs when it costs.

As he talks you realise you're angry, too. You're angry about a Parliament that stopped governing in the nation's interest, and spent 3 years arguing over a thing that could not be done, purely because they'd staked their careers on it. You're angry about allies who behave like enemies, knighthoods for men who hit women, a vice-admiral who consorted with a paedophile rapist yet keeps his pension, and his rank.

You're angry that because the people who took it upon themselves to run the country are unable to do so, you've been asked to re-elect Islamophobes, anti-Semites, incompetents and rabble-rousers so they can have another go at cocking things up, on a starting salary of £79,468 a year. You don't like politicians pitting you against your neighbours because of how they pray or the colour of their skin.

You're perplexed about schools that have to shut down one day a week, about a NHS winter crisis that lasts all year, about a minimum wage which isn't enough to live on. You thought all that crap was supposed to be over, by now.

You remember how you were promised electoral reform in 2010 and it never materialised. You wonder about the worth of a system that tells the critically ill to get up and work. You wonder how disabled people can have a better life without the allowances they need to pay for independent living.

You realise that many veterans are disabled. And they are given the same crappy treatment as everyone else, and often have to fight harder to be compensated by the employer who put them in harm's way.

You think about at your local postmaster, corner shop owner, launderette, binman, cabbie, cleaner, nurse, teaching assistant, council operative and heaven knows who else and wonder how, precisely, we'll manage without migrants, and who'll be coming up with the "points-based system" you're told is such a great idea.

Perhaps you look at your own bloodline. Perhaps you look at the history books. Perhaps, in the words of those who talk of sedition, treachery and surrender, you hear the echoes of bad people from bad times.

You think about the fact 14.6 million people who could vote last time didn't bother. You remind yourself there's more than a million people missing from the electoral register - who should be on it, could be on it, but don't see the point.

You stand there, feeling angry, and think about how 414 years ago a war veteran with 10 years' fighting behind him, who worshipped the same God in a different way, who felt oppressed and angry about promises his rulers had made and broken, stood in the undercroft of the Houses of Parliament with 36 barrels of gunpowder, some coal and firewood, and matches in his pocket.

You think about how that veteran was seized and dragged before the king, how he and his fellow plotters were tortured with the rack and other instruments for 10 weeks to produce confessions, and how after a show trial they were taken to the yard outside Parliament so the politicians could watch as they were hung by the neck, cut down while still alive, castrated, disembowelled, and cut into pieces.

Perhaps you know enough to remember that despite injuries so bad he could barely sign his own confession, Guy Fawkes was brave and quick enough to jump from the scaffold before the executioner could stop him, breaking his own neck and saving himself the extra agonies the state wanted to inflict. You wonder why we still celebrate the capture, torture and death of that man with a bonfire and fireworks, why we have forgotten that it was once laid down in law we had to do so whether we agreed or not, and that for centuries his desperation was used to persecute others who shared his faith.

You wonder how we all forgot why he was so angry, or that after he was gone the oppression for people like him simply got worse, and lasted for more than 200 years. You remind yourself we live in a country where Catholics were banned from marrying senior Royals until 2015, all because Henry VIII took against them.

Perhaps you'd also wonder what the authorities would do to that Afghanistan veteran if he was caught red-handed with his bomb under Parliament, and how it would compare to what they would do if he was Muslim.

You look over your shoulder at the door, and you're glad no-one's come along yet. Maybe you wish him luck, and tell him that as Fawkes said on the rack "a desperate disease requires a dangerous remedy".

Maybe you will try to talk him out of it, or go to find a policeman in the hope he'll get help and the people who put themselves above will finally listen to those left below. Perhaps you're prepared to be optimistic about his chances of getting the help he was promised, and that he needs.

Me? I think I'd quietly turn around, close the door, stick my elbow in the fire alarm and then let him get on with it.

The rise of UKIP shows we're sleepwalking into a scary place - and mainstream politicians are completely to blame

April 30, 2013

It is a truth universally ignored that when politicians fail they blame someone else.

When the voters don't turn out it's because they're lazy or it's raining – it's never because the politicians on offer were as inspiring as a mouldy bath towel, and twice as wet. When their financial policies lead to an economy as lively and vibrant as a mangy old mongrel living in a dustbin under a bridge, it's the fault of the previous administration – never the people who've had control of the finances for the past three years. And when fringe political parties gain attention, public support, and coverage it's the fault of, oh just about anyone rather than the fleabitten wets in Westminster.

Two days before local elections, a minor party is getting so much airtime it not only looks like it might humiliate the government at the polls but is being so rapidly disinfected by the spotlight of media scrutiny it might have no-one left to vote for on Thursday.

The most recent polls have given the UK Independence Party its highest-ever rating and predict it could be on course to steal 100 seats. At present it has just seven. It's such an underdog that if the predictions came true it would be like the Spanish Armada all over again. And because it's fielding so many candidates with a party machine that is not really used to it we keep finding out UKIP's wannabe-councillors include the kind of people so dense or bigoted we'd cross the road to avoid them.

At the weekend it was Leicester's Chris Scotton who had been Facebook-liking "ethnic banter" and the streetfight-prone English Defence League. Last week it was Anna-Marie Crampton of East Sussex, who reckons the Rothschild banking dynasty "use the Jews", caused the Holocaust and engineered the Second World War. UKIP's candidates have been linked to the BNP and National Front, suspended, investigated, insisted their computers must have been hacked, and derided by Ken Clarke of all people as "loonies".

So why's it popular? It's been going since 1993 and hasn't changed the anti-European record once. It doesn't even have a tax policy. We all know that no-one sane can discuss Europe for more than five minutes – this lot have been at it for 20 YEARS. It's led by a chain-smoking, twice-married stockbroker in frightening trousers who survived not only a plane crash but his pilot's later threats to kill him, and whose gravelly-voiced appearances on TV and radio are better for a laugh than serious debate. And none of us can name anyone else in his party.

It's got to the point where 'sources' defend their dodgy candidates by saying "he's a braggart and a fool, but from what I understand he's not a bigot" and the leader says "not all of them have got Neo-fascist pasts." Just some, then. And we'd all be thrilled to elect braggarts and fools who have no idea what they want to do with our money beyond not giving in to Fritz.

It's hardly a recipe for success, is it? How on earth has a man who dresses and talks like Rupert the Bear after a bottle of whisky got within a sniff of power? Unless those terrifying corduroys possess magic powers a billion times stronger than my lucky pants there's only one clear answer: it's because every other party is cack.

There are a few loons in their ranks too of course – Tories who think children of colour will 'escape into the forest' and form a 'sexual volcano', Labourites who diddle their expenses, and most of the Lib Dems. The simple fact is, the main parties are all the same. They're filled with rich people in nasty suits making scripted remarks with the combined life experience of reception class at nursery school.

Yesterday Ed Miliband, out on the stump for local elections, spoke to voters from on top of an austerity soapbox. He was as uninspiring, grey and poor at public speaking as the last politician to stand in his suit on a soapbox, which was John Major, and about as loveable.

Cameron and Clegg are simply privileged men of high forehead and low achievement, and Osborne out meeting the people looks like an 18th century French aristocrat who's lost his hanky. They're career politicians without the wit to know that in order to win public support they need to differentiate themselves – not just with their policies ('BORROW! SPEND! YOUR FAULT!') but in their characters.

Clegg, Cameron and Miliband can't do that for the simple reason they don't appear to have any character beyond that of blustering back-stabbers whose achievements in the past three years include not protecting the NHS, a capital city on fire, secret arrests and an attack on all our rights and freedoms.

When UKIP win a bunch of seats on Thursday – or when it's the BNP again, book-burning Lefties, or heaven forbid George Galloway and his ilk – the suits in Westminster will blame voters who are racist, scared or stupid. If they want to know who to blame all they have to do is look in the mirror. And if they have any sense, slap themselves in the face[24].

Fringe, minority, extremist politics gain ground only when the mainstream loses the attention and support of the people. We're sleepwalking into a bad and scary place. One where there's more than just scary trousers – one where there's frightening people with frightening ideas.

Only the apathetic think apathy is someone else's problem.

[24] In the 2013 local elections, the number of UKIP councillors increased to 147 in what was described as a "political insurgency". A year later it received 27.5% of votes in the EU elections, and produced 24 MEPs, then gained two MPs via party defections. In a later general election, that dropped to just one MP. Leader Nigel Farage resigned, unresigned, then resigned again. In 2016 to prevent a haemorrhage of Tory votes, PM David Cameron called a Brexit referendum which was criticised for populist, dog-whistle politics. In the wake of the decision to leave the EU, support for UKIP declined. In May 2022 it lost its last 3 local councillors. And none of it had to happen.

What Nigel Farage said and what he meant: He's only racist when he's tired

May 19, 2014

Dear UK Citizen[25],

Dear retired colonel who reads the Daily Telegraph, who is the only person doolally enough to believe this tosh.

My recent, widely-reported comment that people would be concerned if a group of Romanian men moved in next door to their house has caused a predictable storm of protest and accusations of racism.

My recent radio boo-boo whereby I said my European bilingual wife and children are entirely acceptable but other European bilingual people WHO ARE A BIT SWARTHY would frighten the life out of the neighbours has caused me to look like such a nasty nana I've been told to write a letter explaining it before I can go to the pub.

Let me be clear.

Let me say a bunch of stuff that sounds clear but isn't.

UKIP is not a racist party, and our immigration policy, far from being racist, aims to end discrimination against non-Europeans.

Look! Some of my best policies are black!

---

[25] During a 2014 election campaign, Farage gave an interview saying he'd feel "uncomfortable" if a family of Romanians moved in next door. He later said: "I regret the fact that I was completely tired out and I didn't use the form of words in response that I would have liked to have used." A few days later UKIP took out a full page ad in the Daily Telegraph, in the form of an open letter from Farage, which is translated for Mirror readers here

Just don't ask what discrimination I'm talking about, as I'd have to admit people from Jamaica, Pakistan, India and other non-European countries are already here in much higher numbers than Romanians.

And even if I won an election I couldn't do anything about this, as it's a Commonwealth thing. And even if I won in Europe I couldn't stop the Romanians either, because I'd need 33% of all EU seats to block legislation and, let's face it, I only turn up to work when I feel like it.

The vast majority of Romanians who have come to the UK wish to better their lives and would make good neighbours.

I've been told to say here.

But there is a real problem, an unpalatable truth that our political class would rather not discuss.

But there is still a reason to vote for me, even though I've been a member of the political class for 15 years and have been discussing this same thing that whole time.

Since the fall of Communism and the awful dictator Ceausescu, Romania has struggled to complete a full transition into a western democracy.

A democracy like ours, where in recent weeks my candidates have claimed the Holocaust was a voluntary sacrifice by the Jews, tried to get peaceful protesters arrested for hate speech, flipped the middle finger at voters, offered to deport Lenny Henry and had their businesses raided by immigration officials hunting for illegal workers.

Silly Romanians don't know what they're missing!

When I visited the country I was truly shocked by the living conditions and social exclusion of a large Roma minority.

I looked at gipsies so you won't have to.

It is difficult to believe that such discrimination still exists in Europe today.

And I see no reason why we should help them. Look how nice and thoughtful I am though.

The other huge problem in Romania has been the growth of organised and criminal gangs for whom EU membership has meant greater opportunities.

If I put the words "criminal" and "EU" in the same sentence it sounds a bit like it's Europe's fault.

Under the free movement rules there is absolutely nothing the UK authorities can do to stop such people from entering our country.

There's absolutely nothing I can do about it either without dismantling the entire European project, for which I'd need to be Prime Minister, which I don't have a cat in hell's chance of.

But that's no reason to get off the all-expenses-paid gravy train.

With about 100,000 Romanians currently in the UK, consider these Metropolitan Police crime statistics:

It's 140,000 according to the Office of National Statistics last week, but I see no reason to be exact about dirty foreigners:

92% of all ATM crime in London is committed by Romanians

This was a claim made by a DCI in an ITV documentary in 2012 but has no statistics to back it up, but who cares?

28,000 Romanians were arrested in the past five years in the Metropolitan Police area

Well to be precise it was 27,725 arrests between 2008 and 2012, and it includes people arrested more than once, offences which saw suspects rearrested several times during the course of an investigation, and people who were later released without charge. But still. Romanians!

HARRUMPHITUDE

And across the EU as a whole, Europol figures show: 7% of all crime across the 28 EU member states was caused by 240 Romanian gangs

In fact it's 6.7% of criminal gangs identified by Europol, which doesn't know all of them and which I'd like to disband, so let's not concentrate on this one

We should not be in a political union with Romania, with an open door to all their citizens.

OH EWW IT'S GOT ROMANIANS ON IT YUCKY-POO

We must take back the power to stop criminals from entering our country by taking back control of our borders.

The only way to do that is to leave the EU. Or change the EU rules. For which I'd need to talk to Europeans, and turn up to work, and not be in the pub. ARSE TO THAT.

Then we can give Romanians who want to come to the UK work permits and do the necessary checks.

Which hopefully will be better than the checks UKIP does on its own candidates. I'm tired, are we nearly finished?

When this happens my answer to the questions "Should people be concerned if a group of Romanian men moved in next door?" will be "No".

My answer will be "NO WAY! Romanians? In MY street? Kirsten, pack the golf clubs, we're moving."

It is not racist to want to stop organised criminal gangs undermining our way of life – it is common sense.

It is purely coincidental that racists rather like it.

Yours sincerely,

I'm only racist when I'm tired,

Nigel Farage MEP

PS To the pub!

What has immigration ever done for us?

September 6, 2017

Hundreds of migrants have swarmed to within a mile of my house. I say swarmed because we're supposed to imagine they're a kind of locust, but using EasyJet rather than wings.

These avaricious, Biblically-bad beasties can be seen in the fish and chip shop (Turks), Post Office (Hindu), corner shop (Muslim), TV repair outlet (Polish) and the farms which surround the village. There, they live in rows of mouldy, rusting, single-skinned old caravans with broken windows and ragged net curtains. At this time of year they pick apples, pears, and grapes, and in the winter they prune the plants they grow on.

They maintain the solar panels, repair the generators, drive the tractors, pack the fruit in huge warehouses, and spend hours bent over in a field to get strawberries to Wimbledon and blackcurrants to the Ribena factory. And yes, when no-one's looking I scrump the Ribenaberries.

These uncontrolled hordes work all the hours of daylight and more besides. You don't generally see them in the pub or on the train, because they're cooking chips for drunks who fall off the last train home, shrink-wrapping apricots under fluorescent light or selling milk to someone who forgot to get some earlier.

All those shops are open on Bank Holidays, and most of them on Christmas Day and Easter Sunday which is handy because those are the days people generally wish they had another bottle of milk. None of them speak English as a first language. None of them cause the least concern to locals. And none of them appear to have been noticed by the man down the lane who has a UKIP flagpole in his front garden, who also seems unable to spot bloody-minded rudeness when it's hoisted 20ft into the air.

And that's just within a mile. Further afield in this corner of Anglo-Saxon shire are cleaners, coffee servers, sandwich makers, street sweepers, retail assistants and other unwelcome people. Every single one of those migrants speaks MORE than one language. Every single one is doing a job considered unskilled by politicians whose only job qualification is a brass neck. And they all pay in SIX TIMES more taxes than they take out in benefits.

The village primary school of course is over-subscribed, but that's because education funding has been cut in real terms and the council keeps building houses in a flood plain. The local hospital occasionally kills its patients, but that's because the NHS is getting a 1% budget increase when it needs 4%, doctors are leaving in droves and the nation is missing 40,000 nurses. You're still more likely to survive than die, and that's because despite the Tory efforts to destroy the welfare state it's being propped up by the immigrants. Immigrants don't put unbearable pressure on our public services. Austerity has done that - and without the taxation produced by foreign workers they'd be doing a lot worse.

Jobs aren't stolen by the unskilled European masses, because despite all those jobs being available within a mile of my house I've never seen a single unemployed Brit queue up at the farm gate looking for back-breaking minimum-wage work with the sort of accommodation that wouldn't be acceptable in a detention centre. If anything their presence in the economy creates jobs - it puts money into the system, and makes work for others by increasing demand for other services. Even though we've high levels of immigration, there are a record 31 million of us in a job and 93% of the workforce is British.

The Office of Budget Responsibility thinks migrants help the UK economy grow by 0.6% a year. We're currently growing at about 1.7% annually and have a GDP of £2trillion, so if the OBR is right migrants are worth their weight in gold. Wages aren't suppressed much either. Several studies have shown that while there has been a small drop in wages for care, restaurant and bar workers, it amounts to 1% over 8 years.

The rest of us are finding our income is static, or worth less, because the economic chokehold of austerity has drained optimism, restricted growth, and depressed interest rates. It effectively took an already-crashed car and entered it into a banger race without bothering to kick the tyres and add petrol first.

And immigration has done nothing to harm this green and pleasant land. All those migrants in my village blend in so well that the UKIPper can't see them. They provide cheap labour to farmers who are struggling to make any profit at all because consumers don't want to pay more than a few pennies for an apple. Because those farms are viable businesses, the farmers don't have to make ends meet by selling off fields one at a time to be built on by developers eager to build £500,000 houses only a commuter can afford, which were it to happen would take a wrecking ball to the community cohesion that the thriving pub, chip shop, Post Office and under-pressure school are doing so well to maintain.

And that is perhaps why the government has worked up a policy document, leaked overnight, saying that it will crack down hard on unskilled EU migrants by stopping them coming for more than a year, and then added seasonal farm workers will get a permit. In other words they'll SAY they're stopping immigration, while quietly admitting we need it.

The pub staff, the hospital cleaners, and everyone else will be allowed in only if their employer can make an economic case for them, which seeing as one indisputably exists sounds like extra paperwork to get the same damned thing. Brexit was sold to this nation, especially the not-racist parts of it, by claiming EU immigration was causing us problems. It wasn't, and it isn't, and the government has to pretend it's getting rid of a thing it can't get rid of, because if it does we're buggered.

Fish and chips were brought to us by Joseph Malin, an Ashkenazi Jewish refugee. Chicken tikka masala was invented by a Pakistani who moved to Glasgow. Beer and hops were imported from Europe, sponge cake was invented by an Italian and when James Keiller invented marmalade it was because a Spanish ship carrying oranges sought refuge in Dundee harbour. Immigration has made Britain a more varied, tasty, delightful place to live. As a result of all that, migrants still fancy the idea of coming to work and live here. They're less likely to be Polish these days, as the economic benefits at home have improved, and University College London says they are more likely to be young, single French and Italian graduates working in finance or technology - skilled, in other words, but just as useful as someone prepared to sell you a kebab at midnight.

The greedy, job-stealing, wage-suppressing locusts who are required to pass no entry test before entering into our lives, who prey upon our fears, who thrive on our imagined misfortunes, are the creatures who run the country by running it into the ground. And the net result of all that is not that we'll keep migrants out - it's that migrants will stay away from our NHS which needs them, our Treasury which relies on them, our homes and businesses and lifestyles that depend upon them.

The man with the UKIP flagpole and a distinctly un-British lack of manners makes them feel unwelcome, and they're already staying away. If the best we can hope for of a successful Brexit is a country that is exactly the same as the one we had before Brexit, but with more paperwork and fewer immigrants, that's not a success.

It'll be a bloody mess, and you can bet your bottom dollar Nigel Farage won't be washing the floor.

Brexit cannot cross the Irish border - and here's why it means the UK won't actually Brexit at all

December 4, 2017

Today, Theresa May is meeting Jean-Claude Juncker in an effort to force through a Brexit agreement so we can move on to trade talks.

The only problem is that it's impossible for everything in that sentence to be true. Either they DON'T agree, in which case there will be no trade talks. Or they WILL agree, in which case there will be no Brexit to speak of.

EU sources have told reporters we're "85% to 90% there". What they haven't said is that was the easy bit, and the last part is going to cause an international migraine.

Because you have to find a way for there to be no border between two legally-separate states, after a vote in which borders were demanded, and in a place where borders cause bombs.

It's no wonder the EU is putting its foot down. And it's no wonder that Theresa May has absolutely no idea what to do.

This wasn't talked about much in the run-up to last year's referendum, perhaps because "AAAARRRGGHHH BUGGER" isn't the sort of thing that looks good on a bus.

The Irish border, in places, goes through someone's front room. In others it's a low hawthorn hedge. About 100 people live in an area called The Connons which is in the republic but surrounded on three sides by the province and joined to its mother country by a narrow strip of land just 200m wide.

To add to the fun, the main N54 road between two republican towns crosses into the north and back again FOUR times in just SIX miles.

Irish TV journalist David Blevins reported this week that just outside Clones, in the top right of this map, is a petrol station where half the pumps are in the south and half in the north. It's that wiggly.

You can't change that - you can't knock down houses, seize or cede land, or ignore a road down which traffic thunders at 60mph.

During the Troubles there were 20 border routes. Today it's 275, with 30,000 people crossing every day along with 6,000 lorries. It may not matter much to the UK, but you can be damned sure it matters to them.

When Northern Ireland and the Republic were both in the EU it was doable. The currency and tax regimes were different, but there was an historic common travel area and any problems could be ironed out. It was in part the EU which helped to fix the island's Troubles. When the Good Friday Agreement was signed in 1998, part of the deal was freedom of movement, an end to the razor wire and guard posts at the border, and a promise that both sides would have the same human rights.

But last month the government narrowly won a vote to dump the EU's Charter of Fundamental Human Rights, because Brexit means the UK can't keep it. Uh-oh.

The government says those rights will be rewritten into UK law and possibly improved - but that would still breach the peace deal. Anyone who voted for Brexit because of too many human rights will decide it was a waste of time if we all end up with more.

The only option is to not change the border. Keep the hedge, don't impose controls or barbed wire, and allow people to cross from one to the other. And then anyone who voted for Brexit on the basis of ending freedom of movement is going to find that was a waste of time, too.

A migrant who feels the urge to be close to Nigel Farage will be able to travel freely to the republic and stroll north, where they could claim asylum in the UK or rack up our deportation bill.

So why not just change Northern Ireland's status? Make it special. That not only tears up the Good Friday Agreement for the third time today, but would also mean the Democratic Unionist Wingnuts who prop up Theresa's government would withdraw token from board.

Part of the deal was that the DUP insisted Northern Ireland must be treated the same as the rest of the UK. You can't have a sea border between NI and the mainland, you can't check NI citizens via passport control, and you can't impose trade duties. Even if you can persuade the DUP to let that happen, Scotland would then demand the same.

On top of that, the law which provided the referendum was about the entire UK leaving the EU. If one part doesn't, then the UK hasn't, and the vote has not been upheld. And Theresa's promised she'll uphold the vote.

The government is this afternoon "quietly confident" there's a way around it. They've found a fudge to keep the Irish government and the DUP happy for now, talking about "total regulatory alignment" which means the province trades within the EU rules.

But that is insane, because it means that NI would either lose 85% of its trade with the UK or force the UK to keep the same rules we've just voted to tear up. And it doesn't solve the fundamental problem: that the UK and EU will share a land border which we cannot patrol, notice, or close.

If NI doesn't Brexit, then the Scots won't. The entire United Kingdom could crumble on this point, and there are only two real options left for Theresa to choose between.

The first is to Remain In All But Name: to replicate everything that being in the EU involved. The same trade, same payments, same human rights, same borders, same customs union. NI sells 15% of its goods in the republic, and most of the border crossings are near-invisible - you cannot impose a trade tariff on the Irish border, and if we can't do it there we can't, legally or politically, do it elsewhere. Every import would divert via Belfast quicker than Lewis Hamilton's private jet.

We're halfway down this road already, because a lot of Brexit has been delivered missing the essential Brexity bits. Theresa has had to accept the jurisdiction of the European Court of Justice, we've coughed up £50bn, and we're either going to have to pay to access EU industry bodies, or pay more to copy them with our own which follow their rules.

The problem is that's not Brexit. It's just a very expensive way of Remaining.

The second option is simply to Remain. A Survation poll at the weekend showed 53% of people want a second referendum, and next week Parliament will debate precisely that.

If it gets to the point that Leaving the EU will be EXACTLY like Remaining but cost more, how many of the 52% would still back it? Not enough, I reckon.

And that's the circle Theresa has to square - to Brexit without Brexiting, and to make it look like Brexit even though it won't feel like Brexit. That couldn't be done by Einstein, and it certainly can't be achieved by these simpletons.

Which is why the Irish border, and all its meandering, means that whatever we get at the end of the day, it won't be Brexit[26].

[26] Theresa was ousted because she couldn't fix it; Boris promised there would be no border checks, then imposed them; the current fudge is an 'honesty box' sort of system, which relies on smugglers admitting they'd prefer to smuggle things

Where's the golden goose of good stories gone?

September 20, 2013

Once upon a time there was a fox in need of a story. She looked in the dustbins, and she looked in the celebrity haunts. She looked at Twitter and she hunted through court lists. She read the papers, Googled ideas, rang up her friends and even went along to Parliament to see what they were up to.

But she could not find a good story anywhere. She found lots of terrible stories: things celebrities had tweeted, and things PRs had released, and statements from government ministers about how great they were.

She found a handsome prince locked in a glass drunk tank, and a house made of cheeseburger pizzas, and a lot of people saying silly things about veils. There was a man who thought that women couldn't think, and someone shooting royal guard dogs, and a really terrible video by a Spice Girl.

But the fox was used to stories that were really, really good. Stories about greed, and lies, and wrongs that needed writing. She was used to tales that didn't just excite the reader in their guts but exposed a human failing and gave the world a chance to be a little better than it was. She wanted a story that would make people stop and say '****, really?', that could rock a government, force a resignation, provoke a peak-time interview that everyone had to see.

The fox asked her friend, the policeman, where all the stories were.

"Go away," he said. "I'm not allowed to even look like I'm thinking about talking to you otherwise I have to arrest you and myself and everyone we both know."

The fox asked a lawyer if he knew where the stories were.

"Sssh," he said. "If I told you, I'd have to injunct you from telling anyone by misusing 17 words in the Human Rights Act which aren't supposed to be a privacy law."

The fox thought for a bit, and then went deep into the forest to ask the owl, the wisest creature she knew, why the stories had disappeared. She would have asked a badger, but they were all dead.

The owl blinked at her, and put down the gin bottle, and said: "You silly fox. The stories have not disappeared – they are all still there. There are still politicians cheating on their spouses while running for election as happily-married people, and some of them are even barking on your telly about protecting marriage and policies for hard-working families.

"There are still people being convicted of crimes they did not commit, and guilty people walking free, and judges getting tied in knots in either the law or bondage dungeons.

"There are still things the police won't or don't investigate and need you to sniff them out. There are still cock-ups and unnecessary deaths that you could expose long before a public inquiry gets around to admitting it."

And the fox asked: "So where are they, then?"

The owl said: "They have been hidden by the Troll King. He thought he was hiding away the celebrity tittle-tattle which lots of people were snooty about, but with a scandal and an inquiry and the biggest criminal investigation in British history he's accidentally hidden everything else as well."

The fox thought about this. It was true that there were some things people did not need to know, and some stories which needed to be more gently told.

Yet the point of telling stories – be it around fireplaces in our oral history, in Grimm's Fairytales where they were collected together, in newspapers or online – was to make a point. To show a wrong, or praise a right, and hold things up to the world. To hide away some of those things, at the cost of hiding it all, seemed an unreasonable trade.

It also occurred to her that the net effect was that we were left with precisely the kind of celebrity tittle-tattle which people had been so snooty about in the first place.

"Perhaps there would be other ways of making storytellers behave better?" she asked the owl, who laughed.

"Why yes, little fox, there is," he replied after another slug of gin. "It's called using the existing laws, but all the people we used to tell stories about preferred to stop us doing it altogether."

The fox left the owl to its alcoholism and followed a trail of self-serving politicians to the Troll King's house. She saw a bishop drive up in a Mercedes, and hid behind him as he said the millionaire's house was where God wanted him to be. Inside the house was an amazing sight.

There was a frog, and a golden ball, and a princess trying to work out why she couldn't sleep. There was a girl living in the fireplace being beaten by her stepmother while wicked social workers looked the other way, a paedophile making poisoned apples, and celebrities hacking their toes off so they could wear the latest Victoria Beckham slipper. There was royalty, and plebs, and corrupt coppers partying alongside hookers, wronged women and a fake sheikh. There were even a few storytellers that the fox recognised, and who thought being inside the house made them better than all those who weren't.

There was a casting couch, the truth about the economy, and rumours that the fox finally realised were true all along. She followed them all the to the central room, where there was a huge golden goose. The goose was laying shiny, beautiful eggs, but before they could hatch the Troll King scooped them up and threw them into a massive oven where they withered and died.

"STOP!" said the fox. "This is not a metaphor! These stories need to be told!"

The Troll King cackled, and replied: "If I need to kill one thousand good stories to stop you telling a single bad one, I will."

"Who are you to decide which stories are good or bad?" asked the fox. "We should let people choose for themselves." And with that the fox grabbed the golden goose in her jaws, and leapt out of the window.

She muttered a spell, and there sprung up between every house in the land a magical net which meant everyone was part of everything and everyone could tell their own stories without asking the Troll King's permission first.

The fox gently released the goose, who honked off and laid eggs all over the place for people to find and tell each other about. The Troll King was furious. He shook his fist, and stamped his foot until it went right through the floor, and said: "I'll get you yet, fox!"

The fox laughed. "People have been saying that for 300 years," she said. "Come and try your best!"

And with that the fox leapt into the future, and smiled.

Citizens! Anti-social behaviour is your problem – do something about it

September 25, 2013

Big problems are difficult to sort out.

The economy, energy prices, child poverty, climate change. They're all so vast that it would give you a brain tumour just to think about them, which is why we pick people we don't like very much to be politicians.

But it's small problems which have a disproportionately massive impact on our daily lives. It's the git next door whose telly is turned up too loud, the woman who was rude in the newsagent's, the person at the desk opposite or that BLOODY cat.

We tend to think someone else will sort the big stuff. The niggling bits of nasty we get in the face every day, on the other hand, are ours to deal with. Yet we've arrived at the point we're scared to do anything about it. We won't have a word with the youths on the train, we won't stand together as a street against that family that parked a sofa on the front lawn.

We put our heads down, we endure, and the nasty eats away at our souls until we hate everything around us. Admit it, there are days you feel like barricading the front door or launching a missile attack from the roof, aren't there? Well, in Waltham Forest they think they've found a solution. They're issuing on-the-spot-fines.

So far it's just for littering, urinating or spitting, but there are plenty who think it's a start. Their number probably does not include XXXXX[27], 18, of Hackney, or XXXXX, of Ilford, who have each been told to pay £300 in fines, legal costs and a victim surcharge for gobbing within sight of a council official. Councillors have greeted it as a victory for common decency and XXXXX's granny didn't help by

[27] Edited to remove names - people who commit minor offences have a right to be forgotten

insisting he was "a good child" but currently on remand at Feltham Young Offenders' Institute while awaiting sentence for robbery.

The problem with an on-the-spot fine is this: Not only does an official need to witness the offence, it is likely committed by a little tyke who's never going to pay it, and if you're rich enough you can ignore it altogether. The £100,000 supercars parked on double yellows outside Harrods all summer are proof enough of that.
We can't have crimes that only work for the poor. We can't have crimes people know they can commit if there's no-one in a uniform nearby. That's just daft. What we need is for every single person to be endowed with the power – both moral and legal - to flick another person on the ear for anti-social behaviour.

As well as spitting, littering and urinating this would include:

- Any and all dawdling
- Standing on the left of escalators
- Entering a BMW dealership with intent to purchase
- Forcing others to listen to your taste in music, be it on a mobile, via shoddy headphones, or a sound system in your front garden
- Cyclists who ignore the Highway Code
- The incorrect use of fog lights
- Any attempt to purchase tartan carpet. This includes you, the Queen
- Takeaway food on public transport at any time except the last train home
- FEET ON SEATS. How'd you like it if I wiped my shoes on your arse?
- Entering any public space with a guitar (this would incur a further penalty of having said instrument placed around the owner's neck. Also applies to bongos)
- Use of the word 'methinks'
- Dropping chicken bones on the pavement. Animals eat them, they splinter in the stomach and they DIE, you fools
- Those leggings that are no thicker than tights and force you to regard people's bum cracks/thongs/bad knicker choices
- Swearing in the presence of old ladies or children

- Trolleys left in car parking spaces. If a flick on the ear isn't enough, all misplaced trolleys will be dumped in the transgressor's living room

- People who think prams include an impregnable force field

- Using the word 'hashtag' in conversation

- Being Justin Bieber

I could go on. We all could, let's face it. But then again if we gave people the power to flick ears there'd be some who'd take it too far and begin summary executions of people who hog the middle lane. The fact is there are many tiny things that make living alongside humans rather hard work, but anti-social behaviour makes it more difficult than it needs to be. In the case of spitting, it spreads tuberculosis. With urinating, it attracts rats. The playing of bongos can lead to a murder spree.

In the absence of summary ear flicking, or on-the-spot fines actually related to the amount of money you earn, there is one other solution to anti-social behaviour. And that's for each and every one of us, next time it happens, to do something about it. To take a deep breath, perhaps, and allow for the fact that person might have cut you up because they're rushing to the hospital.

And when necessary to politely point out using 'methinks' means you don't, that you put trolleys back where you found them and if you drop rubbish someone else will come along, pick it up, and drop it right back in your lap again. If we all did it – if we all stopped being scared to say 'hey, life's difficult enough without you making it unnecessarily worse, let's try a little consideration for a change' – then maybe we'd have a thing called social behaviour instead.

Because ignoring it, hating people, letting the world around us get worse, makes us as anti-social as the thoughtless sods who spit in the street and think no-one will mind.

Stand up. Tell them you mind. Don't let it get to the point where council officials are lurking on every street corner with a DNA swab.

And TAKE YOUR FEET OFF THE SEATS.

Are you all right with torturing bad people? Because I'm not

December 10, 2014

Look at the man in this picture. Doesn't he look awful?

The hooded eyes, the veiled sneer. He has hunched shoulders half-turned from the camera, as though he reviles everything to do with us. He's hairy, an animal. He looks like he smells bad, like he's been on the run. He could turn and bite at any moment. The word "feral" just about sums him up.

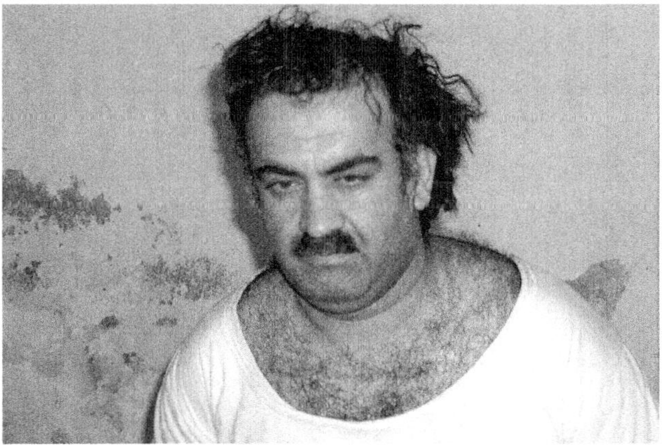

Khalid Sheikh Mohammed in 2003, pictured after his capture by US forces. Licence: Creative Commons

You've probably seen the picture before because it's used a lot to show just what the West is up against in the War on Terror. He is Khalid Sheikh Mohammed, a man usually called the "architect of 9/11". Of Pakistani origin and raised in Kuwait, he joined the Muslim Brotherhood at 16 and studied mechanical engineering in the USA, spending a brief spell in jail there due to unpaid bills.

On release he became a mujahideen in Afghanistan. He married and moved to Qatar in 1993, where he was sheltered from the Americans who wanted to arrest him even then. He travelled to Bosnia, the Yemen, the Philippines, tried to fight in Chechnya, and moved his family to Pakistan. There he made friends with Osama bin Laden, shifted back to Afghanistan and decapitated the journalist Daniel Pearl who was investigating the Al Qaeda network.

He was captured by the CIA in 2003 and confessed to being the man who came up with the idea of a mass plane hijack in the USA. He is, inarguably, a bad man. So it's hardly a surprise that he looks like he's just crawled out of a rat hole, is it? He's an animal, and a nasty one at that. If I asked you now whether you were bothered he'd been waterboarded, you'd probably say "not in the least".

Yesterday America admitted they'd tortured this man and at least 118 others in an attempt to get information from them. You probably still don't care.

The CIA didn't tell the White House what they were doing.

Care? Nah.

Thirty nine of those men were waterboarded without the Justice Department knowing about it either.

Pfft.

Seventeen were tortured without the head of the CIA even knowing about it.

So what?

A number of the CIA torturers had known mental health issues and one had a conviction for sexual assault which, normally, would prevent them even joining the CIA.

Meh.

Twenty six of those tortured were perfectly innocent.

Huh?

The 'stress positions' the suspects were forced to adopt for hours at a time included standing on broken legs with untreated bullet wounds.

Um.

One prisoner tried to chew through a vein in his own arm. Er. The CIA didn't even know who it held or why.

Well…

Some detainees were put in boxes the size of coffins or smaller, which reopened wounds and made them pass out, for up to 266 hours. That's ELEVEN DAYS.

Yes, but they're bad men.

Suspected Afghan militant Gul Rahman was stripped, drenched in water, was deprived of sleep for 48 hours, was subjected to "auditory overload", total darkness and rough treatment, and died of hypothermia shackled to the floor.

But…

Khalid Sheikh Mohammed was waterboarded 183 times.

Yeah, but he was REALLY bad.

In his case the normal practice of pouring water on a piece of material over the nose and mouth was abandoned. CIA agents used their cupped hands to hold water over his mouth, increasing the sensation of dying.

Definitely a bad man.

He suffered convulsions and vomiting. When he refused to eat a lunch of hummus, nuts and raisins it was pureed and forced down a tube into his rectum while his head was held between his knees.

Urgh.

The two psychologists in charge of coming up with these "enhanced interrogation techniques" had no experience of interrogation and later set up a joint company that was paid £52million by the US government for their services.

Oh.

Lithuania, Romania, Poland, Thailand, Algeria, Uzbekistan, Egypt, Iraq and Jordan all colluded with the torture, providing 'black sites' for the secret prisons where it was carried out.

Tsk.

The prisoners were flown through Prestwick Airport in Scotland.

What?

We don't know what our ministers knew about all this because there's been no inquiry in this country.

WHAT?

And not one bit of information that came out of all this was any damned use whatsoever.

All it's done is show America and her allies have fought terror by producing more of the stuff. They have bred, allowed, paid for and overlooked evil acts carried out by people who enjoyed torture for its own sake. It was justified by politicians as an unfortunate means to an end that simply didn't exist. Those nations which abandoned torture techniques – and everyone's used them at some point – did so not because they were mean but because they were useless.

Imagine how you'd feel, locked in a box for eleven days, beaten, screamed at, threatened with your mother or children being raped in front of you, forced through repeated fake drownings and then having your lunch shoved up your arse without so much as a by-your-leave. What would you confess to?

Khalid Sheikh Mohammed confessed to organising 9/11 and the 1993 World Trade Center bombing, the Bali nightclub bombings, a Mombasa hotel suicide bomb, the shoe bomb plot, assassination plots on Pervez Musharraf, Bill Clinton, Jimmy Carter and Pope John Paul II, and planning to blow up the Panama Canal, two New York suspension bridges, the New York stock exchange, several Israeli embassies, Big Ben, Canary Wharf, Heathrow, the Sears Tower and NATO headquarters.

For some reason he missed out blowing up the moon using laser beams attached to the heads of big fricking sharks, but perhaps it slipped his mind.

Torture doesn't work. The information is unreliable. Prisoners say whatever it takes to stop the abuse, try to fool their captors and buy time. You would, I would, terrorists would. That is perhaps why, despite being arrested 11 years ago and indicating a guilty plea to a judge in 2008, Khalid Sheikh Mohammed is still awaiting trial.

It's hard to know what options US politicians had in the aftermath of 9/11 beyond HOO-YAH LET'S GET 'EM because anyone sensibly pointing out thinking first might yield more results would have been lynched. But you don't win a war of ideals by behaving in a less than ideal manner.

You don't prove you're the good guy by being bad.

And if you throw away your principles in the hunt for bad men who say your principles are evil, you will find that a) you've no principles left and b) the bad men win.

The War on Terror is a war about a way of life. Proving that freedom and democracy are better than bullets and bombs. And the only way you win that argument is by giving the people who don't have freedom and democracy a taste of it, and hoping they see your point.

Look at that picture of Khalid Sheikh Mohammed again. The drooping eyes, the flat expression, the hunched shoulders. He looks awful.

He looks like he's been treated like an animal. How would that encourage him to stop acting like one, exactly?

Are you still OK with torturing him? Because I'm not.

Why doesn't the rule of law apply on a football pitch?

March 6, 2015

If I spat on you in the street, I could be arrested for common assault. Especially if there was a policeman who saw the whole thing.

If I happened to do it in Waltham Forest or Enfield there wouldn't even need to be a victim as the local councils have introduced bylaws making it punishable by a fine. Failing to pay that fine can lead to criminal prosecution and a further penalty of up to £5,000.

So how would you feel if I spat on you, in front of police officers and council officials, on camera, but no-one did anything because I was wearing a particular shirt?

"Sorry, sir or madam, but Foxy is in the away strip for Manchester United so you see she's utterly untouchable. Nothing I can do. Move along, now."

Then let's consider I did something even worse. That we bumped into each other on the pavement, there was some shoulder-barging, and I got so upset by it that I picked you up around the waist, held you over my head and then threw you to the floor like Hulk Hogan. Again police officers were among the onlookers; and again they did nothing.

"Sorry, sir or madam, but you see Foxy is now wearing the clothing associated with Worcester City. It's like a shield of steel. She's basically Batfink. Heal thyself and go home."

Imagine I punched you in a momentary disagreement about what side of a white line we both were; if I called you a "f****** black ****" after you made me look silly; or if I tried to stop you getting served by standing in front of you and squeezing your nuts until you cried for mercy.

You'd expect something to be done about it, wouldn't you? Not only would you have been subjected to an attack, but other people saw it happen. If the guilty party isn't punished, they all get the message that it was fine to do that to you, that they could do the same, that £60 nylon shirts made in Taiwan really do make us invincible. But in football it's allowed.

It's not of course - spitting, punching, bodyslams and racism are all expressly outlawed by the rules of the game. Yet when it happens, it doesn't seem to matter much. Body slammer Shab Khan was sent off.

His boss Carl Heeley said he did not condone his actions before doing exactly that, saying: "He's had three or four career-threatening injuries from poor tackles. There's certainly a defence there. We've got to remember that incident wouldn't happen if the Stockport player didn't commit an awful challenge."

Can you imagine being bodyslammed in the street and then told it was your fault?

The Football Association has charged Jonny Evans and Papiss Cisse with spitting after their clash on Wednesday. Evans spat towards Cisse on the ground after a tackle, who then jumped up, wrapped his arms around Evans and spat back at him. In the street it'd be affray but on the pitch it merited nothing more than a telling-off from the referee. The FA has now decided that wasn't enough, but the most it can do is a six match ban. Cisse's been fined a week's wages by his club and apologised, but Evans denied he spat at all. His boss Louis van Gaal believes him and said "for me, the matter is done".

But is it? Is it really? First off, football is a contact sport. There are constant tackles which if they took place in the street would be unacceptable. But if the police were to criminalise someone for each of them they'd never have time for doughnuts.

And sport is by its nature often violent. Boxing involves two men repeatedly hitting each other in the face. Ice hockey can lead to a puck being buried in your skull. Motorbikes, F1, horse riding, rugby, bobsledding - they all carry an associated risk of injury, often at someone else's hands, and occasionally death.

Yet each sport carries rules for how that game is played - where punches may land, or whether they're banned. The sportsmen and women who take part in them know those rules well and if they don't stick to them they don't last. When Mike Tyson bit a chunk of Evander Holyfield's ear in 1997 he was disqualified and it marked the beginning of the end of his career. When Luis Suarez did much the same he got a £75million move to Barcelona.

When John McEnroe cursed at a Wimbledon umpire in 1981 he was fined £1,500; when he did it again in the US open it went up to $17,500 and a two month ban, and he didn't last long after that.

It's impossible to imagine a cricketer taking such umbrage at an umpiring decision he batters an opponent. It's hard to picture Lewis Hamilton being so infuriated by being overtaken that he stops his car, gets out and tries to lamp another driver. And what tennis player, heckled from the audience, would launch a kung-fu kick on a fan?

But in football, and football alone, it's not unusual to see all of those things. Sometimes the police get involved but more often they don't, despite the fact members of Her Majesty's Constabulary attend the matches both as supporters and officers of the law who are only too happy to nick the fans.

Yet there is a forcefield around a football pitch, which puts those 7,140 sq metres of grass in a different country where there is no law, no comebacks, and the worst that can happen is a red card. The problem is we can still see it; the men, women and children who love the game watch their heroes kick, spit, swear and abuse their way around the leagues, and all are taught it's normal.

It's why chants of "get yor tits aht for der lads" directed at female medics, linesmen or commentators are dismissed as banter. It's why bosses don't take concussion seriously. It's why juries, if incidents ever get so far, frequently seem to think "the heat of the moment" is an acceptable excuse for a crime. It's not acceptable. It never is. People have been hanged for things they did in the heat of the moment, and these days they can still be locked away for life.

Some say it's not worth getting worked up about. But every week tens of thousands of people watch a small group of individuals get away with what would be minor crimes if their victim pressed charges, simply because of the shirt they wear.

They are left with the impression that they should do the same when they play at school or in the Sunday five-a-side, that they can heckle women like that when they get drunk or on the way to the game. And they learn that if you're rich or special enough you are above the law. Taken together, it means all those minor, unimportant, heat-of-the-moment, on-the-pitch crimes spread into the world at large like a creeping vine, spread by thousands of thoughtless people who hurt thousands more.

It's high time the police cracked down on the violence and abuse which are already outlawed by the rules of the game but draw so little penalty that players and fans think they can carry on with it.

The rule of law applies everywhere, to everyone, or there is no law at all.

And just imagine what it would be like if what was accepted in the stadium was accepted outside it. We wouldn't call it the Beautiful Game anymore; we'd call it a cancer, and we'd sort it.

Twit Tax: If you fine people for bad behaviour you might just make them nicer

January 19, 2015

Let us take a moment and give thanks for Julie Lawrence. This Cornwall mum has struck a blow for etiquette by issuing an invoice to the parents of a boy who did not turn up, as promised, to her son's birthday party.

Julie made a verbal agreement with Alex Nash's dad Derek that his boy would attend, and had made arrangements at a dry ski slope for all the children she was expecting. Unfortunately the Nash family was double-booked. Not having Julie's number, Derek bailed without telling her and intended to apologise afterwards at the school gate.

In the meantime a presumably-furious Julie had generated, printed and delivered an invoice for a £15.95 "no show fee", which Derek has today been waving at the newspapers and BBC in a state of high dudgeon. You might be forgiven for thinking Julie was over-reacting, that dry ski slopes are rubbish anyway, or that she should have realised not everyone turns up to these things. In fact, Julie just invented the Twit Tax.

Derek has now learned to check the diary first. He's learned to make more effort to track down contact details, to pass a message via the teacher or other parents, to have used his noggin and that maybe, just maybe, people might even be out of pocket because he was a bit thoughtless. Yes, Julie's an arse. She sounds like the kind of party organiser I've spent a lifetime successfully avoiding. But she is on to something, because if you fine people for bad behaviour you might just make them nicer.

After all, how many of us slow down in accident blackspots solely because there's a camera rather than blood on the road? So let's not stop at childrens' parties. Think of all the other things we could, and indeed should in the interests of a more civil society, be issuing Twit Tax invoices for…

It should be legal to demand £4 for having to listen to someone else's music via their car windows, tinny mobile phone speakers or leaking headphones.

It could be followed up, in the event of non-payment, with directional megaphones playing Tom Waits' most experimental stuff at the guilty parties. Any use of the word "banter" would generate a bill of £3.79, an odd number just to annoy the offender as much as they've just annoyed you, and with no change possible. You'd soon find music was turned down and banter returned to meaning "the friendly exchange of teasing remarks" rather than being a catch-all excuse for ignorance and isms.

What else? Well, everyone six inches shorter than their dating website profile pretended should be fined a minimum of £50. Then another £50 for using a picture that was 25 years old, another £50 for not mentioning the personality disorder and at least £100 for wasting an evening of my life because I'm too polite to take one look and then leave.

In fact, time-wasting in general should be taxed at a rate commensurate with our normal salaries. Every cold call that you get out of the bath to answer, every minute spent on hold, each chirpy sales pitch for something you don't want or already have, should lead to an invoice for your time. We'd soon find sales calls got a lot snappier or stopped altogether and in fact WE'D be trying to keep THEM on the line. And think of the penalties for companies running late trains....

On top of that I'd charge £1 for every misplaced apostrophe spotted. If we all did it, the local butcher might finally realise how irritating his "lamb chop's" are and learn the error of his way's. We can probably charge £5 to anyone who uses public transport while carrying smelly takeaway food. GET YOUR FOUL TAKEAWAY OUT OF MY NASAL HINTERLAND, YOU SLOP-FACED SLOB, AND NO DON'T LEAVE THE WRAPPER THERE.

Got a colleague who never gets a round of tea? Fiver every week until they do. Got a friend who "forgets" to ring you back? £2.50 a time, and if they don't get the point they're not your friend. Got shoulder-barged by selfish commuters on your way to work? £3 a pop until they learn some manners.

Like every other social surcharge the Twit Tax would begin as a one-off introduced to deal with an etiquette emergency. But with the world being what it is, and a glut of twits available in the global marketplace, it could end up a crucial part of our financial system. It might even be that politicians would actually encourage us to be more twittish to one another in order to keep the economy going. And we would, inevitably, have to deal with the fact that some of those issuing Twit Tax invoices would themselves be twits about it.

People like Dr Jonathan Levy, who invoiced British Airways for £1,350 after helping a passenger whose peptic ulcer burst in mid-air. Or Nigel Farage, who claims allowances from the European Union and avoids votes while arguing it's a waste of money. Only the way you do it, Nigel, and that's £2 for me having to tell you so.

The Twit Tax is a fabulous idea, and well done to Julie for inventing it. But with the sheer number of twits in the world and the ineffable nature of their twittery I fear it would only make twits of us all in the long run. So if we can't introduce a penalty because it might inadvertently multiply the world's idiot quotient, what can we do instead?

Well, we could try to be more thoughtful. Less like Derek Nash.

People in wheelchairs didn't crash the banking system – so why are they paying the price?

June 30, 2015

This morning, I woke up and got out of bed. I drew the curtains, scratched my bum, and went to the toilet for a wee. Then I wandered downstairs, made breakfast for me and my dog, went back upstairs, ran a bath, washed myself, dried my hair, dressed, and took the dog for a stroll. When I came back home I made a cup of tea, gave the pooch a chew, and settled down to work.

Yesterday I went to the supermarket. This evening I'll make my dinner. If work demands, I'll get myself to the nearest train station and on Thursday I'll probably pop over to my mum's. I expect you do some of the same things every day. Wherever and however you work, you more than likely get out of bed, draw the curtains, scratch your bum and have a wee before starting your day.

As of midnight, 18,000 people don't know how they're going to do that tomorrow.

Now, 18,000 people isn't very many. It's slightly more people than can sit down at Centre Court in Wimbledon. It's one fifth of the capacity of Wembley Stadium. It's 0.02% of the British population – a tiny, almost insignificant amount.

Each of those 18,000 people receives about £300 a week from the Independent Living Fund, administered by the Department for Work and Pensions. It costs £320million a year to the UK, which is about 0.2% of the DWP annual budget for benefits and pensions. Another tiny, almost insignificant amount. The thing is, it's not insignificant if you're one of the 18,000[28].

---

[28] The closure of the ILF was ruled unlawful but went ahead anyway. Replacement funds were introduced by devolved governments in Wales, Scotland and Northern Ireland, but in England the responsibility was transferred to local councils, paid for by a government grant. In 2022, it was announced that grant had been reduced to just £160million a year

Because all of them are so severely disabled that they need help to do all the things we take for granted. They have to wait for a carer to arrive before they can draw back the curtains or have a wee. They have to pay someone to make their breakfast, or put them in a wheelchair, or dress them, bathe them, do their shopping or help them get to work. Some of those 18,000, should they wish to scratch their bum, have to ask someone else to do it for them.

For many it wasn't always this way – perhaps they had parents who used to do all that, and have now passed away. Perhaps they grew up in care and hospitals, where there was help. Maybe they had a partner or children who stuck with them through illness and hard times, and who for whatever reason are no longer able to do what they did. Maybe they used to be as able as the rest of us, but hit bad luck. But now here they are, adults with severe disabilities, waiting for someone to come round and help them out.

That help has been available for the past 30 years, so long as they can jump through all the hoops and paperwork and medical evidence needed to qualify for the ILF. But now as part of the government's austerity drive it's all going to change. The fund is closing at midnight, with just £260 million of the money expected to pass to the Department for Communities and Local Government – which itself has already had a £250m budget cut this year. Local councils will now have the responsibility for assessing and paying for carers for the severely disabled – and local authorities are also facing cuts of up to 6.4% this year. They're also under pressure to freeze council tax, which is the best way for local councillors to find extra cash.

The government has refused – refused , mind you – to ring-fence the ILF money. Councils have been asked what they'll do but only a third so far have promised to pass on the money without any cuts. So that's a £320million fund reduced to £260million, given to a department facing a £250million cut, passed on to local councils facing more cuts, without guarantees the disabled people will get any of it, and two thirds of them definitely won't get as much as they did.

To cap it all, the current arrangements are in place for just nine months before someone, somewhere, will get the chance to fiddle with it all again. We all know what will happen then – it'll be cut a little more, and a little more, and a little more. And so far, none of the 18,000 have been told what their new care package will be. Even though, as of midnight, it ceases to exist in its current form. And for what?

Severely disabled people didn't cause the banks to crash. They didn't run up a deficit, speculate on the Libor rates or foment any terror attacks. They can't even get out of their wheelchairs, for goodness' sake. Their £320m is so insignificant in terms of our spending that we could save more money by making every public official switch to second class post.

Last year the UK government had an income of £648billion – which means we earned enough to pay for the ILF in less than THREE MINUTES. It's simply not worth cutting, moving, axing, closing, or slicing. You might as well say you're going to clear the deficit by painting slightly shorter white lines on the roads. And if they don't get enough care at home, the chances are many will end up in hospitals and care homes which - just for reasons of painful irony - are more expensive, and less productive.

But it doesn't really matter, because even though 20 wheelchair-bound protesters were turfed out of the Houses of Parliament last week for daring to disrupt Prime Minister's Questions we won't have to watch.

When those 18,000 people – one fifth of Wembley Stadium – can't get out of bed quite so often, if at all, when they can't get to the toilet, eat, shop or dress, when they don't see their friends, go to work, pay taxes, or have anything to smile about it'll happen behind curtains that remain drawn all day and all night.

Those people in wheelchairs won't bother us because they won't be at our work, on our pavements, or in our shops. We'll all just scratch our bums, and carry on with our day, while the government tells us it's taking the tough decisions that are absolutely vital to get us back on track.

They're just not telling us where those tracks lead.

I have epilepsy - and I refuse to be afraid or ashamed

March 26, 2018

I have epilepsy.

Damn, but that was hard. I'm not sure I've ever said that before. But then, I'm only just getting used to the idea myself.

When the neurologist told me that I was officially epileptic I had to come to terms with fact I had a disability, and unlike all the conditions where they can fix you up, mine had nothing.

No cure. No new brain. No real prognosis.

"So what does that mean?" I asked the quack.

"You might start having lots of seizures or you might never have another one. We don't know. Oh, and you have double the chance of having a massive seizure which will kill you without warning, but it's only double the minuscule chance of that happening to anyone, so still tiny.

"There's nothing you can do so I wouldn't worry about it," he said. Then he shrugged.

Of all the things you don't want to see a doctor do – cry, bite their nails, snap on latex gloves – trust me when I tell you that shrugging is the worst.

Shrugging means the person who studied medicine for years doesn't know the answer. It means the person who has spent more than a decade fiddling around with brains can't help yours. It means you're on your own, and you might die, and oh f***.

But if I'm honest this wasn't unexpected, and it wasn't as bad as it could have been. You see, to be epileptic means you need to have had at least two seizures and this was my second. I sort of knew how it would go.

One in 20 of us will have a single seizure at some point in our lives – febrile seizures as children, or even geriatric seizures. Children who have it will often grow out of it, and when epilepsy strikes adults it's usually connected with major life events. Like when children and house moves happen at the same time, and things all pile up. With me, it was divorce.

My first seizure happened six months after I got my decree absolute. I'd had a year and a half of sleepless nights, terror, financial nightmares and personal misery. After the decree I began to relax. I started to think about my future, sniff the flowers, that sort of thing.

One day I was walking along the river with my parents, felt a little woozy and sat down. I blinked my eyes and when I opened them there was a paramedic in front of me asking me to tell him my name. Five minutes had passed in which, my parents told me, I'd had a seizure. Foaming mouth, thrashing limbs, the lot. A small crowd had gathered. I had been sitting up and talking for a bit but hadn't been making sense.

I was put in an ambulance and wired up to machines; my blood pressure was through the roof, and I felt incredibly sleepy. They took me to A&E and ran a lot of tests while I tried to make jokes with my parents, and then a very handsome young doctor told me: "You might have a brain tumour."

"I… what?"

"It's probably an isolated seizure, it doesn't sound like a faint, but there's a small chance it might be a brain tumour so you'll need to see a neurologist and have a brain scan to get it checked out."

Mum and dad took me home and, because it was a crisis, we had a cup of tea. "It's not a brain tumour," said mum. "A friend of mine had a brain tumour and she spent six months walking like a crab. Your balance and movement are normal. It's not a tumour."

I Googled it and, yes, single seizures are common. They often happen to people who are really stressed. And they're linked to migraines, which I used to get as a teenager during my exams. Only – here's the thing – I always got the migraine AFTER the exams. I dealt with the stress, and when I relaxed there was a sort of backwash that knocked me over.

So it wasn't epilepsy, it was a side-effect of divorce. It was just me being dramatic and odd like I always am, and as a bonus I could blame it on my ex. #WINNING.

But we still had to be sure it wasn't a tumour, so I had my scan and got the all-clear. The neurologist who gave me the results shrugged when I asked him what caused it, and said there was one more test that could be done – an electroencephalogram, or EEG, which checks your brainwaves.

Fine, I said. Book me in. Knowledge is power, etc.

An EEG, if anyone ever offers you one, is dozens of wires attached to your skull with conductive wet clay. The wires pick up the electrical patterns in your brain while a light is flashed at you. That doesn't sound too bad does it? Until they speed up the flashes to 10 or 20 times a second and you start to feel like Malcolm McDowell pinned to a chair with his eyes forced open in A Clockwork Orange.

A powerful light flashed in your eyes up to 20 times a second for an hour with a nurse saying 'try not to close your eyes' is the closest thing to medieval torture I have ever experienced. It was physically painful, like knives. Tears poured down my cheeks. I left the clinic as exhausted and confused as I had been after the seizure.

A few weeks later the neurologist put on his serious face and said the results had shown a problem. At some frequencies my brain waves had done a funny skip, which meant I was photosensitive.

"Hang on – there were no flashing lights when I had my seizure!" I said. "And I've been surrounded by cameras flashing for years, been to nightclubs, never had any problems. This is DAFT." I'm not sure I didn't fold my arms and huff.

The neurologist explained that flashing lights were a basic test, a bit like poking a dog with a stick. If it bites, you don't know it's a bad dog or if it'd be fine if you didn't poke it. You just know the dog doesn't like being poked with a stick. "We don't know what causes seizures," he said. "But we do know what can trigger them. Alcohol, drugs, overwork, sleeplessness, flashing lights. Just try and avoid all of them." I laughed in his face. I've never done drugs but as for the rest – I'm a journalist, for heaven's sake. And this was stress, right? So long as I didn't get divorced again I'd be fine.

The doctor shrugged, and said: "It might be stress which brought this out – but your brain has always been like this. It's how you were born. You have a 50:50 chance of it happening again."

That's nearly as bad as the shrugging: 50:50 is the same as flipping a coin. Shrug, I dunno, heads or tails. What next doc, trepanning?

Adding to my anger and confusion was the fact that a friend of mine had been killed by this. Raelene was a bright, funny girl who I sat next to in maths, one of the few I'd stayed in touch with when they all went off to uni and I went off to do deathknocks. Then one day I got a phone call to say she'd died. She'd gone to bed one night and never woken up. The coroner decided she'd had a massive seizure in her sleep, her first ever, and it was so severe it had effectively pulled her plug out at the socket. She was 24.

For weeks I found it hard to sleep, not knowing if it would happen to me too. Gradually I stopped worrying and got on with not being normal.

After a seizure the DVLA like you to hand your driving licence in, and your neurologist likes you to live quietly. I had to abandon my car for a year, and half of the stories I'd otherwise be writing, and as a token health kick decided to replace wine with mixers on a night out. The upshot was I drank a lot of vodka orange, and spent a lot of time in toilet cubicles realising that human stomachs don't react well to three pints of orange juice an hour.

I also sat down and started writing a book about how my heart got broken, which did more than anything else ever could to fix both it and me. With every passing year it got further away, a weird one-off. After five years you can forget all about it, the doctors say, and I was five weeks off that hurdle when I had my second seizure.

This time I was in the park walking the dog, standing on concrete, and went down like a sack of spuds. A passing doctor and his wife stayed with me and called an ambulance, put my dog on his lead, but by the time I came round they'd gone and I couldn't thank them. I'd lost five minutes of my life again – one minute I'd been walking along, the next I was addressing three paramedics and seeing in the ambulance window that I had blood all over my face. Back to hospital, back to A&E, this time to have my lip stitched up.

More worried parents, and another chat with the neurologist. I told him life was fairly stress-free these days as I had left my job and gone freelance, although there had been a few sleepless nights at the start which was, ooh, about 6 months earlier.

"I haven't even got divorced," I joked, but the doctor said that every time you have a seizure it makes it easier to have another – they've tested it on mice with electricity, and they need lower doses to cause the seizure every time.

Then there was the "you're twice as likely to die like your mate" conversation and they referred me for cognitive behavioural therapy to make me better at dealing with life events. It was quicker than writing a book if nowhere near as cathartic, and I did another year without my car. I got a disabled person's railcard, and felt embarrassed about using it.

It meant that when the car needed to be serviced and MOT'd, I had to ring the garage to come and get it. It meant that when I interviewed someone I had to explain I would arrive by train. It meant I had to turn down work if public transport was too impractical. And every time I did that, I didn't say why I wasn't driving. I'd just say "medical reasons", and am fairly certain the person on the end of the phone thought I was a drunk driver. There is, for some reason, less stigma in that.

Epilepsy is seen as mildly shameful and unmentionable, a bit like bumholes. Yet this is something which already involves 50 million people worldwide, 600,000 people in the UK, and could potentially affect us all, because each of us has a seizure 'threshold'. Perhaps yours is three bottles of absinthe, an armful of heroin, or four kicks to the head. I'm luckier than most because I know mine is persistent insomnia, and that can often be fixed with a hot bath, some warm milk and, in extremis, publication. I'm also luckier than most people with epilepsy, because my problem isn't so bad that I'm on big doses of pills with side effects that can include miscarriages or birth defects. But the rate of diagnosis is increasing. More of us have seizures now, perhaps because of the pressures of 21st century life. Every single day in the UK, there are 87 people diagnosed with epilepsy and 21 people who die as a result of it.

That's one person every 70 minutes. And those who die are the ones who don't see their doctor, don't take their pills, don't change their lifestyles. People who live in poorer areas with poorer chances. People who do what I did, and pretend the thing they can't see and no-one understands isn't really there. On top of all that, there are almost 25,000 children in the UK whose epilepsy does not react to the normal drugs. Some have responded well to cannabis oil, and there's a campaign by parents who want to see if it will help the others.

So far as we know, doctors have prescribed it to just one child. ONE, out of a group of children that would fill 125 primary schools. The government changed the law in 2018 to make it possible to prescribe it, but with guidance so restrictive you might as well not bother.

Seizures can kill. They can leave you with brain damage. And while 1% of us are diagnosed with this illness, it gets only 0.3% of research funding.

I've been seizure-free now for almost 8 years[29].

I'm lucky that both times I had seizures I had people around me. I'm lucky neurologists know as much as they do and can take pictures inside my skull. I'm lucky to know I was born photosensitive like 3 per cent of epileptics are, and that it's nothing more serious. I'm lucky it wasn't a tumour, or a head injury, or an infection like ME that would leave me with more frequent seizures I couldn't avoid. I'm lucky I can wear sunglasses, avoid nightclubs, forego Jagermeister. I'm luckier than Raelene; I got a reboot.

But I'm stupid too, because for a long time I didn't talk about it. I worried what people would think. I called myself names like retard, spacker or eppy, especially when I was angry that I couldn't do something basic like drive to B&Q without asking for help. I have spent 12 years coming to terms with the fact this thing exists, and I'm still not happy about it. It helps, as always, that I can write things down and show it to others - to spread the word, maybe use it for something good.

But if even I'm in denial, when it's killed my friend, made me write a book, and scarred my face, then the 95% of people who've never had a seizure won't have a hope of understanding it. Today is Purple Day, an event begun to promote awareness of epilepsy, raise money and remove the stigma. So it seems to be a good time to say, I'm not a drunk driver, I've got every right to this railcard, and please let's do something to stop the shrugging because it really gets on my nerves.

Research has shown up to 18% of untreatable epilepsy could be solved with surgery; that high-fat diets can help children with frequent seizures; and that sleep is

[29] 10, huzzah!

vital to help the brain cleanse itself of neurotoxins (who knows, perhaps that's my trigger). Epilepsy has no clear cause, and can disappear by itself. It's not my ex's fault. It's probably genetic, as are the migraines which returned in my 40s, and which my dad and nana also used to get. My family are under strict instructions to let neurologists have my brain after I'm dead and don't need it anymore, in case it helps the research.

If someone has a seizure, it is physically impossible for them to swallow their tongue. Don't put your hand in my mouth, because I'll bite it. Just cushion my head and let me ride it out. Cover me with a coat or blanket if you can, because I'll probably wet myself and would appreciate a smidge of dignity when I come round.

Get plenty of sleep. Drink, but not too much or too often. Don't take drugs when you've no idea what they'll do to your wiring. Don't underestimate stress; it's a killer.

You only get one brain, so look after it.

Epilepsy shouldn't cause fear and stigma for any of us, and stopping that starts when we cease pretending that it only happens to other people.

So. This is me. I have epilepsy. I am not afraid, and I am not ashamed.

Boris talks about betrayal of Brexit while he betrays a British mum going mad in an Iranian hellhole

May 22, 2018

It's fitting that Boris Johnson chose Valentine's Day to set out his dream of Brexit.

His record of lies and unwilling apologies aside, there could be no better time for him to demonstrate just how much the blond bombshell loves himself. This is a man not only seeking to seduce an entire country, but who believes that it's genuinely possible - that by telling you to dump the EU and with a vow he'll stick by your democracy forever, you will all be persuaded to let him screw you.

He won't want you to notice he has promised you the painfully impossible, because if you Leave you'll need to amputate Northern Ireland first and there isn't enough anaesthetic in the world. He won't tell you the EU is too big to ignore, that the alimony makes Leaving uneconomic and he's always been quite happy to ignore democracy when it suits. And he's especially not going to tell you during this dimly-lit seduction there's another woman. One whose hair is falling out, one separated from her child, one enduring torture as he treats you to a wink with a rose between his teeth.

The photographs of Nazanin Zaghari-Ratcliffe before she was sentenced to 5 years in a Iranian jail for false allegations of trying to to topple the regime show a delighted, healthy, new mum. A photograph of her now would show something different. She's since spent 22 months living in utter terror, arraigned for crimes she did not commit, denied a proper trial, and denied her basic human rights.

According to lawyers for the charity Redress she spent 8 and a half months in solitary confinement in cells as small as 1.5m x 2m square. She was blindfolded, ordered to wash in stinking sinks, and denied light and fresh air. She was taken out of the cell only for interrogations and at one, where she was allowed 30 minutes of walking a day, she had to do it blindfold. Her family didn't know where she was for 2 days, were told she'd be released a week later, and didn't get to see her for 40 days. At that meeting she was too weak even to pick her daughter up. That was in June 2016. Just one month later, Boris was made Foreign Secretary.

Nazanin suffers claustrophobia. She's had panic attacks, palpitations, teeth problems, chronic back pain, arthritis in her neck worsened by sleeping on the concrete cell floor and a breast cancer scare. She went on hunger strike early in her incarceration, and when her mother visited with Gabriella to beg her to eat she collapsed. She can't sleep without sleeping pills. She says she feels lost in an "ocean of mistrust". She's been diagnosed with "advanced depression".

She is not James Bond. She's not trained to withstand hard interrogation. She's a junior charity administrator who once worked for a trust providing journalist training, and she never worked on any projects it ran for Iranians. She has not been allowed a single visit from the British consul in Tehran. She's been in jail for 682 days, 581 of them with Boris at the Foreign Office, and he hasn't even managed to persuade the Iranians to let an official see her.

At the end of last year this man, whose job includes helping British nationals in trouble in foreign countries, did the opposite by publicly stating Nazanin HAD been training journalists. And that's despite the fact that, not being a journalist herself, she wouldn't have had much to say about how to be one. Nazanin was immediately threatened with another 5 years' jail and broke down in her cell. Boris was forced into one of his rare, blood-from-a-stone apologies, and finally agreed to meet her husband to discuss the campaign to release her.

It was followed by a trip to Iran where Boris claimed he'd held "frank" and "forthright" talks with the regime. Ayatollah Alamolhoda responded by calling him "a clown" and "a womaniser" so presumably it didn't go well. Nazanin's file was labelled for early release, but it never came. Her husband has resumed the campaign, saying she's being used as a political pawn and he can wait no longer for governments to extract digit from backside.

In the time that Nazanin has languished in a series of unsanitary cells smaller than the average British bathroom, Boris has written thousands of words about Brexit, been involved in untold Tory leadership plots centred on Brexit, castigated his fellow MPs for Whats Apping their unhappiness about Brexit, got the Yemen and the Lebanon mixed up, passed comment on the mummified corpse of an aged female relative and suggested building a Brexit bridge across the Channel that would close in every light breeze.

In the 22 months she has been jailed there have been 5 full Parliamentary debates on Nazanin's case. But according to Hansard, Boris has spoken about her just twice - both in November last year, when he was forced to apologise, and then apologise more sincerely, for worsening her situation. There is no reason the MP for Uxbridge, the Foreign Secretary and the leader of the Brexit campaign can't do all those jobs with the same commitment. But Boris is fully committed to the aggrandisement of Boris. There's no gain for him in Nazanin's case, so he'll keep it at arm's length until he can find a way to take credit, just as he did with Crossrail and the London Olympics.

Instead he concentrates on selling you a dream of Brexit, ignoring all the facts and realities of the thing and likewise not mentioning that Brexit is denying Nazanin the best chance she has of freedom. The EU-US Iranian nuclear deal, aimed at giving the regime trade in return for an end to their weapons programme, was abandoned by Donald Trump after he took office. The EU's might is now the only force in the world capable of bringing the regime to heel, and were it willing to go in to bat for Nazanin it could be almost guaranteed she'd be released. But there is no point in fighting for the citizen of a country that has voted to Leave; still less for a nation whose foreign relations have boiled down to Boris saying "go whistle".

I'm not arguing to overturn Brexit for one woman. But Nazanin is just one of hundreds of Britons jailed around the world who need the support of the EU and won't get it, and there'll be thousands more in the years to come. Then there's people with international marriages and child custody disputes, business wrangles, job searches. Can you really be sure one of them won't be you?

The truth is that foreign relations and Brexit are incompatible, in the same way as the Irish border and customs checks. Nothing this man is selling you can be delivered, and the steaming hot lunch he finally serves up is going to cost more than you realised.

There is no way this charmer will pay the bill or still be there in the morning. There'll just be another mug, another desperately suffering victim, another example of how one man's ego can break a woman's heart[30].

[30] Nazanin was finally released on March 16, 2022, after the UK paid a longstanding £393 million debt. She had been detained for a month shy of six years

27 reasons why Boris Johnson is not a feminist crusader, a defender of free speech, or making a joke

August 10, 2018

It says a lot about the size of the hole you are in when Mr Bean feels compelled to ride to your defence[31].

But while Rowan Atkinson is trying to dress Boris Johnson in the Speedos of comedy, while removing the trousers of shame and not exposing the private parts of disgrace, on a beach populated only by people who cannot see what he's doing anyway, there is something else afoot.

One rather badly-written newspaper column by someone who recently flounced out of government complaining about a plan he had no alternative for, having done the most to push the country into a position where it needed a really good plan, has held our attention for a solid week.

The column was not about the plan. The column was, theoretically, about why banning burqas is wrong. The column also, in reality, stirred millions of people to talk about how they agree with the author that burqas are a really funny letterbox joke, tools of female oppression, security risks, aids to criminal endeavour and an example of how political correctness has gone mad and we're not allowed to say anything anymore. That Boris is a man of the people, stating an uncomfortable truth. So let's take these things one at a time.

1. Boris was only making a joke

Atkinson wrote to The Times to say: "As a lifelong beneficiary of the freedom to make jokes about religion, I do think that Boris Johnson's joke about wearers of the burka resembling letterboxes is a pretty good one... you should really only apologise for a bad joke." Leaving aside for a moment the sad truth that Rowan has yet to say sorry for *The Thin Blue Line,* Boris wasn't making a joke. A joke is a thing which causes, if

[31] In a brief period between resigning as gaffe-prone Foreign Secretary and becoming gaffe-prone Prime Minister, Johnson wrote a newspaper column which managed to offend everyone

not laughter, then a wry grin, snort of recognition or at the very least a flippant gesture in response.

Johnson wrote: "I would go further and say that it is absolutely ridiculous that people should choose to go around looking like letter boxes; and I thoroughly dislike any attempt by any - invariably male - government to encourage such demonstrations of 'modesty', notably the extraordinary exhortations of President Ramzan Kadyrov of Chechnya, who has told the men of his country to splat their women with paintballs if they fail to cover their heads."

Perhaps there are those who find the idea of vigilante paintballers funny. Boris, however, says he has a "thorough dislike" of it. Not a joke, no punchline, and more importantly any humour to be found is on the side of those who fire pellets at uncovered women, which means if you think this was a joke you have more in common with a Chechnyan thug than Oscar Wilde. Sorry Mr Bean, but no.

2. Boris was standing up for women

Johnson has a long and glorious history of belittling and undermining women, regardless and sometimes because of their clothing. In 1996 he wrote about his "Tottymeter" at Labour conference went off whenever "a young woman delegate mounts the rostrum". He wrote about pinning a Pirelli calendar over his Telegraph desk and that later, amazingly "they made women feel embarrassed, I was told". After leaving The Spectator he advised his successor when in dealing with publisher Kimberley Quinn: "Just pat her on the bottom and send her on her way." He has written about female drivers and "taking them from behind"; spoken of female volleyball players at London 2012 "glistening like wet otters"; said female students attended university because "they've got to find men to marry"; and finally said Hillary Clinton "resembled a sadistic nurse in a mental hospital".

And if you want to dismiss this as mere bantz, while Mayor of London he axed the role of Women's Advisor, and cut £90,000 and five jobs from the domestic violence task force. He argued over funds used to tackle rape, and abolished a childcare unit for single parents.

More recently, he has spent two years undermining Britain's second female Prime Minister and arguably the only one in history with a task as tricky as Brexit, has apparently made the situation of a British mum languishing in Iranian jail worse AFTER he intervened, had to apologise for his "inadvertent sexism" in referring to his opposite number by her husband's title, and in his personal life has not managed to be faithful to a single woman he has been publicly and romantically linked with. In short, he shows no sign of being a feminist.

3. No woman in a burqa has yet robbed a bank

MEN have put on burqas to cover up their identities while carrying out crimes or fleeing them; but no woman who ordinarily chooses to cover her face has blown anybody in Britain up. The people who HAVE done so are male, British, and in several cases born into Christian families. A point worth bearing in mind when anyone claims it's the lady in a niqab we need to worry about.

4. It's political correctness gone mad

Political correctness requires us to be considerate to other people. It is merely the practice of good manners. Try switching the words. Would you say that telling people they look like letter boxes or bank robbers was good manners? And would you say that, if someone was criticised for rudeness after doing so, that it was good manners gone mad?

5. It's all about freedom of speech

Calling people names is legal. Belittling clothing choices is fairly common. But it is also pretty rude, and while we all have the freedom to be rude to people we all, generally, do not express most of this rudeness because we have either politeness or empathy. So I may very well think that Boris is fat, ugly and porcine, but I would not say so, and certainly would not do it to his face. I would assume that such an act would make me sound unpleasant, be quite unkind, and may make the object of my jibe feel upset. I have the freedom to say these things, but I choose not to because it makes the world a less nice place.

Boris DID do it. The freedom to offend can be easily defended if it sparks valid and intelligent debate - as with the Life of Brian, perhaps, Charlie Hebdo cartoons, or Spitting Image caricatures - but if all it sparks is racist online vomiting, then its benefits are harder to spot and frankly leaves everyone the poorer for it. Sometimes, rudeness is just rude.

6. Boris isn't racist

Boris Johnson has been accused of racism more often than Donald Trump has been accused of Russian collusion, and with considerably more evidence. He has written of Africans giving "big white chief" Tony Blair "watermelon smiles" and that the Queen was greeted on foreign trips by "flag-waving picanninnies". It took him six years to apologise for that. He said the Turkish president had sex with goats, said Barack Obama was "part-Kenyan" with "an ancestral dislike of the British Empire", and said the Conservative Party was as cannibalistic as people from Papua New Guinea.

When he was editor of the Spectator and one of his columnists wrote a column about "black thugs", claiming West Indians "multiply like flies", death threats were issued to a leading black lawyer and Scotland Yard was called in to investigate. There are female converts to Islam who cover their heads - but when Boris talks about burqas, crime, correct identification and being able to assess a person's motives, the only thing people see is the brown people doing it.

7. Boris is a man of the people saying it like it is

"I'd like thousands of good schools as good as the one I went to, Eton."

"I suppose with houses and assets then I guess I would be a millionaire. But so are a lot of people."

I'll leave those there.

8. Rudeness is amplified in a newspaper

9. Newspaper columns have an impact when they're written by politicians

10. Politicians who were in Government a month ago are listened to

11. Ex-Government ministers who write newspaper columns do it to say things that they think will get them back in power

12. A politician who gets into power because they normalise rudeness to a group of people is A Bad Thing

13. If an ex-Government minister wrote a newspaper column saying black people all looked like wheelie bins, he would be cast into the outer darkness

14. If you or I went to work and said a Muslim colleague looked like a bank robber, without any evidence they had ever robbed a bank, we would be disciplined, fired, shunned and probably sued

15. Likening a group of people to street furniture or criminals would be considered funny only if someone laughed

16. Even Hatey Plopkins and Stephen 'Pretend I'm Called Tommy' Yaxley-Lennon aren't laughing, because they can't

17. If no-one is laughing and everyone is offended, either at the column or the reaction to it, then it's not a joke

18. No Muslim woman has yet said Boris was right and she does look like a bank robber

19. The column has, so far, not caused a single veiled Muslim woman to throw off her headscarf

20. The only woman who has thanked Boris so far is Nadine Dorries

21. The column's main impact has been for the word 'Boris' to be said, repeatedly, in every office, home, pub and coffee shop in the country

22. If you want to help a woman, start by being nice to her

23. If you want to help a woman being oppressed by men, have a go at the men

24. Boris Johnson has shown himself to be a man of integrity the same number of times that the rest of us have shat a golden cucumber

25. No-one has had time this week to remark upon what a complete balls-up Brexit is and how it's all Boris' fault

26. No-one has noticed that Boris just victimised a group of victimised women

27. It wouldn't be OK for Corbyn to tell Jews they were c***s. It wouldn't be OK for the PM to tell Donald Tusk he looks like a paedophile.

It should not be OK for the former Foreign Secretary to say women who cover up are victims, while punching them in the face and shouting: "LOOK AT ME! VOTE BORIS!"

But he did, didn't he?

No, Boris Johnson is not about to save the NHS. He's about to make it worse

August 5, 2019

The relationship between a Prime Minister and the National Health Service is do or die.

The health of a PM's career is inextricably linked to that of the nation. If they care for the NHS, they care for us. If they don't do that, we die, and they'll soon find themselves short of voters. Boris Johnson's relationship with the NHS is abusive. He has demanded more money for this grand old lady, using logic that collapsed in the time it took for someone to stick it on the side of a bus. Despite the fact everyone knew £350million wasn't available for her upkeep, and never would be, he kept repeating the promise until the UK Statistics Authority sent him a stern letter requesting that he desist.

Perhaps resenting this black mark upon his character, perhaps in the belief that polishing it will render his many other flaws less visible, or perhaps because he is genuinely seeking to restore his reputation, Johnson has today promised £1.8billion for the NHS. Not only is £1.8billion a bigger pile of money than £350million, it is also a bigger lie. An inverted pyramid of panhandling poo-bah, if you like.

1. The money doesn't exist

2. It's still not £350million a week

3. Even if it was, it's also not enough

But numbers, right? Let's hurl around some big numbers, millions, billions, hundreds of fizzillions, and it all goes in the headline, where people will just see the big numbers and think better of the man they persist in calling 'Boris'. I hate maths, but not as much as I hate people lying. And if maths has one thing over words, it's that it cannot lie. So let's take this one painful sum at a time.

When the Vote Leave campaign did its bus sums, it used a gross figure for the amount sent to the European Union as part of our membership. It did not take into account the rebate for about a third of the total, which Margaret Thatcher had negotiated. And they didn't factor in those things the EU gave us in return - farm subsidies, infrastructure projects, bus stations and regional investment.

The claim was knocked down during the referendum campaign. It was proven false before, and immediately after, the vote. But a year later Johnson wrote again in his newspaper column: "Once we have settled our accounts, we will take back control of roughly £350 million per week. It would be a fine thing, as many of us have pointed out, if a lot of that money went on the NHS."

This assumes we will give the EU the £39billion we owe. Which if we do not pay, it will demand in a future trade agreement. And which, for his latest sums, he has pretended is in his pocket. But the billions Johnson has recently promised for police officers, hospitals and schools are billions he has no control of. The real figure we spent on the EU is nearer £250million a week . And it will be dwarfed by the economic cost of any sort of Brexit, estimated at anywhere from 3% of GDP with a deal, to 10% without one. In other words, it will cost a minimum of £1.9billion a week - a deficit 5.4 times greater than the profit we were promised.

Added to all this is the fact that the money Johnson is pledging isn't real. It includes £1billion the hospitals already have, and which they got only by making cuts to services that amounted to more. After which, they were told not to spend it, which made those cuts effectively greater still. All that Johnson has done is tell a small proportion of hospitals they can spend money they earned as a result of losing a larger amount of money. His £1.8billion cash injection could therefore be more accurately described as a multi-billion pound cash EXTRACTION. A cash-ectomy, if you like.

Then we have the revelations this weekend that the Tories have swiped £4.2billion from NHS maintenance budgets to pay wages. The absence of spending on buildings means the repairs that were needed have got worse, and will now cost £6billion. On top of all that is the £30billion a year black hole in NHS spending, the lack of a national social care service, 100,000 vacancies and migrant NHS staff departing these shores at unprecedented levels because of Johnson's dodgy, undemocratic, and as-yet unsuccessful referendum.

If you look at Johnson's dealings with the NHS, his empty promise of £1.8billion must be compared to a minimum £151billion he and the government he was part of have taken from the NHS. Or, in simpler terms, the Prime Minister has cost our health service at least 83 TIMES what he has promised to give it.

Throw in the harm any sort of Brexit will do to the economy at least in the short term, and you can multiply that by many billions more that should have been available for NHS spending and will instead be lost in tariff subsidies, a mass slaughter of the lambs and an inevitable rerun of the austerity we all hoped was over.

If Boris Johnson's relationship with his mother followed the same pattern as that with the NHS, he would have persuaded her to abandon her pension, personally brought down the government he wanted to write her a cheque instead, and increased his own spending to the point where the only solution was to steal money from his mother's purse.

Now it is finally his job to provide the money, he's found a few pennies down the back of the sofa that his mother had lost already and presented them with a showman's flourish. An act which should merit calling the police, not a thank you. He expects this to restore his reputation. He expects it to bring him votes.

Anyone who thinks better of a son for treating his mother this way is a fool. Anyone who thinks better of someone treating THEIR mother like this would be a matricidal maniac.

And any voter who thinks better of a Prime Minister who behaves in this manner towards the NHS in which we are all birthed, bandaged, scanned, screened and saved on a daily basis, is asking for an earlier, grubbier, and more painful death. It was bad enough before Brexit, but with Boris Johnson's input, we'll soon be screaming blue murder.

He said Brexit was a matter of do or die. So this is the easiest maths of all - if we Brexit, he's toast[32].

[32] Despite having 'got Brexit done' - by his definition - Johnson's poll ratings by the time he left office were his lowest ever, at -53

Boris Johnson's government has killed thousands in a viral Dunkirk. They cannot lift lockdown safely, because they left it too late

April 17, 2020

In Italy, it took 35 days. In France, it was 37. And in Spain, it took 40.

In the UK, the government waited for 53 days from the date of the first confirmed coronavirus case before announcing a lockdown. In those 7 weeks, thousands died before their time.

Boris Johnson stood before the nation on March 11 and said: "I must level with you, level with the British public - more families, many more families are going to lose loved ones before their time." And then he waited for another 12 days before doing what was most needed to limit the tragedy, in which time he was probably infected with the virus himself.

Now the government, led in his absence by Foreign Object Dominic Raab, is discussing how to end the lockdown that costs an estimated £2billion every day, and 5 dead domestic violence victims every week. But thanks to how they've handled things so far, there is no way they can do it without killing more.

According to the World Health Organisation and just about every medical expert with their head screwed on, all countries need to meet 6 basic criteria before they can lift restrictions.

The first is that the bug is under control. The only way of knowing if this is the case is with widespread testing, but we have minuscule amounts of testing. Second is the ability to detect, isolate and trace every single new case. For which you need, oh yes, widespread testing.

Third is cutting the risk of outbreaks in care homes, where there is, ahem, near-zero testing. Fourth is preventative measures in workplaces, and fifth is controls at the borders which 15,000 people are crossing every day without testing.

Finally, we need community engagement, which is the only target we're currently able to meet and which, with every day of cocking about, gets shakier.

The Tories are currently besieged by a toothsome Keir Starmer, who is asking for a lockdown exit plan he knows will mean them admitting their mistakes, and economists claiming money matters more than lives.

And yesterday, the persistent running sore which is Iain Duncan Smith lost his last marble and claimed that while "increased testing and tracing will be essential", the country "cannot wait for these to determine when we unlock". Essential, yet simultaneously non-essential. He also insisted we "must not rely solely on epidemiological models". Heaven forfend epidemic experts should tell you how epidemics work, hey Iain?

If he had his way, a government which insisted it was following the science and didn't, thereby making things worse, would try to make things better merely by abandoning the pretence. Unfortunately, IBS' ability to irritate the digestive processes of the Conservative Party means his madness is often heeded when it should be laughed out of town. If they listen to him this time, thousands more will die.

The first confirmed case of Covid-19 in the UK was on January 31. On the same day, the first cases were confirmed in Spain and Italy.

When Johnson was pressured to impose a lockdown, he said he was following the science. Helen Ward, Professor of Public Health at Imperial College London, says that because science had little idea how to tackle coronavirus its best advice was to test, trace, and quarantine. On March 11, Johnson made his dire prediction, yet on March 12 it was announced all testing and tracing would stop.

Four days later, an Imperial report predicted 250,000 deaths in the UK. The government waited until March 23 to impose a lockdown; coincidentally, it came 24 hours after the Sunday Times had quoted the PM's chief advisor Dominic Cummings saying the policy was "herd immunity, protect the economy and if that means some pensioners die, too bad". No10 denied the report, but the damage was done: people believed the Tories were following the science that suited them, not us.

China kept coronavirus a secret for 6 days, and thereafter was so sparing with its information that its own doctors and scientists were arrested, the WHO was conned, and half the world lulled into a false sense of security. Its habitual secrecy has led directly to the infection of 2 million people and, at time of writing, the deaths of 146,898.

The exponential growth of a virus means every day of delay made the problem worse by an order of magnitude. Where once governments thought they could mull over the options for hours that stretched into days, now they have horrors that increase in minutes instead of hours. We cannot exit the lockdown soon, because we didn't start it early enough. We will need weeks, maybe longer, to not only scale up testing capacity but to get those tests to the people that need them, in care homes, in key worker hubs, and in the community.

That decision - that white flag of surrender - gave us the lack of testing, a lack of protective equipment, lack of the right medicines, an uncontrolled spread in care homes, exposure of key workers, deaths of bus drivers, carers, nurses and doctors, and a reaction from those citizens who've always felt ignored that they might as well ignore the lockdown.

The problem with surrender is that it's very hard to reverse. Oh, you can insist you never meant it, that you were taken out of context, or a victim of a smear campaign. But if you've demobbed the troops it takes time to get them back on the field, longer to organise them, and victory is further away.

Everyone loves a war analogy, and Johnson likes comparing himself to Winston Churchill. So this is his Dunkirk - a lack of leadership and assumed superiority, coupled with allowing the enemy to dominate the air, leading to a deadly retreat ameliorated only by the heroism of a handful of people.

Churchill needed 4 years and global co-operation to go back and try again. He also needed to admit his failings, marshal his forces, and ask the rest of the world for help. Unless Johnson comes out of recuperation a changed man, able to admit his cock-ups and fix them, he will not do that. The people he has promoted to government are not able to do that. Most have been self-isolating from logic for so long they don't even know how to spell it.

They want to lift lockdown, but are unable to make it safe. They'll blame someone else, and arrest those who grow disillusioned. But governments only ever spill the blood of others, and voters tend to notice when there's so much of it they cannot leave the house.

Brexit: Boris Johnson is smashing your house up in order to swat a fly. It won't end well for any of us

September 7, 2020

If Aesop wrote a fable to satirise Boris Johnson's attitude towards Brexit, it would be about the man who blew up his own house swatting a fly.

Sadly for us all, the Greek slave-storyteller did not commit that particular morality tale to parchment, which means that when Boris Johnson studied the Classics he never so much as glanced at a metaphor for self-defeat. What a different world we might be living in, had he done so: one which made a smidgeon of sense, or in which Prime Ministers were capable of remembering lessons from childhood.

Welcome, instead, to Planet Brexit: a place where a man really HAS just blown his house up trying to swat a fly, and Boris Johnson is about to do the same with an actual country.

In the Dordogne, a man in his 80s grew so enraged about the buzzing of just one of many trillions of insects that he dug out an electric swat and thrashed it about so thoughtlessly that it came in contact with a gas canister, and exploded part of his abode. The man lived, but the fly - whose ancestors survived meteors, dinosaurs and ice ages - is probably still buzzing happily about.

And in Westminster, a man in his 50s got so bored with things being hard to understand that he dug out a withdrawal agreement he'd resigned over, rewritten, declared perfect, fought a general election for, and then relied on for 9 months of talks, and said it was pants.

We had forgotten all about Brexit, which seems about as relevant and recent as Ancient Greece. But once upon a time, 52% of those allowed and bothered enough to vote decided to leave the European Union, and that involved agreeing how to do it. This withdrawal agreement proved more contentious than Johnson's notoriously chequered love life. The plans for it caused Johnson to resign as Foreign Secretary, and sparked a no confidence vote that Prime Minister Theresa May won. She wrote her agreement, and failed to get it past Parliament 3 times. Her government was found in contempt for failing to publish the legal advice about it, perhaps because the lawyer said the agreement was rubbish, and that she hadn't asked for advice until after she'd written it.

Johnson then fought a leadership campaign promising an "oven-ready" Brexit deal on the basis of a new withdrawal agreement. He won, rewrote it, and then shut Parliament illegally so it could not be discussed. After being forced to reopen it, he crowed to the House of Commons: "They said we could not open the withdrawal agreement, and we did. They said we could not get rid of the backstop, and we did. They said we could not get a new deal, and we did."

(NARRATOR: We didn't, and we still haven't, but it's still not his biggest lie.)

Parliament voted for his deal, but also for more scrutiny of it than Johnson was prepared to allow. He demanded, instead, a general election, and was asked in the House of Commons if he'd campaign on the basis of his agreement, or try to change it.

He replied: "I can tell the House that we have an excellent deal for the whole of the UK and that we will campaign on the basis of that deal." In other words, there was a fly, but he planned to open the window. A new Parliament voted for it, the EU ratified it, Johnson signed it, and he told the Queen to sign it. Then negotiations restarted, using that deal as the blueprint for talks.

It is *that* deal he has just torn up. The expensive, painful one he didn't want anybody to look at and which has been law since January. The one which has formed the foundation for every Brexit building block that has been laid since - millions of pounds worth of border infrastructure, business investment, civil servant hours, and compromises already agreed with the biggest market on Earth.

And he's done it over the one problem he, and Brexit, have always had - the border between Northern Ireland and the Republic. It's been called the backstop, a border of varying flaccidity and location, and today it's a "loose end". But, in its fundamentals, it's the fact that almost everyone forgot there is a border we cannot control, and if we don't control it we cannot leave the EU.

If we patrol it, the country will go bang. If we don't, Brexit will go bang. It's that simple: do we split the union and restart sectarian war, or do we allow the EU to control who and what enters and the country? Johnson has decided he'd rather explode the United Kingdom than reverse out of the ideological cul-de-sac he's stuck in.

Leaving the EU, its market and rules, means creating an edge - somewhere beyond which it cannot go. A point where goods are checked, tariffs applied, passports scanned, and people assessed. That demands a deal. Without one, there's no edge, no rules, no guarantees. We cannot even strike other deals - under World Trade Organisation rules, all our borders must be controlled first. The agreement Johnson resigned over was one in which the border was NOT checked, and the EU could oversee the island of Ireland. The one he wrote was one in which that border was STILL not checked, but we made a new border with the mainland which we checked instead. Today, the government plans a new law which says we won't bother to check that border EITHER - meaning there'd be no checks anywhere.

Neither the EU nor UK are legally able to create the edge they both need on the Northern Irish border. Either the EU has to treat the whole island of Ireland as part of the UK - effectively, evicting the Republic from the union - or the UK is treated as though it were still part of the EU, even after it's voted to leave. In all directions, madness lies.

Johnson is probably just bluffing to force through the last details. Any law he'd propose may get voted down or amended by Parliament anyway. But it's the umpteenth time he's lobbed a bomb into the talks, the umpty-teenth time Northern Ireland has been a stumbling block, and there are only so many times either the EU or the 1.8 million people who live in his flammable bargaining chip will wear it.

And there you have it - a man so irritated by a fly in the ointment he is prepared to blowtorch his own face in order to kill it. Unless he gives Northern Ireland and its unwilling citizens away, that border will never exist, and never be controlled.

Brexit was not possible on any of the terms he suggested, whether on buses, in Parliament, or on paper, but he's trying to convince you he's doing a thing that cannot be done.Which is why we have the posturing, the thrashing, the inevitable declaration in a month's time the fly has been exterminated, even as the country begins to break apart under the twin pressures of a virus that cannot be beaten and demands for a Brexit that can never exist, and we all start to wonder how, exactly, this man ever appeared intelligent.

Remind yourself that this is his deal he's complaining about, his promise he's breaking, and his legacy he's creating. Remember the lesson of the old man and the fly, and ask yourself: is he going to explode his home, or yours?

The North is revolting against Boris Johnson. Last time this happened, we got Robin Hood and Magna Carta

October 9, 2020

Picture, if you will, a conference of barons. They angrily complain of the arrogance of a ruler in London, of being taxed, criminalised, and abused by the authorities. They demand open justice, standards of proof, and something in return for the money that has been taken from them.

Eight hundred years ago, such landowning lords rode horses, quaffed ale and planned on parchment as they marched their armies south to threaten the king. Today, it's Andy Burnham on a Zoom call with Steve Rotheram, as Manchester and Liverpool get together to gang up on London.

It's not clear where our modern power-brokers stand on quaffing or equestrianism, but their problem with Boris Johnson is precisely the same as that of their medieval predecessors: they're ruled by a prat.

To recap: the Plantagenet dynasty, also known as the Angevin empire, ruled England and most of France. A brilliant military leader had several sons who spent decades fighting him, and each other, for power. The one who was most vicious, duplicitous, and unhinged was the final survivor: youngest brother John, who was such a terrible king that no heir has been named after him for the best part of a millennium.

He taxed and warred same as his brothers, but was despised for his military and political failures. He went cap in hand to the French, signed away almost every European territory, and rather than reward his lords for service punished them mercilessly - torturing his prisoners, and taking their children as hostages.

He is said to have personally murdered his 15-year-old nephew, while drunk, and thrown the body in the Seine. The wife of one of the potential witnesses was jailed with her son and both were starved to death. When their cell was unlocked, her corpse was found knelt over her dead boy, having gnawed at his cheeks for sustenance. He lost his money, his crown jewels, his land and his battles. In short, despite having sabotaged and betrayed every previous king, John was no damned good at kinging.

John's incompetence, rather than his cruelty, was what led the northern barons to rebel. They marched, warred, took castles, were besieged by the king's forces, and forced John to surrender - signing Magna Carta, a peace treaty aimed at resolving the issues. Having signed it, John immediately reneged on it, got the Pope to declare it unholy, and went back to war. He was king, and everyone must do as he said. Does that ring any Withdrawal Agreement bells with you?

John died, to widespread delight, from dysentery, his guts turned inside out as he writhed in agony. The knights who ruled on behalf of his young son reissued Magna Carta, saw off a French invasion, and generally saved the country from going down the toilet with him.

And 804 years later, local leaders are up in arms about someone ruling by decree, rejecting all criticism, and taking away people's hard-won rights while claiming something they cannot see makes it reasonable.

There's a difference between one man raised to be a tyrant and another taken by surprise with a pandemic. But both Boris and John enjoyed some early wins before breaking their contract with the populace - an unwritten agreement that people would be ruled by rulers who knew what they were doing. Covid-19 has shown up the Prime Minister's habitual laziness, lack of preparedness, and showmanship as the shallowness of a man remarkable only for what he's been able to get away with, just as wearing the crown showed John's unsuitability for it.

In 1216 Prince Louis of France convinced half of England it'd be better to have a Frenchman in charge; coronavirus has persuaded a good chunk of modern Britain that a micro-organism would be a fairer arbiter of who lives and dies than the PM. And while our 13th century politics centred on failing to control France, that of the 21st centres on failing to control just about everything. The disease then was *droit de seigneur* - today, it's *droit de twit.*

Britain was a sitting duck for covid. We had existing epidemics of obesity, diabetes, poverty, respiratory and heart disease, health inequalities, deprivation. We've still got rickets, for heaven's sake. But we also concentrated those problems in the north - in the former industrial heartlands that have been left economically worse-off, where housing is worse, where money has been sucked out of local councils and where the poor, the sick, and the immigrant were more likely to be corralled.

Once Covid got in, the North was always where it would end up. Those terribly unfair lockdowns that have targeted the Labour-voting areas least able to withstand them, are also the only tool the government has to protect them from a disease that is more of a risk in Burnley than it is in Brighton.

Boris, like King John, is trying to overcome an enemy by ignoring it. Trouble is, the enemy, for him, is those northern barons - and Nicola Sturgeon in Scotland, or Mark Drakeford in Wales - who he can't even be bothered to talk to. It is either cowardice, arrogance, or an unwillingness to engage with those who are not, politically, his friends, but it all leads to the same place. A fractured country, a dysfunctional power structure, and civil unrest.

The only upside to John's rule was that it gave rise to the legend of Robin Hood, perhaps based on the life of his childhood friend Fouke Fitzwarin. The two quarrelled, John seized his estates, and Fouke fled to the forest as an outlaw while fighting the king's forces. At the same time, hundreds of other hooded forest outcasts, when they appeared in court, were given the pseudonym Robehood or Robynhod.

Rebels multiplied, under John, just as coronavirus is spreading under Boris, but a reviled ruler gave rise to a revered hero. Johnson must be smarter than the king whose name he shares - fight the enemy without, not make more within.

Neighbours, everybody needs good neighbours... but the Boris and Rishi fairytale is going to end in tears

February 7, 2022

If there's one thing that Boris Johnson is disciplined about, it's control. Specifically, not being subject to it.

Wedding vows, lockdown rules, basic morality, the Ministerial Code, his own manifesto: the default response of the Prime Minister to all of them is "PAH!" Which is why it's interesting that, a week after the worst week in his premiership since the previous worst week, which was only the week before, the PM is now submitting himself to the control of his Chancellor of the Exchequer.

In a single weekend, Rishi Sunak's mates have moved into No10, expensive policy announcements have been binned, and the crime of fraud which has taken £10billion off the taxpayer on Covid alone has been downgraded to a harmless infraction of little consequence.Unfortunately, this whirlwind romance is headed for some very big and pointy rocks.

The first is that the cost of living crisis, which is already a crisis, is going to get worse with food costs predicted by millionaires to rise another 5% in April. No-one knows what to call something worse than a crisis, but the dictionary will probably need updating to include something like "crisaster".

The second is the energy crisis, in which the taxpayer has been forced to compensate corporate giants for not being able to steal money immediately, and instead letting them steal it over 5 years. Prices are likely to rise again in the autumn, and because 9 months was too long for billion-pound firms to wait, the government may allow an extra price rise in the summer to tide them over. Presumably, we'll be calling this "frobbery".

If Boris thinks Her Upstairs is difficult to live with, he's going to flip when he finds out that Rishi is the sort of spouse who'll give him £200 towards the housekeeping, and then ask for £222 back by exerting some below-inflation fiscal drag on state pensions.

On the face of it, their relationship is rooted in shared politics and a mutual love of money. But while one partner is a hedge funder who's got more money than the Queen, the other never carries cash because he can't hold onto it for more than 5 minutes.

Both of them seem unable to spot a party when it involves 30 people, soft drinks, beer, renditions of Happy Birthday, a society wallpaperer, an official photographer, a strategically-sly cake, and a police investigation. Both, according to reports, are also capable of enjoying all that in the space of just 10 minutes before "getting on with the job", which is a polite way of saying you burped all afternoon.

But there's little else these two have in common. One is a spender, the other a spaffer. One drinks beer, the other power. One is vain enough to arrange photocalls on staircases so he doesn't look as short, while the other has just one suit and no comb.

Today, we're told that a major announcement on Boris' big promise to use the £12billion National Insurance increase to bring down NHS waiting lists has been boiled down to a website, so that you can stop ringing the doctor to find out about your appointment and just throw the computer out of the window instead.

Officially, the plan "isn't ready yet", and unofficially Rishi's blocking it until he's PM and can announce it himself. And therein lies the problem with this partnership: only last week, Johnson's friends were telling him to kick Sunak out, on the grounds he was trying to steal his job.

Imagine a bride trying to get the groom sacked, withholding cash while giving it to rich mates, giving Princess Diana eyes in TV interviews whenever she's asked about parties.

Picture a groom so desperate to keep the house that he'll overlook their differences, let her take total control, and start measuring up for curtains he will never get to see.

Think about a relationship in that much trouble before its second anniversary. It might work in an Australian daytime soap, but it ain't going to last in a world where people don't come back from the dead after 5 years lost at sea.

Johnson thinks he's saved his skin by ceding control to his most ambitious enemy, and boasts it would now take a Panzer division to get him out of No10. Sunak, meanwhile, is quietly lining up his tanks in the Downing Street garden, which he has always had a great view of from his No11 office.

The PM is being infantilised by enemies saying his wife wields all the power, and potentially criminalised by his friends claiming that she has nothing to do with his work, but nevertheless attended a lot of work events.

And the only PR expert who can be persuaded to enter the fray is someone who considers the PM "sexually incontinent", throws Benny Hill salutes at world leaders, quotes Gloria Gaynor, and on his first day gives the press the headline: "He's not a COMPLETE clown."

But the fundamental flaw with this great "reset", which is probably more of a breather to allow Rishi to liquidate assets, is that it involves trying to instil discipline in a man who has spent a lifetime shucking it. The fact he needs to be taught the self-control of a toddler is why he lives in Errorsborough - a town twinned with Débâcle.

Fans may think these two have found the perfect blend of bluster and billionaire, but it'll last only as long as it takes for Johnson to take back being out-of-control, and Sunak deciding that his tanks are ready to evict.

Badgers are making us look stupid – so let's kill them all!

September 2, 2015

It's been a difficult few years for all of us. There was a banking crisis, billions of pounds worth of bailouts, belt-tightening and blame.

Winter stopped being cold, summer stopped being sunny, people who wore white tie at 11 appeared to be the most normal and competent lot to run the country and our own citizens started blowing us up. But it's all right. Because finally we know who's responsible for it all.

Badgers.

Those stripy-faced devils are responsible for all the ills that have befallen Blighty. It's badgers who breed two or three cubs every year, contributing to a population explosion. It's badgers who take up all the school places, and insist on GP appointments during the hours of darkness because they claim to be nocturnal – more like they can't get out of bed.

And have you ever seen a badger at work? Course not. They're all on benefits, the ligging scroungers.

I wouldn't be surprised to hear there was a badger in the Alma Tunnel when Princess Di was killed. And someone told me it's the badgers who are after Julian Assange, or at least that's what Julian thinks and I'm prepared to take that as evidence. They probably gave Sue Perkins that brain tumour, too. BASTARDS. They're not even Anglo-Saxon. What native Brit has a black and white face? They've probably scuttled through the Channel Tunnel or hidden themselves behind engine blocks in order to get into soft-touch Britain.

Why didn't they stop in France, eh? Why come here, unless it's to send us all to kingdom come? There are great swarms of badgers, lurking on the Continent, sharpening their claws and coming over here armed to the teeth with infectious diseases.

They sneak in and breed in YOUR garden, creating stripy little timebombs determined to destroy the British way of life.

Luckily our government is prepared for this ground-dwelling menace and is happy to spend £7,580 per badger to shoot them on sight. Do not question this, citizens! It's for your own good. Do not question why shooting one corgi-sized animal outside its home address costs as much as a small family car. Presumably, they put up quite a fight.

They go all "YIPPEE-KIYAY MOTHERF*****!" and start lobbing grenades while thinking regretfully of a quiet Christmas Eve with the cubs.

Do not question why it costs £5,000, plus an Easyjet flight to Zurich and the cost of a final meal, for a human being to commit suicide at Dignitas and 50% more to put a single bullet in the face of a short, fat, slow-moving omnivore.

Do not ask yourselves why we as a nation pay our most severely disabled citizens £109.30 a week in Employment Support Allowance, but spend £145.77 a week to pop a cap in a stumpy-legged creature who nicks the occasional chicken. Especially don't ask yourself why we have to kill them at all.

The main reason is that they can infect cattle with bovine tuberculosis, a disease which more often than not does not kill cattle who can go their whole lives without developing the full-blown disease. It does not make the meat unsafe to eat, and the milk is safe to drink as well so long as it's pasteurised.

The problem is that back in the days of yore milk wasn't pasteurised, and everyone who drank infected milk got TB. So, in the days of yore, we decided it was a good idea to kill badgers. The fact that a century later it is no longer necessary to kill badgers is, frankly, seditious talk and I don't want to hear any more of it.

It is likewise treason to mention the fact that rules forbidding the export of perfectly-safe milk and meat products from infected cattle should be changed, if not for the badgers' sake than for that of sanity. You should never mention that slaughtering infected-yet-healthy cattle has cost the taxpayer £1billion in the past decade and is a complete waste of time, money and life.

Likewise, don't let anyone hear you say the main cause of infected cattle is other cattle, and their movement between farms. And if I hear anyone point out that dogs, cats, alpacas, foxes, goats, pigs, deer, and llamas also spread TB but for some inexplicable reason are not being culled I shall report them to the nearest police officer.

You are especially not allowed to mention previous governments have spent £23million on vaccines but they're being held up by testing rules which could take another decade. If anyone publishes the fact that the National Trust and RSPB already vaccinate badgers on their land and it's actually more effective than shooting badgers dead they ought to be deported. And it would be akin to mooning Kate Middleton to point out that killing badgers costs £7,580 a time and vaccinations cost £660 each including trapping and staff costs.

Because, you see, the badgers have asked for it. They went out dressed in short skirts, got drunk and willfully coughed over cows an infectious disease that isn't that harmful and could well have come from a domestic cat anyway and in so doing did the worst thing it's possible to do.

They made the government look stupid. Because it didn't change the stupid rules, or challenge the stupid people, or speed up the stupid vaccines, or spend their stupid money on the right stupid thing, they decided to blame the badgers.

Which makes a change from blaming the disabled, the poor, and the single parents and the teachers and the GPs but is, just the same, pretty stupid.

They have now compounded this stupidity by spending £4.4million on killing 558 badgers over the course of a year, not a penny of which will stop bovine TB or be repaid by reducing compensation paid out to farmers.

Because at a time when we've had a banking crisis, billions of pounds worth of bailouts, and belt-tightening which has been used to justify spending less money on children, health, education, roads, green energy, the disabled and carers, it's more important to find someone else to blame.

In this case, Brock. The only creature clever enough to have figured out how to eat hedgehogs.

Which makes perfect sense if you're Mrs Tiggywinkle and absolutely none to anybody else[33].

[33] In 2022 Defra announced an expansion of the badger cull, which was predicted to bring the total number of badgers culled since 2013 up to 200,000. Brexit should have given us the power to set our own bovine TB rules, but we didn't because we still need to export beef, and the EU can't yet differentiate between infected and vaccinated cattle. Sorry Brock, Brexit didn't help you either

Dear the Labour Party – why do you make it so difficult?

November 18, 2015

Do you know what the easiest thing in the world is? It's easier than falling out of bed. It's easier than picking a fight with Katie Hopkins. It's opposition. Of any sort.

See, the person who's got a big idea has done all the hard work already. They've done maths and sweated over the press release and told their mum and everything. All an opposer has to do is give it a bit of a kick. Make the pedestal wobble. Cause the still-wet mortar to shift. Put a dent in it with something as simple and easy and cheap to get hold of as a few well-chosen words.

And if anyone says "worl, whatchew got that's better?" you can pluck just about anything out of thin air and add a bit of small print about it being subject to change if the sums don't work out. It doesn't matter whether you're arguing with a mate in the pub or standing in the House of Commons opposite the Prime Minister. All you have to do is look mostly sane and ask the right questions.

Which is why, the Labour Party, you're making such a hash of it.

It's not just that you voted in Ed despite him being slightly less electable than a confused aardvark. And it's not just that to replace him you decided to have "a broad debate" about "the direction of the party" which ended up with Jeremy Corbyn and the ever-deepening hole you seem to inhabit. It's this - not only have you got the easiest job on Earth but you're making it as hard for yourselves as you possibly can.

Look, the people running the country look like they've left their periwigs and corgis in their second-best carriage. They cut tax credits for the working poor while food banks multiply like Charlie Sheen's ex-lovers and cut the emergency services in the middle of an international terror crisis. They don't have a strategy for dealing with ISIS even though they've been bombing them for two years, their computer systems are as susceptible to cyberattack as a ZX Spectrum and the power stations keep being turned off without anyone bothering to turn on a new one.

On top of that they've had their first five years of honeymoon and are stuck into the second term in which hubris and backbiting always combine to produce rebellion and laziness. They don't do their sums, they don't think it through, and the Prime Minister doesn't even intend to stick around. Not only is opposition the easiest job in the world, but opposing this lot is the political equivalent of lying on a sunbed ordering another cocktail while somebody rubs your toes.

And yet you make such hard work of it. You don't know what you think about Trident. You don't know whether hypothetical terrorists spraying citizens with guns should be shot. You don't know how much of a nod is enough, and you don't know enough to keep Ken Livingstone away from anything too sharp, like a defence review or a microphone. You don't know that giving Diane Abbott a job doing anything is as welcome to most of the country as recruiting Camila Batmanghelidjh to be Shadow Chancellor of the Exchequer. And even those of you who DO know all that don't know what the hell to do to stop it.

Yvette, Dan, Alan, Chuka and the others just sit there looking glum, rolling their eyes when they think no-one's looking and hoping Corbyn's spade-based efforts to reach Australia without a plane ticket will burn him to ash without any effort on their part. The Corbyn fans who joined the party in large numbers tell themselves and anyone on Twitter who hasn't blocked them yet that this is all fine, there's nothing wrong and if you don't agree you must be a spy, crowing madly like Comical Ali as Baghdad falls.

Meanwhile The Voter – who incidentally is the person you need to get on-side with, something you seem to have forgotten – thinks you're doing worse than Ed Miliband was FIVE YEARS AGO. So I'm going to make this easy for you. I'm going to use simple words and clear instructions.

First, say that ISIS is bad. Second, say that terrorists spraying bullets should of course be shot if the police called to deal with them decide that's the best thing. Third, put somebody with a passing experience of defence in charge of your defence review and put Livingstone, Galloway and Abbott in separate padded cells. Or perhaps a shark tank. Either/or. And fourth, CATCH YERSELVES ON.

Jeremy Corbyn is never, with the best will in the world, going to win a vote that puts him in Downing Street. Replace him with someone who will. NOW. Not next year, or after the EU referendum, or at some point when Yvette or Chuka finally summon up the blood.

Corbyn is a complaint. He is the result of a number of people saying "I don't like this" without thinking any further. He is, ironically, a perfect bit of opposition while simultaneously being incapable of presenting any himself.

You have an open goal, if only you would climb out of the funfair barrel you are stupidly swimming around in and learn how to kick the flipping ball. All it takes is for one person among your MPs to say “enough of this shit” and 51 nominations from their colleagues, followed by the Labour Party membership coming to its collective senses and voting to win rather than excavate the Earth’s core to see how far from reality you can get.

It shouldn’t be so difficult as it apparently is. It’s just a case of sanity, and deciding you’d like to experience some. If you don’t do it for yourselves, then do it for the nation.

It’s the easiest thing in the world.

Dear America: Please don't put Donald Trump in charge of the free world[34]

August 7, 2015

Dear America,

How are you? Feeling okay? Got a temperature? Some kind of strange blockage in your bowels that can't be explained? That would be Donald Trump, the man who in defiance of all reasonable human expectations is the front-runner for the Republican nomination to run for President.

Let me say that again: the front-runner. The human equivalent of Red Rum in the human equivalent of the Grand National, if the prize for running fastest around Aintree was getting your hooves on 1,800 nuclear warheads. And this is despite the fact that he makes a horse's arse look gifted.

Now, I appreciate you'll think this is nobody else's business. I agree there will be many who think a billionaire is the embodiment of the American Dream that you, and many others in the world, hold dear. And I can see why you'd think a Brit giving you their opinion would rankle your 1775 sensibilities. But hear me out, just for a second. We don't tell you what to do these days - we even let you cock up the important business of brewing a cup of tea with little more than a sigh - so please treat this as less an instruction and more of an intervention. One without tanks, if you can imagine such a thing.

PLEASE DO NOT VOTE FOR DONALD TRUMP.

Don't vote for him to win the Republican nomination. Don't vote for him to win the Presidential race. Don't vote for him to win the X Factor or a church raffle or even Best Pony In Show. Every nation has its share of idiots, and I appreciate we've

[34] They did

exported some to you. And America has given the world some wonderful things, not least the word "moron" and an awareness of what can be done with a cigar. But nobody wants Donald. Not you, not us, not humanity in general.

Allow me to explain:

1. It's a terribly important job

This doesn't just affect you - the Leader of the Free World is able to start, or stop, a world war. He or she can dish out aid, salvation or retribution to most of the planet and the rest of the planet don't get a vote. We're all relying on you to get this right, or at least not so wrong that the whole place gets had backwards by a complete liability with banjo strings for hair. The Free World cares very much who you choose, and if you choose Donald Trump there's every chance he's going to find a way to charge us for it.

2. He is not the embodiment of the American Dream

He's a billionaire real estate developer who was the son of a millionaire real estate developer, and four of his businesses have been declared bankrupt - the most recent of them just last year. This has caused other people to lose hundreds of millions of dollars, which for most people would make him more of an American Nightmare. He is also one of the least intelligent trolls on the internet, and they don't need any encouragement.

3. His last name is slang for fart

You may think this is a minor consideration, but if Ol' Fartypants gets into the White House you will find he is as socially unwelcome as an extrusion of intestinal gas that hangs around for five years.

4. Think of the problems that will arise if everyone starts voting for the Tit With The Hair

5. The purpose of opposition is too important to give the job to a clown

Sarah Palin should have proven this to you already, but just in case she didn't: Whether you are Democrat or Republican, you should want the opposing candidate to be competent, capable and a contender. Firstly because the better they are, the better your side has to perform in order to win and therefore the greater mandate they will have, and secondly because on the off-chance the other guy wins you don't want him to behave as though he were an ADHD-afflicted, penis-obsessed cretin who has to graffiti his name on everything.

6. You will become the United States of Trump

Donald Trump is the man behind Trump Financial, Trump Sales, Trump Restaurants, Trump Tower, Trump Buffet, Trump Bar, Trump Catering, Trump Ice Cream Parlour, Go Trump online travel website, a Donald J. Trump line of menswear, Donald Trump the fragrance, Trump magazine, Trump University, Trump Golf, Trump home furnishings, TV company Trump Productions, Trump the Board Game, Trump Chocolate, Trump Books, Trump Model Management, Trump Shuttle, Trump Ice, Trump Vodka, Trump Mortgage, Trump Steaks and something called the Trump Institute, where presumably he's developing plans for the Trump Underground Lair, Trump H-Bomb and to rename every planet in the solar system as Trumps 1 to 9.

Do you think he might be over-compensating for something? Just a smidge?

7. He keeps being asked if he's a criminal

This is the man who settled out of court in 1975 after being accused of refusing to rent property to black tenants, who was investigated but not questioned in 1979 over bribery, questioned but not charged in 1981 over racketeering, and has not responded to claims that he built Trump Tower with concrete supplied by two New York mafia crime families. On top of all that, he's been accused in divorce documents of raping his ex-wife Ivana, which he denies. Donald has never been charged, has said "I have a great relationship with the blacks", and is quick to sue. He could be purer than the driven snow and innocent of any wrongdoing. But if he ends up in the White House these accusations will keep being reanimated and there'll be bugger all legislating done if he's mired in personal lawsuits.

8. He has absolutely no sense of humour

Donald has spent years asking to see Barack Obama's birth certificate to see if he was really American. So comedian Bill Maher demanded to see Trump's birth certificate to see if he was fathered by an orang utan, as that was the only other thing in nature with the same hair. Donald announced he would sue for $5million, and then changed his mind when he realised he was acting like an ape.

9. He's a bit like Nigel Farage, but with unlimited piles of cash

Donald credits himself with starting a debate on immigration by claiming Mexican immigrants were "rapists and drug mules", wants to "build a wall" along the USA's 1,933-mile southern border, and responded to criticism from a female journalist by telling her she had "the face of a dog!" He says he's allowed to tell a female Apprentice contestant he wants to see her on her knees, and call women fat pigs, on the basis that "political correctness is killing this country". He didn't mention what good manners would do to it. Nigel, for all his faults, has not done any of those things - but then again he does seem to have an internal censor of sorts that keeps him on the edge of hatefulness without ever quite going all the way over. Donald on the other hand doesn't just believe in Bongo Bongo Land, he's thinking of buying it and renaming it Trumpo Trumpo Land. And those are just the first things I can think of from the top of my head.

I know Britain has a long record of voting for people who later turn out to be daft ideas, but the important thing to remember is that they seemed a sensible choice at the time of voting. You can't say that of Donald. You can say he's odd, you can say he's over-privileged, you can argue that he's not as good a businessman as he'd have us all believe. But more than anything else you can, without fear of lawsuit, also point out that he's not a long way from barking mad and a HELL of a long way from a sensible choice for anything short of testing hairspray on the far side of the moon.

He's amusing, he's interesting, he adds a thousand-fold to the gaiety of the nation if not the happiness of anyone with dark skin or a vagina, but the rest of the planet would really like it if you remembered what happened last time you voted for an idiot and try, very hard, not to do it again.

Thanks for listening[35],

Lots of love,
Blighty

PS While we've got your attention, it's best done with BOILING water and you put the milk in FIRST.

[35] They didn't

Don't ban Donald Trump from the UK – let him in

December 9, 2015

Donald Trump is an obnoxious, hateful, ignorant bumhead.

Quite literally – I imagine the hair around his exhaust pipe looks about the same as that on his bonce. But that's not a reason to ban him[36]. If anything, it's a reason to invite him on a state visit with all the trimmings. Because if you ban him, he's still there. Still on Twitter[37], still in the world, still Trumping away.

What would be the point of banning Tyson Fury from BBC Sports Personality of the Year? He'd still be an uneducated misogynist only of use if the flooding forces us all to live in caves and brings back sabre toothed tigers. What's the point of banning eggs having their tops sliced off on children's TV? The alternative is eggs having their heads bashed in with a spoon. And most of the things and people we've banned already – fundamentalists, drink driving, class A drugs, Cliff Richard songs – are still there.

So let the Donald in. Lay on a plane. Send Kate Middleton to welcome him at Heathrow in full evening dress and a tiara, because that would make most people remember their manners.

And then show him around.

Take him to Marks & Spencer, founded by a Polish Jew from Belarus. Send him for a morning jog with Mo Farah, Olympic gold medallist born in Somalia. Take him for a swim afterwards at the London Aquatics Centre, designed by Baghdad-born and British-honoured Dame Zaha Hadid. Oh, and drive him around in a Mini, invented by a Greek born in Turkey. Get him to sing nationalist anthem I Vow To Thee My

[36] The announcement of an impending state visit by the US President was greeted with more outrage than previous visits by undemocratic tyrants who seized power. The Libtards had him sized up about right

[37] In 2021 he was suspended from Twitter after the attack on the US Capitol, and in 2022 allowed back - although he has yet to take up the offer

Country, written by Gustav Holst who was born in Cheltenham of Swedish, Latvian and German descent. Introduce him to a mad old git from a Danish-German family born in Corfu and explain why Prince Philip was allowed to impregnate the Queen.

Take Donald for a curry and a Cobra beer. Explain, using the beer mat and simple diagrams, how it became the nation's favourite dish and quashed a lot of racism at the same time.

Then take him to Beachy Head and contain the urge to push him off. Instead point out France, where immigrants aren't so welcome and coincidentally they have more terror attacks than us.

Once there, Donald will say that all these immigrants are the reason we don't have an empire. It's why half our capital is a no-go area and if only we all had guns and better-groomed bum hair we could be more like America.

Tell him that, since his idea of banning Muslim migrants to the USA was to stop gun massacres, it wouldn't have stopped Chicago-born Syed Farook pouring bullets into his co-workers in San Bernadino last week. Nor the other 349 mass shootings in the US this year, most of which were carried out by the mentally ill and the Christian fundamentally-inclined.

Point out that, by his logic, all American-born Muslims would need to be deported for safety's sake, and that it would be his job to go and tell Muhammad Ali and Mike Tyson.

Then sigh, take him to Trafalgar Square, glue his feet to a paving slab and invite him to say whatever he pleases. It will be less than 30 seconds before someone Vines[38] themselves shouting: "YOU'RE A COCKWOMBLE, BRUV!" In under a minute, someone else will have started repeating whatever he says in a silly voice. The Donald will fluster and bluster. Tourists will take photographs. Children will point out the flaws in his argument. Pigeons will poo on him. Nelson will, as ever, look down on him.

Yes, camera crews will turn up. Journalists will write it all down and repeat it. They'll be accused of making it worse. There'll be a handful of idiots who say to themselves "Hey that Donald doesn't sound like other politicians! I'd vote for him, if only I could get out of this padded cell and forget that he sounds like a satellite dish picking up Kim Jong Un's brainwaves". But most people will hear an idiot shouting to himself, and laugh at him.

And that's the most devastating thing you can do to anyone who wants to be taken seriously.

---

[38] A social media format allowing six-second looping videos, which launched in 2013 and closed in 2017

You can't have freedom of speech that applies only to people who think like you. It's not particularly free, and it's not that useful either. When the likes of Trump – and every nation has a Trump, we've got about three last time I looked – speak it's absolutely brilliant for the rest of us. First, our usually apathetic opinions get a kick up the bum. Second, we realise the freedom to hold them has to be fought for. And third, we always win in the end.

Everyone who's ever suggested segregation has been proven wrong. Every nation that split people according to their genes changed its mind. Everyone who ever voted for fascism – and my word, but there's been millions – came to regret it. If Donald Trump is out in the open, at least we know where he is. If he attracts people who agree with him, at least we know who they are.

Can you imagine how worrying it would be if we didn't?

The time to worry is when The Donald goes quiet. The time to panic is when you don't know what he, and hateful fascists like him, are up to. And the time to ban things that need arguing with is NEVER.

(And if that's not enough – take comfort in the fact that about 30% of Trump's supporters aren't even registered to vote. The most popular candidate for Republican voters is actually Ben Carson – a man who believes the Holocaust would not have happened if the Jews all had guns, there are "too many vaccines", and that the pyramids were built to store grain. Remember – there's always Hillary[39].)

---

[39] Misplaced optimism on the author's part

"Hey Barack! It's Donald. HELP!"

November 14, 2016

Now we know why Barack Obama and Donald Trump looked so uncomfortable in their first meeting at the White House.

According to the Wall Street Journal: "Mr Obama walked his successor through the duties of running the country, and Mr Trump seemed surprised by the scope."

Even Trump's aides - who are supposed to be the experts here - were "unaware the entire presidential staff... had to be replaced", it added. After what must have been an epic facepalm, "Mr Obama realised the Republican needs more guidance. He plans to spend more time with his successor than presidents typically do".

So what might that "guidance" be like? Here's the first, imagined phone call between the two...

War of the Worlds theme rings out

"Hi Donald."

"Oh hi Barack! How did you know it was me?"

"You have a special ring tone."

"Oh COOL! Is it All The Single Ladies?"

"No."

"Is it that Robin Thicke one?"

"No. Look, anyway how are things going? I know we agreed you could have my number and call if you needed any guidance but it's day one, Donald. Aren't you busy settling into the Oval Office?"

“Not really, Barack. There’s a damn great eagle in here and I.T. haven’t given me a password to log on yet. Where are you anyway?”

“Hawaii. Where I was born. Remember?”

“Oh yeah. Hey, remember that wall I was going to build? I got some bricks! And a cement mixer! From the same people who built Trump Tower.”

“Weren’t they allegedly mob fronts? Who allegedly protected your construction site from a city-wide strike for reasons no-one can fathom?”

“Yeah! Same guys!”

“You’re going to need very big pre-cast slabs of concrete to build that wall, Donald.”

“OK that’s what we’ll do. Make ‘em and drive ‘em down and then stand them all in a row.”

“You would need slabs about 40ft high and 10 inches thick, that would be planted 7ft in the ground. It’s uneconomic to move them thousands of miles. You’d have to make the slabs near the wall.”

“Sure, sure. We can do that. New jobs. The best jobs. Make America Great Again!”

“You don’t understand Donald. Concrete is made from aggregate you have to quarry. There aren’t enough quarries for that near the Mexican border. The nearest concrete facility is in fact Mexican.”

“Bummer.”

“And because a lot of the border is inaccessible desert and mountains you’d have to build some roads to get the work crews out there. And then dig 7ft into rock to put the slabs in, put some razor wire on the top, cameras, staffing. The total cost is projected to be $15billion.”

“We’re going to borrow lots of money though. Make America Indebted Again!”

“Donald, you can do that. You can borrow some money. And you’re going to have to spend quite a lot of it on concrete and on recruiting a LOT more border guards because those guys all get pensions, you know.”

“I know this! I know this! That’s so we can deport all the migrants I got people worried about, isn’t it?”

“That’s right Donald, that’s what you said. You wanted to deport 11 million people. More recently you said it’s 2 million to 3 million, so I’m not sure how many you want to deport now.”

“As many as we can, Barack. DRAIN THAT SWAMP. “

“OK Donald, 2 million would mean 1,369 deportations a day, 365 days a year, throughout your term of office. That would need a lot of immigration officials, two jumbo jets a day, a suspension of the legal appeals process and removing the entire bottom tier of the US economy. No gardeners, no nannies, no garbagemen, no fruit pickers.”

“Well we can give those jobs to Americans!”

“Yes you can. But it would also mean fewer cars being bought, fewer goods and services, a lower tax take and probably a few more vigilante groups rounding immigrants up ‘to be helpful’, so probably some criminal justice costs too. Oh, and all the decent baristas would be in Cuba.”

“My head hurts, Barack.”

“Mine hurt every day for eight years, Donald. Mainly because I kept hitting the desk with it whenever some dumbass on Twitter said my birth certificate was a fake.”
“Whatever. Hey you know that Chinese guy?”

“Which Chinese guy? In the canteen?”

“No, no, the one in China.”

“There’s a lot of Chinese guys in China, Donald.”

“The one in charge. The boss. I’m going to really piss him off and put 45% tax on everything he sends over here! Great, huh?”

“Is that a good idea Donald?”

“It’s a great idea! It’s one of mine! Everyone says it’s the best idea EVER.”

“That would start a global trade war with every nation raising or lowering tariffs in order to attract the best goods and services, with knock-on economic effects for the Earth’s 6 billion inhabitants, diplomacy and global conflict, Donald.”

“Well, OK, OK, all right then how about this? I’m going to make it easier for people to access and pay for two- and four-year technical and vocational college courses so they can all get better jobs.”

"That's a great idea Donald."

"It is? You think so? WOW. I totally like thought Ivanka was stupid when she suggested it."

"Are you going to do it while you're in court defending Trump University against allegations of fraud by taking money for a course about your business secrets that didn't actually reveal any?"

"Huh. Knew it was a dumb idea, I TOLD her. Anyway guess what guess what guess WHAT. "

"What?"

"I got Vladimir coming for a sleepover!"

"That's great Donald. He didn't want to come over when I lived there."

"Ha! I knew it. I'm so much more popular than you. LOSER. "

"I won more votes than you. Twice. Even Hillary got more votes than you and you told everyone she's a witch."

"Well me and Vlad are like best buds now. We're going to fight ISIS."

"And how are you going to do that, Donald?"

"We're going to shoot all the guys with beards and not let any guys with beards into the country because they're so like backward."

"Have you ever met any Amish people Donald? You should get up to Pennsylvania and say hi."

"Hey Barack what's that thing under your desk?"

"What thing? The waste paper basket?"

"No, no, the thing, the thing under the desk."

"The carpet? The chair? The plug socket?"

"The red thing."

"DON'T TOUCH THAT BUTTON DONALD. BAD. NO. NOT THE BUTTON."

"You sure?"

"I'm sure. How about your tax cuts? How's that going?"

"Oh I'm going to give a multi-billion dollar tax break to billionaires."

"I'm sure that's not what you promised Donald."

"Oh yeah I said the middle classes but it'll be billionaires too, so that's cool. And corporations. And I'm going to close bits of the internet that ISIS uses. And scrap most of your dumb doctors and nurses thing. And, and, and I'm going to keep Guantanamo Bay open and send Hillary there."

"Oh right. Hey Donald, guess what I just worked out?"

"What?"

"It sounds like America is going to have a big wall to keep people apart, no money, a thriving black market economy, mobsters, little contact with the outside world, perks only for those who can afford it, and internet censorship. There might even be some white supremacists in there. You know where else is just like that?"

"No, where?"

"Supermax jail, Donald. You're putting America in jail."

"No, I'm just going to put the webby guy in jail."

"Is that because he hasn't given you a password yet?"

"No the other guy. The guy in the webby stuff."

"You're going to have to help me out. Where did you see him?"

"He's in the corridor. He runs after me all the time. He's got webs all over his clothes. And there's this guy with pointy ears on a mask, and some dude in blue pantyhose is drinking whisky in the kitchen."

"That's Spiderman, Batman and Superman, Donald. You can't put them in jail. They're the good guys. Well, Superman will be better in a bit."

"They keep chasing me!"

"That's their job, Donald. Without superheroes America would have pretty much nothing else going for it."

"Oh yeah? How about the French toast?"

"That's French, Donald."

"The cars?"

"Japanese."

"Our iPhones!"

"Made in China."

"DAMMIT, BARACK. This is so HARD."

"I know, man. That's partly why we have a year and a half of presidential hustings so we get the absolute best candidates who know their stuff. Something must've gone wrong this time."

"Yeah well guess what, I'm only going to get paid $1 for this job."

"I heard that. Is that on top of the corporation tax breaks, billionaire tax breaks and inevitable financial scandals?"

"Screw you, Barack. I don't need your 'guidance'. I totally know what I'm doing. I'm going to make America great again!"

"Are you spelling that G-R-E-A-T or G-R-A-T-E?"

"You're FIRED Barack."

"We've been over this. You can't fire someone whose contract expired."

"Oh yeah, I forgot. Hey Barack?"

"What?"

"Can I call you tomorrow?"

CLICK

Like every Mafia boss, Donald Trump is a cheap crook, a terrible businessman, and an awful parent. But will it make any difference?

September 28, 2020

In 1995, as a non-graduate trainee journalist on my local paper, I earned £7,000 a year. That's £134 a week, £26.92 a day, or £3.36 for the 8 hours I always worked more than.

And do you know, I STILL paid more income tax than Donald Trump. That year, and every year since.

But then, I was also learning my trade. And so was Don - a craft that his future biographers will inevitably call The Art of The Steal. Trump has always run his empire like a Mafia enterprise. It operates on blood ties, threats, the promise of enrichment, and demands of total loyalty.

But after he expanded the organisation to cover the entire continent, it began to implode. Investigators picked off his capos one by one, the made men started making deals with the feds, and the phrases we kept hearing were "pleaded guilty", and "tax fraud". It went quiet after his consigliere Michael Cohen went down, blabbing about Stormy Daniels, charity fraud, pay-offs, and potential deals with enemy gangsters across the water. But it's still bubbling.

Trump doesn't mind too much, because it makes him look like a Corleone. The problem is that he is not Marlon Brando, or Al Pacino. He is what would happen if flat-footed Fredo accidentally became the boss of bosses - corrupt, dumb, and fattened by decades of feasting on his own ego.

Research has shown that, had Trump invested all he inherited from his father in the stock market and "spent his career finger-painting", he'd be richer. He's actually managed to lose billions during a 50-year career in real estate, the one industry which constantly outperforms the stock market.

His tax returns, leaked to the New York Times, show he has hundreds of millions of dollars of property assets and they're losing millions more. A suspicious taxman should investigate, and probably already is, whether they're losing quite what is claimed. And, according to today's revelations, he not only fancies his daughter Ivanka but has also exposed her to criminal accusations of tax fraud over paying her firm "consultancy fees" on hotel deals when she was already his employee.

A terrible businessman, a rotten parent, a man at the heart of criminal tax conspiracies which take money out of the pockets of every single American: just like every other Don, except this one's dumb enough to take a job which makes it more likely he'll be busted.

Five weeks before an election in the UK, a nation which considers mutual support of the NHS a matter of faith and nationhood, such revelations would devastate the culprit. In the US, which has spent two centuries bitching about taxation and government overreach, it's neither a surprise or an electoral problem.

To Democrats, it's a disgrace. To Trumpkins, it's canny accounting. To none of them is it the sort of thing that equates with a lack of decent healthcare, or indicative of duplicity even though Trump has often claimed he pays lots of taxes and says he is treated unfairly by the Inland Revenue Service. That much, at least, is true - the average American who did the same would have been jailed years ago.

What matters, to both sides, is that Trump is a godfather. One they can either despise as a criminal, or one whose gang they want to join. The only way to puncture the fantasy everyone in America shares of Trump as a powerful, capable overlord is to prove his incompetence - the bad decisions, the losses, the childlike inability to see why lying is going to get him in more trouble, not less.

That's not going to happen in 5 weeks. Nor will the Great Trump Tax Fraud be dismantled by the army of law-enforcement personnel crawling all over it in time for America to go to the ballot box. For this vote, taxes do not apply.

Instead, race matters. The economy, jobs, America First, and whether those shy Trump voters of 2016 will still quietly pick the Klan-sympathiser or, perhaps just as quietly, choose a long-in-the-tooth lawmaker with a reputation for decency but not much else. The polls, as four years ago, are close enough to go either way. There are suggestions that even in the event of a Joe Biden win, Trump will gerrymander the electoral college in swing states to win a nomination the votes don't justify.

But if you want to know what's really going on, ask the bookies and the shopkeepers. Trump's odds have narrowed since August 1 from 9/5 to 6/5, or from a 35% to 43% chance of a win. Biden has gone from 65% to 53%, but is still favourite, and the televised debates are about to begin.

Meanwhile gun makers and sellers say they have seen an unprecedented boom in arms sales - a first wave due to the pandemic, in March, and a second in June as the Black Lives Matter protests kicked off following George Floyd's death on May 25.

So you have a narrow victory for someone, in a nation that is both armed to the teeth and torn by race hate. Whoever wins, there will be riots, maybe even a fragmented civil war. Biden would accept a fair defeat, but Trump will litigate, lie, throw shade, refuse to transition and do all he can to stay in office - not just because that's the sort of baby he is, but because the White House is all that's keeping him out of jail.

He has $300million of loans coming due in the next 4 years, coupled with a dysfunctional family, a decreasing number of lieutenants, and constant criminal investigations. Time is running out. At 74, and morbidly obese, there's a reasonable chance he'll die before he has to make good on any of it.

But make no mistake - Trump wants to die a president. He will call himself President-in-Exile if he has to, or stoke a Facebook-crazed militia into armed insurrection[40] if that'll work, but he'll carry on doing what he always has, and leave America with the bill.

[40] Just don't ask me which horse will win in the 3.30 at Epsom

Everything you know about pregnancy is a lie - this is what it's really like

December 5, 2015

You have been lied to.

Blame the media, blame the Illuminazis, blame Nigel Farage. But pregnancy is not what you thought it was. Pregnancy, we have been told, is 9 months of joy with a bit of sickness at the start and some discomfort at the end. It's not.

That's a lie. And, having got pregnant and thereby stumbled across this fact, I can tell you it's the biggest cover-up since Adam put an apple core behind his back and said "Eve told me to do it". And because I'm a reporter, I'm going to tell you the truth.

It starts, as so many things do, with boobs. At first they hurt. Then they itch. And for three months your nipples are permanently erect, like you're caught in a Force 9 gale in a nightie. Before any male readers start daydreaming, that's not sexy. It's agony. It's like having invisible piercings reeled in by an angry fisherman 24 hours a day. I imagine it's about as grim as having a three-month erection, and just as difficult to find the right clothes so that no-one else ends up with eye injuries as a result. If you see a scowling woman rearranging her bra in public while walking like a crab and muttering about nipples, she's either newly pregnant or a tramp.

After the nipples comes the sickness, we're told. Well, I had none. I just had, for four months, the sensation that I was ABOUT to be sick. That feeling you get in the loos at 2am when you weigh up a strategic vomit and carrying on against the benefits of your duvet. Hot spit was the main symptom. Constant, increasing gallons, of hot spit, which is caused for no good reason by pregnancy hormones. I didn't vomit once, but wish I had. It might have been easier.

Once pregnant your ovaries produce progesterone, a hormone which encourages the uterus to hold on to the new embryo. For reasons best known to itself it also causes your bowel to slow down to the speed of an old man in a Fiesta going the wrong way up the M1. There is pain when you poo, pain when you don't poo, pain when you eat, pain between eating. You eat Weetabix three times a day, drink water, eat fruit. If you're lucky, your bowel speeds up to the pace of a sloth stuck in the wheels of justice. You get a bump even though the baby is only the size of an olive: a bump consisting entirely of poo.

Enough details. Let's just say that it's not good, and it's not right.

You can't take a laxative. You can't take a pill for anything. Progesterone also causes increased production of mucus. Not just sufficient to protect the baby from bugs, but enough to fill your head and leak out of your ears. You can't take a Sudafed for the pain. And there's two things that make the snot worse.

First, the baby's taking all your water to make blood so you get dehydrated. The snot filling your skull is as dry as beef jerky, and as chunky. Secondly, the extra blood a pregnant woman has zooming around her system makes the capillaries in your nose burst. A lot. So you not only have the discomfort of blowing your nose 87 times a day, but also of passing through your nasal cavity great bleeding snot scabs that the Ghostbusters special effects team would pass up as too icky.

Remember the thick, horrible scabs on your knees when you were five? Like that, but green. The blood issue means you get bleeding gums when you brush your teeth. It's very common to then get gum disease. In days gone by women were said to lose a tooth for every baby - today it means lectures from the dentist.

All of the above seems so much worse when you're not sleeping. I expected this bit to come at the end, when I'm too big to lie comfortably. Ha. I WISH.

Every night for three months I woke up at precisely 2.45am. At first it was a desperate need to wee - when the baby is teeny and the uterus is inside your pelvis it pushes on the bladder - but once the baby had grown out of the way I woke up because of a hormone spike. It felt a lot like having three espressos. Why my hormones felt the need to do anything at 2.45am I don't know. Even after the clocks went back, they still did it at 2.45am, leaving me staring bug-eyed at the ceiling composing letters to the manufacturers of Nytol suggesting they extract digit from backside and make something to ease this hell. After two weeks it felt like I was clinging on to sanity by my fingernails. The solution? Going to bed at 8pm, for a few hours' extra kip.

Bye bye, prime-time TV. Bye bye, social life.

All of this would be bearable if I could drink. But not only does all the medical advice agree that it's bad idea during the first three months, your taste buds start malfunctioning like a wonky supermarket trolley. Beautiful white wines I would normally adore smelled wonderful and tasted like piss. Gin smelled great but tasted like battery acid. Tea seemed slimy. And butter, my dears, tasted like rotting, rancid, human flesh.

I've stood in mass graves. I've seen bodies splattered across the countryside by trains, shot to pieces, drowned and left to rot in the sun. It's a vile, indescribable smell, and I had it IN MY MOUTH every time I ate anything with butter in it. That's sandwiches, cakes, buns, almost everything in every restaurant, scrambled eggs and toast.

On the day I discovered this problem I made three batches of eggs on toast, certain eggs or milk were off. I fed a bit to the dog, I nibbled a bit myself, and then acutely aware that manky food can cause problems for the baby began to panic. Mum turned up to find me in floods of tears rabbiting about killing the dog and, bless her, ate scrambled egg out of the kitchen bin to prove it was fine.

I've stopped going to the pub. The social machinations required to avoid alcohol while not telling anyone you're pregnant were just too much to deal with. "What do you mean you're not drinking? Is it the Apocalypse?"

But I've particularly enjoyed being told by people the only explanation for whatever I've written that day is that I'm drunk. NO, I'M NOT, BUT THANKS FOR BRINGING IT UP.

Now the baby is fully formed and my taste buds are firing properly again I've allowed myself half a glass of red wine once a week. It reminds me that I'm me - a vital rebellion against the forces of occupation currently turning my wardrobe into a selection of strained elastic. Oh, and the boobs are a problem again. I don't like these new ones I've been issued. They're too big and the nipples look like they've melted.

It feels like I'm carrying a set of bagpipes around with me. I have to wear a bra at night so they don't get stuck in an armpit. I WANT MY OLD TITS BACK.

And all this is despite the fact I planned to get pregnant, am happy to be pregnant, and looking forward very much to not being pregnant. I've been very lucky and had the perfect pregnancy. All the scans and tests show the baby is well, and I've had it easy compared to many women.

Which is not to say that it doesn't still feel weird. I've been taken over. I don't feel like the me I always thought I was. The wriggles I can feel in my tummy are a cross between hunger pangs and the squits. I used to run up escalators. Now I stand on the right, wheezing like a rusty traction engine because pregnancy means a 20% oxygen deficit.

I stand outside Timpson's and inhale the smell of shoe polish like it's crack. I only eat dark chocolate. When I come up to London you can find me plastered starfish-like to the side of a sushi bar, gazing at all the raw seafood I'm not allowed to eat.

And don't get me started on scallops. I love scallops. In butter. With white wine. ARGHHHHHHHH.

I'm now at the stage where every meal or cup of tea causes hiccups and burps. For hours. To the extent my oesophagus feels like it's got rocks in it. I'm starting to wish I had shares in Rennie.

I don't know how to answer the question "do you have children?" Despite having for years the rock-hard bladder of a news reporter who can sit 24 hours on a doorstep sustained by a Scotch egg and carton of Ribena, I'm now weeing within 20 minutes of every cup of tea. And do you know the biggest lie of all? The absolute whopper? They tell you human pregnancy lasts nine months. It doesn't. It's ten LUNAR months because OBVIOUSLY women are werewolves, and as a bonus the bit you weren't expecting is right at the end when you're proper annoyed.

It's all proof, if any were needed, that if God exists he's a man. No woman would put another through this sort of crap unless they'd at least run off with their husband first. A woman wouldn't design pregnancy hormones to taste like corpse. She'd make boobs a matter of personal choice and heaven only knows the evolutionary benefits of not being able to poo straight for almost a year.

Perhaps this is my fault for not paying enough attention. Maybe I tuned out when my friends were pregnant, and didn't ask the right questions. My best friend - a mum of three - said to me: "I've genuinely forgotten it all. If we didn't, the human race would die out." My mum said: "Everything with children is a phase. It passes and you forget it because the next thing that happens is even worse." Then she laughed. I think she feels it's revenge.

She's right of course. There's going to be screaming, crying, staying out until 3am binge-drinking and refusing to come home. And goodness only knows what the baby will get up to while I'm doing all that. I'm not bothered too much about the birth. I'm not looking forward to passing something the size of a pumpkin through my most sensitive parts but there's drugs and doctors and all the evidence says it can be done.

What puts me in a panicky tailspin is the thought that, afterwards, I'll be a mum. I'll have to be the person who is the constant source of comfort and advice. Who loves no matter what, who endures the worst anyone can do, who is the centre of another creature's world. My mum is brilliant. How can I possibly be as good at it as her? She says I'll figure it out. And she's usually right, so let's hope so.

I promise not to be a boring columnist who writes nothing but baby crap. I promise not to lose my opinions. I promise not to mention it too often, unless it's relevant. I also promise the next time someone asks me a personal question about it to point out that they wouldn't poke their nose into my gynaecology under normal circumstances, and that just because I look like a Weeble is no reason to forget your manners.

And lastly, I promise to take a notebook into the delivery room. Mum and all my mates swear blind they've forgotten what childbirth feels like, but I'm certain they're lying.

The hell of being heavily pregnant in rush hour

February 24, 2016

HEY YOU! Yes, you! I'd like a word.

I appreciate that you're a very busy person with things to do. Perhaps you're incredibly important, wrestling with the great philosophical questions of our time, or consumed with thoughts of a loved one currently in hospital. I'm prepared to be open-minded about the reasons for your behaviour. I can understand and sympathise.

BUT SHIFT YOUR ARSE OUT OF THE PRIORITY SEAT FOR THE PREGNANT WOMAN OR I WILL KICK OFF AS ONLY SOMEONE WITH A BLADDER THAT IS NO LONGER THEIR OWN CAN.

I've been stood here for five minutes. I've sighed. I've patted my tummy. That's not a big lunch in there, you know, it's an eight-month-old foetus which seems to have 17 elbows. It's like being in the front row of a One Direction concert.

An elderly lady across the way has offered me her seat. A gentleman of 50 or so has ORDERED me to sit down. Two teenaged girls have had a long whispered discussion about whether I'm really pregnant, or it's, like, TOTES embarrassing to discuss it because it's all vaginas, innit?

But your seat is the one I want, because you are the person who barged past me to get on this train in the first place.

It's not that long ago I would regard pregnant women on public transport with a jaundiced eye myself. Partly because I had no experience of it, and partly because I had a LOT of experience of standing up in high heels with throbbing feet while a lady in flat shoes got to sit.

I never resented her getting a seat, but I did think it would be nice if, while everyone was being so thoughtful, it might spill over to the stressed journalist who'd had a 12-hour day, six 10-minute bollockings and one inflamed bunion because she had completely ignored her mum's advice about high heels. But then I've learned a lot, being pregnant. Let me tell you about it, since you're already sitting so comfortably.

Firstly, if an omnipotent being planned things this way then he's either a raging misogynistic sadist or so utterly barking he shouldn't be trusted with cutlery, never mind galaxies.

Secondly, once you get past the first five months of painful breasts, nausea, chronic constipation and being elbowed in the ribs on rush hour public transport by people who think you're merely a little pudgy, there's another five months of enormous and painful breasts, chronic constipation made worse by iron pills and being ignored by people who act as though by carrying an extra human being you are somehow less of one.

And yes, that makes 10 months. That's how long pregnancy lasts - 10 LUNAR months. Anyone who repeats the 9-month lie gets a cynical remark about werewolves.

Let me state at this point: I'm not doing anything a gazillion women haven't done before, I don't ask for extra-special treatment or want to be wrapped in cotton wool. I've spent recent weeks working as hard as I can, as I'm self-employed and don't get maternity leave, and my days off chainsawing logs and digging over the vegetable patch. A wilting flower I am not.

That's why I'm on your rush hour train. I've been working, doing those same 12 or 14 hour days with 50% more blood to haul around than usual, not enough haemoglobin for me and the baby (hence the iron pills), and a bony mass which, if it didn't have a heartbeat, would be mistaken for a 1.5lb tumour the size of a honeydew melon.

Everything, I should add, is fine. She's well-behaved so long as she has daily doses of chocolate, and should be with us in six weeks or so, after which I expect her to ignore all my wise advice about bunions.

But she wees. A lot. Far more than I ever have. A few years ago I went on holiday with a friend, leaving my house about 4am for an early flight, transferring at a second airport, landing at our destination then driving up-country for several hours before finally getting a bowl of ice cream and into our room about 20 hours after we left home. I went to the loo, and when I came back she very thoughtfully said: "That's the first time you've used the toilet since we left your place."

I had a journalists' bladder – hard as nails, and capable of sitting on a doorstep all day without emptying. I was proud of it. It was a GOOD bladder.

Now the poor thing is being squidged by a small skull, punched by two tiny fists, and filled by four kidneys. It empties every time I cough, sneeze, or stop concentrating.

She demands toast AS WELL AS breakfast. She seems to like poo a lot because she holds up my digestive processes like a highwayman who can't get enough of it. And despite warning emails from well-meaning pregnancy websites about "empty calories" and "healthy snacking" she currently requires a diet that is 80% glucose and I'm eating Double Deckers like they never went out of fashion. (FYI, they're not "empty" calories. They're packed full of fun and enjoyment. Baby laughs at your sunflower seeds and demands cake, bitches.)

And, of course, she WEIGHS. She's just a few pounds but the extra blood is a lot more, along with a swollen uterus and boobs that appear to have been donated by Dolly Parton's plastic surgeon. These combine to make my walk up the station steps slower than the little old lady you just elbowed past. I can't make it without clutching the handrail you just wiped your snotty hand on.
And as for slopes, oh don't get me started...

Even a gentle rise in elevation means the baby pushes right down on my pelvis. I get pains in my cervix. I have to put a hand under the bump and try to lift it up to relieve the pressure – while holding on to something else, carrying my workbag and laptop, and avoiding the Commuter Dodgems. I can't roll over in bed without earth-moving equipment. Getting out of the bath is like a walrus trying to beach itself. I can't leave my knickers on the floor because, frankly, they'll stay there. Oh, and I burp. I burp ALL THE TIME. Mum says I never burped even as a baby, yet now I'm burping like Rab C Nesbitt after a particularly vicious vindaloo.

The hormones which loosened my pelvic muscles also loosen the sphincter between my stomach and oesophagus, with the result that everything in my stomach – acid, a glass of water, a nice dinner – can exit whenever it pleases.

I can't lie flat in bed, I can't eat a normal-sized dinner, and last week I vomited while brushing my teeth before bed.

It's also playing on my mind that at some point I have to pass a mass of bone and gristle through a much smaller part of my body that is used to being treated nicely and is packed with a lot of nerve endings. I told you anyone responsible for designing this system hated women, didn't I? If I ever meet him he's going to get his ear bent and a football filled with rocks shoved through his cock.

So here we are. You're sat comfortably, I'm stood with all this stuff going on and a temper on a short fuse, and I've resorted to The Stare. You know I'm staring, the rest of the carriage knows I'm staring, and while I don't expect you to give a toss about my baby I do think your mother should have taught you some manners.

There are some perks to being heavily pregnant, I'll admit. Lots of people DO notice and are sweet. I can legitimately demand the most comfortable seat in any pub, restaurant or strangers' home. When hungry I can usually find substantial bits of food under a boob and I can balance a full wine glass on my belly.

It's just the rush hour. It's just people like you. It's just the fact you know I'm here and are avoiding eye contact in case the alien bursts out of my stomach and eats your face. That, or you're so immersed in your own life you haven't noticed the grumpy, annoyed woman glaring at you who can't even have a fat gin and tonic when she finally gets home and is anxious for the day she can teach her daughter to pour one for her. The way I feel right now, it'll be before she starts nursery.

Oh, why, THANK YOU! That's SO KIND! How THOUGHTFUL. I'm getting off at the next stop but have a Brownie point for finally realising my backside needs a rest more than yours does.

Oh, and two tips for the future: please do the same for non-pregnant commuters in high heels when you see one, and if you ever know anyone who gets pregnant buy them one of those bean bags you can heat up in the microwave because those things are LIFE-SAVERS for an aching back.

And enjoy the rest of your commuting. I'm not setting foot on a train again until I have a pram with which to smash your ankles to smithereens.

Oi, Jamie Oliver! Breast isn't always best

March 19, 2016

George Osborne was distracted by them during his Budget speech. Susan Sarandon isn't allowed to get hers out. And according to a man in my ante-natal class on Wednesday they are the only way you can bond with your baby.

We all know that MEN think breast is best. But what does Jamie Oliver say?

Now his wife is pregnant for the fifth time (LEAVE HER ALONE!) he wants to tell us how important boobies are to the whole process. "I think the most upsetting thing for me at the moment is breastfeeding. We have the worst breast feeding in the world," he said, ignoring places like Syria where breast feeding amid barrel bombs and people smugglers is probably worse.

Some people say Jamie shouldn't interfere when he doesn't have boobs.

This is silly, not just because he's got a bigger pair than most females I know but because he's about as right as Jeremy Corbyn at a We Love Chairman Mao party. Breast, you see, is NOT necessarily best.

1. Breast milk has more sugar than some formula milk

In a cupboard in my house is a carton of baby formula ready for when my child arrives in a few weeks. In every 100ml feed it makes there is 6.8g of sugar, or lactose, and 67 calories. In human breast milk the same figure is 7.2g, and 75 calories. Seeing as Mr Oliver says "parents who give their children energy drinks might as well be giving them cocaine" I can't help but think he hasn't thought this whole breast feeding campaign through properly. Or perhaps he has, and his next move will be to suggest a tit tax.

2. There are no rules about what goes in to breast milk

Whereas there are LOADS of rules about formula. Labelling laws, peer-reviewed scientific research, trading standards, those dreaded EU regulations Nigel Farage complains about. It's not toxic or poisonous. It's not something that a big corporation scraped out of the bottom of a fridge. On the other hand, a breast feeding mum could eat nothing but Turkey Twizzlers dipped in Jamie's pasta sauce for a month and there's not one law that says she CAN'T feed it to her baby.

3. Jamie's science is REALLY questionable

Jamie says breast feeding mums who do it for six months are 50% less likely to get breast cancer. In fact, they are less likely to die from breast cancer. But perhaps that's because those who breast feed for six months are also more likely to be middle class. According to a study published in the British Medical Journal, breast feeding mums are more likely to be well-off. And research from the University of Leicester in 2013 found that wealthier breast cancer patients get diagnosed earlier while poorer ones delay going to the doctor. So while it's right to say breast-fed children are less likely to have infections, obesity and diabetes, it's even MORE right to say they're also more likely to go skiing.

4. 'Natural' is not the same as 'a good idea'

It is natural to feed your baby. It is also natural to die in childbirth, but these days we try not to. The 'natural' rate of maternal mortality is reckoned to be about 1,500 per 100,000 live births. In the UK, it's 8.2. Hands up everyone who wants to go back to doing it 'naturally'? Thought so.

I've been lucky enough to see a lot of the world in this job. I've interviewed women with a baby on one hip, a toddler on the other and a third on the way whose boobs simply can't do what's 'natural'. I'll never forget the father in Niger who had to choose which twin was going to die, because his wife had enough milk for only one. This week I heard a dad-to-be in my ante-natal class claim corporations selling baby formula in the developing world were a disgrace. Having been there – which I suspect he hadn't – I'd say it's a disgrace they're not handing it out for free.

5. The official advice changes

It's not just Jamie. The World Health Organisation, charities and the government all want us to breast feed more. But when my mum was having her children the official advice was to use tinned Carnation milk. I was bottle-fed on the stuff. It's got more sugar than breast or modern formula milk, but I'm neither obese or sickly. Evaporated milk is still popular as baby food in many places, particularly deprived areas or those with poor diets. A 1995 study in Newfoundland claimed that it was a harmless 'third-best' alternative after formula, so long as you added some iron to it. And I'd happily feed it to mine.

6. Breast feeding hurts, chaps

The leaflet for my ante-natal class this week the leaflet said it would include "advice about bottle and breast feeding". The only time bottles were mentioned was to point out they made no difference to bonding. The remaining two hours were devoted to showing us how to get a baby to latch on (difficult), what to expect (pain each time until the milk comes down), leaking (yuk), mastitis (YOWCH), hand expressing (oh come ON) and why only you should feed your baby.

The pressure to breast feed is immense. The common sense is not. There was nothing about maternal choice. There was nothing about other people helping out. There was no answer why, while many new mums start breast feeding, 80% of them are on bottles within a few weeks. I'll tell you why – it's so someone else can do a feed. It's because breast pumps are a bit rubbish, your tits hurt, and once the rose-tinted glasses of new motherhood get covered in puke you realise the 21st century is a much better place to live than any other.

7. Do what's right for you

If you've the time and inclination to spend six months to two years breast feeding your children then go right ahead. If you've neither then that's fine too. You have to choose what's right for YOU, not Jamie Oliver.

I have epilepsy so mild I don't need medication, but I do need enough sleep. With a new baby that'll mean having a night here or there where I can take a sleeping pill while someone else is on duty – and I can't breast feed while doing that. I'm self-employed, which means I don't get six months off. I work both at home and away, often at short notice. There's no guarantee I could express enough milk to feed a baby while I'm gone, especially not in the 10 minutes' warning I'd get.

And my mum is my childcare. I don't want her stressed trying to get a breast-fed baby to take a bottle, or for the baby or me to be stressed either. So why shouldn't I skip the mastitis and use formula from day one?

For almost 10 lunar months a small creature has dictated what I eat and drink. She's taken over my body and I'd quite like it back. I want to eat curry. I want to drink champagne. Both are supposed to be fine but have led breast feeding friends to have terrifying hospital dashes with their babies. So what's right for me is bottle-feeding, having read the label, listened to advice and made a reasoned judgement based on the needs of me and my baby. And what's right for Jamie Oliver is for someone to pat him on the head and say "wind your neck in, sugartits, and get back to the kitchen".

How can anyone forget childbirth? Very easily, it turns out...

April 18, 2016

"Oh, I can't describe it," said one friend. "It hurts, but you forget about it afterwards," said another.

Every one I asked to tell me what childbirth was like swore blind they'd no real idea, although they'd all been through it. Even my mum, who's experienced it more than once, told me: "I can't remember. But TAKE THE DRUGS."

As the months of pregnancy passed and I got closer to it, the more this collective amnesia bothered me. How can anyone simply forget a massive life event? Childbirth is a major physical trauma that still kills 830 women worldwide every single day. It can't be that forgettable. Perhaps it's so appalling the human mind simply blanks it out, I thought, like a motorway pile-up. Or maybe there's a conspiracy of silence to ensure the continuation of the species and I haven't been inducted yet.

I've been a journalist so long that it's more of a diagnosis than a job. So I decided to find out whether all these mums were psychologically scarred to the point of subconsciously editing their own memory banks, or simply lying to me. I packed a notebook and pen in my hospital bag.

"I shall take notes," I told myself. "Then I'll tell everyone. That'll solve it."

** *WARNING: Readers of a delicate disposition are advised to stop reading at this point. Go and make a cup of tea or something* **

First, it must be said that every birth is different. Each baby arrives in their own way, and what follows is based upon one birth alone. Some mums will nod along, others will think it's gibberish, and a few will count their blessings it didn't happen to them.

It began, as interesting things often do, at 3am.

I woke up, went to the toilet, got back in bed and thought I was going to the toilet again. Then it happened a second time and I thought "oh". The midwife said it sounded like my waters had broken and to drop by in a few hours. So I washed my hair, changed the bedding, tried to explain the situation to the dog, and headed over to my folks' at about 6am.

Mum took me to hospital at 8am, they confirmed everything was fine and told me to go home and wait. Then it stopped. I felt a bit of a nellie.

About mid-morning I started to feel mild tightenings at the top of my tummy. Then they became twinges radiating out from my back, half an hour apart. I paced. I sighed. I helped mum move some garden furniture and when she said "you shouldn't be doing this" I pointed out all it could possibly do was hurry things up. Sometimes the pains were eight minutes apart; at others an hour. It was like watching a particularly temperamental kettle not really boil.

I had a snooze and watched the evening news. Occasionally I winced as a contraction peaked. If you're a woman, the pains were like those you get on the first day of a heavy period. If you're a man, I imagine it's something like having your balls squeezed by someone who doesn't like you. They got more intense. I had a bath, which helped. Then they stopped. Then they started again, stronger than before.

I had to lean on something and pant through a wave that started as a period pain then rose to be inexplicably bad before tailing off. Each one took 30 to 60 seconds and rendered me speechless. As soon as each was over I could walk and talk normally. We rang the hospital. "Come in when you have three in 10 minutes," they said. "They should be toe-curling and so bad you can't ring us yourself." At about 10pm, realising I'd been at this for nearly a whole day and was already knackered, I went for a lie down.

At 10.15pm I started screaming.

Not a "gosh, I'm being strapped to a railway line by a dastardly man in a top hat" sort of scream. More the kind you might hear from a female grizzly bear with her foot in a trap. Deep, guttural, wordless pain. Mum rang the hospital. "Bring her in," they said.

There followed what I know for a fact is a 15-minute drive at reasonable speeds to the hospital. It was probably nearer 10, because my poor old dad undertook it while his daughter was sprawled on the back seat bellowing like a wounded bison. It felt like an hour. Finally, there were people in blue uniforms with lots of lovely drugs.

"You can't have any drugs," they said. "There's been an emergency and the anaesthetist is in theatre. You can have some gas and air until he comes out. Maybe some pethidine."

It was a Friday night, it was 10.50pm, and my cervix was 4cm dilated.

It needs to be 10cm for the baby to be born, and the midwife said with a first child it normally increases by 0.5cm to 1cm an hour. "So another six to 12 hours? Blimey," I said. "Good thing I brought a book."

Ninety minutes later I was 10cm dilated and hollering for opiates like Lord Byron on a bender.

With a slower progression your mind and body have time to acclimatise to the pain. THIS was the childbirth equivalent of warp speed, and it HURT. It felt as though one of those medieval two-edged battle axes was being swung upwards from the floor into the base of my spine: a splitting, skeletally-deep pain. From there it radiated sideways across my back and around my front. The space between contractions was long enough for me to gasp a sentence, no more. Like "where's the doctor?" or "EPIDURAL, PLEEEEEASE".

Then the baby's heart rate halved and the midwife sounded an alarm. Suddenly the room was filled with doctors, fresh from theatre. The baby sorted herself out, and the obstetrician said I was close.

"Epidural," I gasped. "Too late," they said. "The baby will be here in 20 minutes. You can do this." But I couldn't.

The gas and air made me feel drunk. The pethidine made me woozy. I still hurt. Each contraction was unbearably bad. I apologised to my mum. A lot. For everything. I didn't swear once. Not because I didn't want to, but because I could hardly speak. I pushed and pushed and pushed, just like you do when straining for a poo. The midwife kept yelling encouragement but nothing was happening. By 2am I'd had enough.

"I can't do it," I said. "Yes you can," she told me. Half an hour later I was pulling wires out of my arm and throwing them across the room, screaming "I CAN'T".

The midwife wasn't to know this, but I never say "I can't". If even I, who thinks there is always a way even if it involves tilting the Earth on its axis, am saying something's not possible then things are officially screwed. The contractions were weakening too. If the baby didn't have help she would die.

Suddenly a dozen people in blue popped up out of the floor and began scurrying around. It was like being in a Smurf pub for final orders. The anaesthetist came in. "Where have you been?" I asked. "No, no allergies. Yes, that's my signature. Fine. HURRY UP."

I continued grunting through the pains as they handed mum some scrubs and rolled me into theatre. "Can you sit up for the injection?" they asked. I hauled myself upright and then, bliss. If only I'd had this three hours ago, I thought. I lay back down and stared at the white-bearded anaesthetist above me.

"Will you marry me? I love you," I told him. I think he'd heard that before.

I looked round for my mum. She was alone at the side of the room, trying to stay out of the way of the medics. She looked scared. A nurse gave her a stool to sit on and brought her over to hold my hand. The obstetrician looked up from between my legs. "Right, give us a push," she said. Unable to feel or do anything from the waist down, all I could do was think about pushing.

"Great," she said. "One more and we'll have the head and a third one and your baby will be here."

Think about pushing. Look at the ceiling. Giggle about Smurfs. Think about pushing again. "There you go," said the doctor, and plonked a baby on my tummy.

This may seem silly, considering nine months of pregnancy, but I was surprised. A theoretical, unseen thing was suddenly here, waving her limbs around, autonomous, existent. She took one deep breath and bawled her head off.

"It's a baby," I said, stupidly. Mum cried, and cut the cord. Then the nurses took her away to check her over, and the doctor started fixing me up.

"Is she all right?" I asked mum, straining to see over my shoulder. "Fingers and toes?"

"She's beautiful," said mum. "Everything's perfect."

The baby came back for a cuddle. She stared at me with big grey eyes. I said hello, and stared back. That was nine days ago and I'm already starting to forget.

The memory is simply being overwritten, as though there's capacity only for what's important right now. The next day pain was replaced by paranoia, because no-one told me she was going to poo molten black lava within a few hours and she didn't have a nappy on.

Due to the pressure to breastfeed, no-one told me how to use a bottle so a midwife had to show me the mechanics. The day after that it was getting her to burp before sleeping. I had no idea what a baby's burp sounds like, and trying to figure it out after 43 hours of no kip at all is a bit much. Then it was coming home from the hospital, introducing her to the dog, a thousand other things which replaced everything that happened on that long night.

Obviously, I never got the notebook out of my bag.But I can tell you in four words how childbirth feels. It was like pooing out a train.

Not a dinky miniature steam version. Not a Flying Scotsman, not an Intercity, not a long, winding, grinding thing filled with annoyed passengers.

It was a double-decker bullet train going at 200mph right through my pelvis for 24 hours without stopping for level crossings. And it is forgettable because other stuff is more important.

Like, hiccups. And poo analysis. Or why night burps are different to day burps, and if she's drinking like Oliver Reed now what this means for the world's gin supplies when she's older.

Over time the memory will go altogether, until one day she asks me and I'll say: "I can't remember. But I DID write it down for you, and yes a gin and tonic would be a suitable apology."

It was the most appallingly painful thing I've ever experienced. I should be mentally traumatised, but I'm not - perhaps because it's being erased. What matters now is that my baby and I are alive and healthy, and without that doctor and her team we wouldn't be. The important thing is that she's here and has her whole life ahead of her.

The world has tilted on its axis, but I can't tell you how it happened.

Iggle Piggle's dead and Mr Tumble's a murderer - read this and you'll never see CBeebies the same way again

September 29, 2017

In a city near you is a park with a pond with an island in the middle. On it lives a small girl called Teal. Her only possessions are an umbrella and a blanket and she sleeps in a tree. She is friends with a turnip.

In any normal world this would herald a call to the police and the immediate descent of a dozen safeguarding specialists. Especially when you consider there's an adult male in a corduroy cat suit sleeping in a BED in a HOUSE at the bottom of the tree and her parents are probably frantic with worry. But not on CBeebies. Oh no. In this strange, drug-inspired reality the twisted individual in a cat suit is just giving the little girl a welcome chance to float around on bubbles made by an elephant seal who, inexplicably considering our weather, lives in the lake.

The Adventures of Abney and Teal could be renamed The Corduroy Catnapper and it would make more sense. But this is CBeebies, where television programmes aimed at the under-6s seem intent on teaching them to run away with odd men, fear adolescence and do terrible things to music.

Elsewhere on children's TV resides Peppa Pig, leader of a porcine cult not unlike how the world would be if Napoleon, the tyrannical oinker from George Orwell's Animal Farm, had succeeded in building his totalitarian pig-state. Pigs wear clothes and ride bikes. Pigs of one status are not friends with pigs of a different status. Some animals are more equal than others and granted the right to language, emotions and windows in their homes, but tortoises, parrots and ducks are at the bottom of the caste system and able only to quack, squawk or mope.

Not only does the sight of Peppa render children mute and still, but they are encouraged to dress in cult-badged clothes, play with cult-badged toys, and force their parents to hand over all their income in return for peace of mind. They are conned into doing so by occasional in-jokes that go over children's heads and which the adults believe are "just for them", like a wolf asking casually what building materials an animal has chosen for their new house.

This is a ploy. You are in a cult. It should be called Peppantology. Thank heavens Tom Cruise hasn't seen it yet, that's all I can say.

Then we have Bing, an intensely-annoying rabbit in dungarees who is four times the size of Flop, a walking beanbag who appears to have taken him hostage and spirited him to a town filled with exotic animals kidnapped from all over the world. Flop is voiced with sinister calm by Thomas Cromwell himself, Mark Rylance, a man who is no stranger to Shakespearean malice and always sounds One More Incident With The Toothpaste away from a stabbing.

Bing is rarely allowed outside. When he does, he is under the strict control of Flop or watched carefully by other beanbags. He is forced to repeat whatever he's learned that day at the end of every episode, and seems not to have noticed that there are no grown-ups. This is presumably because all the animals are ritually slaughtered by the beanbags when they reach adolescence, and you can just tell this is the blood-spattered Act III that Flop is building up to.

I could go on, and I will. The fact the Teletubbies have eaten living children and will show you them in their stomachs. The fact they have their own time-space feedback loop which means they have to relive the entire episode the moment the episode has ended. The fact Lucy stays up all night at a zoo which inexplicably is open all night long and will be wrecked for school the next day, the fact Peter Rabbit is a career criminal whose recidivist woodland gang must be making Beatrix Potter do 78rpm in her grave, the fact Dipdap is being terrorised by a pencil with a mind of its own, the fact the Timmy Time theme tune is the most pernicious ear worm known to man and the eponymous young sheep of the title is blissfully unaware of the inevitability of the slaughterhouse.

I only watch it in hope of catching the longed-for episode where his cat, owl and dog friends reveal the harsh realities of farming life to Timmy, in much the same way as older children can always be relied upon to tell younger ones there is no Father Christmas. Then there's Charlie and Lola. Two children in need of a social worker if ever there were.

Presiding over this horrorshow like an evil clown is, well, an evil clown. Mr Tumble has made a multi-million pound fortune with his ever-growing franchise of awfulness, centred on a lightly-handicapped man in pyjamas with a spotty bag and obsession with sign language. I don't know if I'll ever need the hand movement for "gerbil", but it's stuck in my mind for ever.

He has more programmes on the BBC than Chris Evans and Jeremy Vine put together. There's Something Special where his alter ego Justin Fletcher gallivants around the countryside with two child companions doing things like narrowboat journeys or a trip to the beach, like a dull Doctor Who. There's Gigglebiz where he mostly dresses in women's clothing to not be funny. There's voice parts in half a dozen other programmes and, top of the grim heap, is Justin's House - a house in the Match of the Day studio where he lives with a gay robot and a leftover from The Muppets.

The slapstick and storylines are bad enough, but he saves the worst for last with an audience-participation singalong. On the stage whatever jobbing, desperate, bit-part actors have sunk this low help him through a few verses in a particular musical genre, with the watching children singing their own part. The last two I have been subjected to were Bryan Adams-style rock complete with air guitar, and rapping. The only reason my eyeballs are still in place was because there was no sewage-covered spoon within reach of the sofa.

The problem is this man is like crack cocaine for toddlers. Mr Tumble's Big Book of Counting is flung at me twice a day for a read, despite the fact its pages have been ripped to shreds. His Hide and Seek literary effort is so well-known that my cub can find everything before I've read the bit about looking for them, and then wants to do it AGAIN. And the Mr Tumble doll, with light-up bow tie and a chuckle like someone really proud of doing a poo, is regularly hidden at the bottom of the toy box in the hope that the household addict won't sniff it out.

Even that's not why I loathe him. I hate him most because every female character he portrays is fat, a liar, a thief, or a lipsticked sociopath. His men are bumbling idiots, but in his world women seem plain evil.

In the addiction's early days I dreamed he'd got into my house and was hiding in the shadows behind the door, wearing gloves with knives on each finger and waiting to murder us at his own, chuckling pleasure. And if you picture Pennywise, the clown from Stephen King's IT, taking children on narrowboats, murdering music itself or dressing up as a greedy aunt in cow horns it all seems to FIT, doesn't it?

The world has changed since I watched reruns of Captain Scarlet and the Dukes of Hazzard. And all right, Count Duckula was odd, Thundercats the result of post-nuclear feline evolution and Penfold was never really explained. But children's TV was mostly rooted in reality - Scooby Doo might have been a chatty Great Dane, but camper vans existed and so did goody two-shoes like Fred and Daphne. The weirdest things got was a squeaky gopher bothering to acknowledge the existence of Philip Schofield, but perhaps Holly Willoughby performs the same task now.

But we never had something as hallucinogenic and worrying as In The Night Garden, with Iggle Piggle plainly representing the consciousness of a child in a morphine-induced dream state on the operating table as his life slips away, taking his blanket through a garden of Hoo Hahs on a Ninky Nonk before sailing over the horizon in a boat which, if it's not on the River Styx on its way to the underworld, certainly ain't coming back.

Watching children's TV - or just listening with one ear while I'm doing something else, in the same way a parent is always listening for a scream or a thump or a suspicious silence - makes me actively yearn for Bing to be skinned, or at the very least given a good slap. I worry Teal's parents left her there, want Peekaboo to shout his own name at the Twirlywoos JUST ONCE, and can't hear the Peppa Pig theme without thinking of sausages.

The psychotic world of CBeebies is undeniably teaching our children to never grow up. If you don't become a dead-eyed CBeebies presenter who's one alphabet song away from a rampage, you'll be like your own crazed-looking parent who keeps insisting we have to watch Hey Duggee again because it's the only offering of that benighted TV channel that can keep a grown-up sane.

All right, it's a dancing dog in a Scout uniform leading a group of Beavers called Squirrels who are really a hippo, a rhino, a mouse, an alligator and an octopus, but it makes more sense than everything else.

Duggee hug make it all better.

This is why having your own firework display is the most idiotic thing you can do

November 2, 2017

Are you an idiot? I'm sure you are not. Well, actually I just hope you're not.

I can't know for certain and, this being the internet and a country where a third of us are happy to have a wonky shopping trolley careering around the corridors of power, there seems to be an abundance of idiocy at present. Anyway. YOU'RE probably not an idiot, even if HE is. Or that's what you tell yourself, while idly buying some explosive chemicals you're not qualified to deal with and then igniting them close to your own face.

And why not? After all, the children love it, right up to the point they eat something which makes a green flash and is also used in rat poison, shove a lit sparkler up their brother's nose, or get scalped by a rocket that daddy set light to just a few feet away. But that all happens to other idiots, of course. It doesn't happen if you read the instructions and are sensible, and never mind that gusts of wind can't read and children are never sensible, especially when it's cold and they've just eaten a partly-pig by-product with nuclear sauce and their little brother's being annoying. So don't you worry about the fact that the people most likely to be injured by fireworks are children.

CHILDREN LOVE GOING TO A&E! IF IT'S OPEN!

And if the doctor in charge isn't too exhausted from 90 hours of repairing screaming, burned children on trolleys in corridors already this week, and isn't already burned out by a pandemic and a decade of intentional government destruction

You've done it before. No-one was hurt. Who cares? Well, the veteran down the road with post-traumatic stress disorder from conflicts on three continents who has to relive it all with every pop and bang. He might care. Around one in 25 service personnel are diagnosed with PTSD, and others are never diagnosed and instead try to numb the problem with drugs, alcohol, domestic abuse or criminality. So there are a lot of people around them who might care, too.

That guy in your street who seems a bit weird might be absolutely fine with your fireworks, but then again it could push him over an unnoticed mental precipice into a crisis in which he hurts himself or someone else. But don't let that stop you making him think he's back in a war zone. The kids'll love it!

Then there's the elderly couple, one of whom has dementia. And the family with the autistic little boy. And the person on shifts who just wants an early night because they've got to start work at 3am in a casualty department filled with burned children. And no, they can't just expect it on November 5. Because it's any night, any time, for a fortnight.

And then there's the animals. Well, they're only animals. Balls to them! So what if pensioners, the odd kid, the veteran, the hard worker and that yappy dog at the end of the street don't like it? THE KIDS LOVE IT.

According to the RSPCA, 44% of UK homes have a total of 5 domestic pets. That's 12 million dogs, 12 million cats, and another 27 million budgies, rabbits, goldfish, gerbils, snakes, tarantulas, lizards, and anything else that might qualify. At the same time, there are 11.7 million children. If you're being logical about it, what the pets want outweighs the little irks with sparklers by some margin.

Then there's the wildlife. The sparrows, pigeons, tits, choughs, starlings, robins, swans, ducks. The foxes, hedgehogs (not many of them left, either, check your bonfires before you light them), rabbits, field mice, and any badgers that have so far escaped their state-sponsored slaughter. Not one of those creatures knows about Guido Fawkes, the anti-Catholic dogma of the 17th century or Chinese inventions involving saltpetre. Whether in the field, under a hedge, inside a house with the curtains drawn, quaking behind the sofa or with a blanket put over their cage, these animals are all shitting themselves because you decided the children would ADORE it if you set light to some chemicals within easy ignition distance of the home you haven't paid for yet.

According to Churchill Home Insurance, 2 million British homes have been damaged by fireworks, with an average price tag of £307 each - with damage including broken windows, smashed roof tiles, and fences catching fire. And that's WITHOUT the fact that your home insurance almost certainly won't cover the millions you might be sued for if you burn a hole in your neighbour, a guest, or the property next door.

Then there's the environmentally-unfriendly chemicals you are cheerily igniting in close proximity to the people you love most in the whole world. Barium is used to make the green colours. It's used in rat poison, welding rods and fluorescent lights.

Get too much in your system and it can lead to hypertension, muscle weakness, respiratory failure and seizures.

Many fireworks contain arsenic, which can cause nausea, vomiting, profound diarrhoea, haemorrhagic gastroenteritis, heart problems and delirium. Get it in you and you will need your bowel "irrigating", which sounds like a lovely way to spend some family time. Firecrackers purchased in the EU can legally contain 4mg to 9mg of phosphorus, even though the lethal dose for humans is just 1mg. You can absorb it through your skin and it causes liver failure - that's if it's not the sort that explodes on contact with the air first. After Brexit, the UK government had a chance to ban the stuff, but instead chose to 'take back control' by not changing the rules at all.

Perchlorates, a firework accelerant which can cause thyroid problems in humans and is used in the manufacture of methamphetamine, has been found in high concentrations in lakes where fireworks are regularly set off. They're not very nice for the fish, either.

But, by all means, pop down your local store and buy some of this stuff, because YOU'RE not an idiot and you KNOW all this and the KIDS LOVE IT.
Don't, whatever you do, stop to think about the wisdom of explosives being sold in a garden centre or newsagent's, or how you're helping to make it more likely that an 18-year-old with a low boredom threshold will also be able to buy a Super King Size Whizz Banger for a very affordable £10. Don't think about how some troubled youngster might use the cheap, accessible and flammable materials you have made it easier for them to get their hands on.

Don't think about the cats and dogs with bangers tied to them. Don't think about the disabled woman who gets a firework shoved through the letterbox. Don't think about the irks who let off fireworks inside shops, at people they mock, or even at firemen who risk their lives to put out the fires they've started. And especially don't think about the firefighters.

Don't think about the fact the fire and rescue service in England had its budget slashed by almost 14% in the past 5 years, and has lost a fifth of its firefighters since 2010. There are thousands fewer people to come and sort your misfired rocket out, while the number of non-fire incidents they are asked to deal with has jumped by 28%. Don't think about the 40,000 people who fire crews saved in 2019, and how different that number would be if idiots stopped playing with explosives. Why should you stop to ask yourself who's going to come and put out your house if it's on fire, or your neighbour's house?

Don't give a moment's thought to who will give you first aid, who'll carry your granny through the flames, who'll douse the car and damp down the hedge and do it all night long for an untold number of idiots who keep saying "BUT THE KIDS LOVE IT!"

It's not like the fire brigade also have to cut people out of crashed cars, pump out floods, mop up chemical spills, halt industrial disasters, burrow through collapsed buildings, rescue animals, remove children's heads from park railings or extinguish fires which aren't the homeowner's fault.

Don't worry about any of that. Instead give your children a sparkler, which burns at a temperature 5 times hotter than cooking oil. Heck, give them three at once because that's almost a welding torch, and who wouldn't let their children play with one of those? Set off the biggest rocket you're allowed to buy, and keep your fingers crossed that the translation-from-the-Chinese instructions didn't have any mistakes in it and the 150mph missile goes where you want it to.

Fire an explosive shell at 20m so that every animal within a 10-mile radius loses their lunch, why don't you. Don't think about the fact most firework injuries happen in people's back gardens, most of them are inflicted on children, and they are most likely to damage the hands, eyes and face. Don't think about the vapours, the poisons, the strontium, the copper salts, the overworked doctors, the understaffed firefighters, or the knife's-edge mental state of your nearby war veterans, vulnerable humans or terrified family pets.

Don't bother to think about the fact people who aren't idiots go to professional, public displays because they're not stupid and it's only a tenner, it's over in an hour, you're less likely to get burned to death, and everyone can relax.

Don't think about the fact that doing it in the wrong place, or at the wrong time of day, could get you a £5,000 fine or 6 months' imprisonment. Nor that, despite massive petitions and public demands for a licensing regime, Boris Johnson's government shelved a report on it in 2019, and shows no sign of doing something that would stop your children having their faces burned off. Tell yourself that, because YOU think you're not stupid, the best thing you can do this weekend is to buy some explosive chemicals you're not qualified to deal with and ignite them in your back yard.

Because if you're very lucky, you'll just burn your own face off, and the rest of us will be relieved of one idiot.

THE KIDS'LL LOVE IT.

Tell your children the truth about fairytales - they're lessons in morality and adults usually miss the point

November 24, 2017

Once up on a time, a long time ago, it was entirely acceptable for a princess to be indecently assaulted.

Usually, she married him. The king, who was short and fat, and the queen, who was tall and beautiful, thought that was lovely, and so did all the fairies who were surprisingly common. Not common like peasants, of course - common as in unavoidable. In fairytales no young girl can go 5 minutes without some fairy or other meddling in her fate, usually with the ultimate aim of ending her burgeoning sense of her sexual self as soon as it flowers by chaining her for life to the first prince who comes past.

All such young girls are of course aristocratic, and although they have perhaps fallen on hard times the class system is always restored by fairies, fate, or f***ing a prince and hang on a minute...

North Shields mum Sarah Hall has come in for some stick after asking her son's school to take Sleeping Beauty off the curriculum, on the basis it ends with a prince sexually assaulting an unconscious woman.

The problem is that both Sarah and her don't-tell-the-children-life-is-awful detractors have missed the basic point of fairy stories - they're morality tales used for millennia to tell children what dangers to look out for. As such, reading Sleeping Beauty to youngsters is a GREAT idea, and should be done by every school in the land as part of mandatory age-appropriate consent classes.

Since becoming a mum almost two years ago, fairytales have come back onto my radar with vigour, and they're horrifying in all the wrong ways. Blood, guts and horror should always be included. The original compilation of oral fairy stories by the Brothers Grimm are bloodthirsty in the extreme, which is fine for children who are often worryingly keen on capital punishment for even minor offences. But when a prince on a horse finds a group of seven dwarves in a forest, wailing around a glass coffin containing what they insist is the corpse of their unpaid housekeeper, the morally-sound thing to do is to ask if they've checked her pulse and possibly begin resuscitation.

It is NOT a good idea to break open the container and frot the carcass.

That's before we get around to the unpaid domestic servitude, or why they are now 7 People Of A Different Size Who Shouldn't Really Be Mining In Those Conditions. There's no need to be what the frothing old gits of the world call politically-correct - but who these days wants their daughter to grow up to be a housewife? Who wants their son to snog dead people?

That's before we get to the story of Rapunzel, a vain Kardashian-type wench who spent so much time grooming her hair she didn't notice she was being groomed by a lad who claimed to be a prince and impregnated her, much to the annoyance of the evil witch who had locked her in a tower to ensure this type of thing couldn't happen. There's so many questions any enquiring child should ask of that story. Why didn't Rapunzel get traction alopecia? Why, if her hair was strong enough for a prince to climb up, didn't she tie it to the bed leg and lower herself down, then cut it off and make her escape?

Why is the mother-figure who'd rather this dim child wasn't systematically abused an evil witch, rather than her guardian? And why, in the name of Pete, didn't the witch just zap the prince rather than go through all the tower rigmarole?

The true purpose of political correctness is to instill basic good manners in people by way of social shame, and there's no reason any sane parent shouldn't point out that Jack is a lazy beggar who should have listened to his mother, and that one should never rely on the appearance of beanstalks to solve your problems. You might also like to point out that while the giant is turning the castle upside down to kill the little sod it's no different to us hunting down a spider, and the giant might be nicer if Jack didn't nick his stuff. And as for Cinderella... if the shoe fit so well, how come it fell off? Hussy did it apurpose.

There are some fairytales that need very little tweaking. The story of the Twelve Dancing Princesses is a current favourite in my house, and as a massive Strictly fan my daughter thoroughly approves of young girls dancing to their own strange beat whether the adults like it or not. I tell her it's called Twelve Dancing Feminists, and try to skip over the bit where a magician commits several stalking offences to follow them to a party, squeals about it to their dad and then gets GIVEN the oldest princess as a reward.

Unfortunately the good work of the Brothers Grimm is entirely undone by the joint efforts of Walt Disney and an 18th century French bint called Gabrielle-Suzanne de Villeneuve, who wrote Beauty and the Beast in which a man is turned into an animal by his own arrogant rudeness (good) but must be saved by the love of a good woman (oh, for pity's sake).

1. I think the beast learned his lesson, don't you?
2. Telling women they can save men from their demons is a recipe for a lifetime of bad boyfriends. Belle should cut him loose until he's sorted himself out, and we all know it.

Hans Christian Andersen did a marvellous job with the first 90% of The Little Mermaid, about a very silly girl who pined after some boy she glimpsed once, ignored her entire family's advice, drank something she couldn't be certain about and endured the incredible pain of splitting her tail in two only to see him marry somebody else. Unrequited love really does suck. Hans cocked it up though when the mermaid turned into foam upon the waves and was cursed to 300 years of wafting about before she could earn an immortal soul. Plainly, she should have entered the 200m freestyle and taken on Michael Phelps.

In the same way I wouldn't read Red Riding Hood without telling my daughter she must never wander into the woods alone, I couldn't do it without telling her wolves lack the opposable thumbs necessary to don a nightdress and if you're in trouble it's best to find an axe yourself rather than wait for a woodcutter. And the criminal record of Goldilocks: breaking and entering, trespass, theft, and criminal damage followed by not the tiniest sign of remorse. Lock the petty, perfectionist little recidivist up, m'lud, and throw away the key.

But by and large we want our children to grow up not trying to find the perfect partner, who looks great on horseback or has a golden ball or who arse can feel a pea through 20 mattresses and is rude enough to complain about it.
We want them to be the sort of person who says "why would anyone use 20 mattresses?" and look underneath to see what they're up to.

We'll never get the future humans we need if we don't. Fingers crossed that Meghan Markle will be the sort of princess who takes names rather than taking any crap[41].

[41] Well, she was

Liz Truss is growing a custard pie - and it's all over her face

October 7, 2022

Everyone likes pie, the thinking goes. Let's offer them more pie. It's a theory that's worked for every politician since the first amphibians crawled out of the swamp and realised there was no pie, but they'd get to be in charge if they promised pie tomorrow.

Unlike the rest of life on Earth, Liz Truss has not bothered to update her thought processes to cope with global market forces, the inevitability of narrative, or the fact that the proles will eventually cotton on. Which is why the pie she keeps muttering about is on her face, and not in our bellies.

The good news for Liz is that the pie is, very definitely, growing. It is growing mortgage rates, inflation, food bills, rents, strikes, ambulance queues, despair, disgust, the national debt, a sense of crisis, NHS waiting lists, and excuses. If it carries on, this winter we'll also be growing blackouts, suicides, marriage breakdowns, hunger, malnutrition, deaths, domestic violence, crime, and a Labour poll lead in triple figures.

By spring, if her growth plan continues, we'll have grown drought, tax avoidance, more deaths in the Channel and more Tories telling anyone who'll listen this lot are stark staring bonkers and can't be trusted with a spoon, let alone foodstuffs. Liz says she will give everyone more of that, but won't share it fairly. Instead, the poorest people will lose more of their income on energy and food, while getting a minuscule tax cut that does nothing for them, and bankrupts the Treasury. The richest people will get more money to put in the bank, where no-one but bankers will ever see it.

But then Liz doesn't like telling people what to do. She doesn't like public information campaigns about how to save energy, or junk food policies, or green levies. She doesn't like being told what to do, herself, particularly if it's by the anti-growth, lunatic Left coalition consisting of the Bank of England, the World Bank, the International Monetary Fund, the Office of Budget Responsibility, and, er, podcasters.

Instead, she'll keep growing the pie made from gravel and hate which you've been forced to chow down on for the past 12 years, with very little to show for it unless you're in the business of selling shepherd huts to prats. And she'll make you eat more of it.

The good news for us is that the pie she's growing, once you gnaw through the vile crust of people who struggle with Key Stage 1 maths, is that it also contains an increasing number of reasons to vote for someone who has evolved the ability to stand upright for more than 10 seconds.

Keir Starmer could stand at the bar chugging beer for the next two years, and he'd still win a landslide. Ed Davey, a perambulating version of the painting in Nick Clegg's converted loft space, could answer every question from now until the vote with the word "marmalade" and still become the main Opposition. At this point, the f***ing cat could do the job better. Yes, they're evil to the bone, but at least they understand that if the servants don't eat, the cat becomes risotto.

The problem is that the pie she's growing for us is made of shit, while the pie she's growing for herself is made of custard.

Which is why top Tories are, right now, in discussion with senior Labour figures about how to get the numbers for a Parliamentary vote against the budget, why rebel backbenchers don't care if they lose the whip, and why people who voted happily for Brexit and Boris have suddenly noticed there's a liar in No10.

Truss has tanked her party, vindicated Labour, given millions of voters a fistful of reasons to chuck her out, and lost not only the next general election, but probably the next three. If a clown was asked to destroy the Conservative Party, he couldn't do a better job than the current Prime Minister.

Which is why we need her to keep growing that pie - so it makes a lovely big splat, when she gets a face full of it, ASAP.

Liz Truss is basically Brexit - expensive, bonkers, and doomed

October 20, 2022

Word has it that yesterday Downing Street witnessed a 90-minute "shouting match" between the Prime Minister and the Home Secretary.

Few, if any, of us could ever manage a full hour and a half of yelling, but it says a lot about the times we inhabit that it is entirely believable that Suella Braverman, who is stone-cold barking, went at it hammer and tongs with Liz Truss, who is known to City boys as 'Daggers' because they think she's two stops *past* barking.

Apparently the row was about immigration. Truss wants more of it, because it's necessary for economic growth and to appease the Office of Budget Responsibility. Braverman wants none of it, because people voted to take back control of our borders with Brexit. And therein lies the totality of the reason that we are where we are - an impossible idea meeting practical reality, with screaming attached.

Times columnist Matthew Parris called Truss "a planet-sized mass of over-confidence and ambition teetering on a pinhead of a political brain". Former Labour spin doctor and self-made mental health expert Alistair Campbell reckons she suffers from the Dunning-Kruger effect, in which the people who know least about something overestimate their ability to understand it.

But I'm going to pin the blame on Brexit, and here's why a vote held six years ago about something this woman campaigned against has delivered us a slow-motion political pile-up which has bounced off numerous walls and is about to come to a juddering, limb-strewn, bloody stop.

That vote was won by emotion triumphing over caution; the wish to punch David Cameron on the nose, coupled with a belligerence about how the country wasn't working in everyone's favour. The fact it came after six years of crippling austerity, and THAT contributed to the unhappiness, is something that is only now starting to come into focus, when we're horrified at being offered more.

Half the nation felt poor; they voted to change it. Get rid of the immigrants, they said, and you'll be rich. The opposite was true, but those who sold the vote will never admit it. They cannot. They still believe it *is* true, like fairies at the end of the garden and the magic porridge pot. That's why Braverman was hollering in No10, like a toddler told the bribe of cake involved no actual cake. That vote delivered Theresa May, a robotic incompetent with the political skills, and warm, open manner, of a brick. And she was the high point.

Because she noticed the Northern Ireland border the pixie-fiends in her party conspired to throw her out, and replaced her with Boris Johnson, an amoral, shambolic tramp who had about as much personal charm as a walking laundry heap. His grubby tenure left smears all over the nation's institutions, a serious dent in the finances, and Schrödinger's Northern Ireland border. It both did and did not exist, depending on who you were speaking to at the time.

With each convulsion, the Conservative Pasty sicked up its basest, most blinkered non-thinkers, and put them in charge. They were appointed to government not for skill, not for party unity, not to recognise this wing or that and pull everyone together, but on the basis of whether they believed in Brexit.

I believe in humans; but that doesn't make them all capable of untangling string theory. And this lot, dear Reader, couldn't untangle a duvet.

So here we are with Liz Truss, a woman who voted Remain because she believed David Cameron and now backs Brexit because she believes he was wrong and she is right even though she's been so wrong so often that 'Trussterf***' is about to enter the dictionary.

And while the world watches, bemused, as she crashes the car, the economy, and the government, puts her party through the mincer, and smashes her head repeatedly on the wreckage while wearing a broad smile and telling us she's not a quitter, few people have stood back and wondered how this lunatic served in public office for a decade.

She was appointed by three Prime Ministers, all trying to appease the wingnuts but ending up emboldening them. She survived a host of junior ministers who despaired of her, whole armies of civil servants who tried and failed to get detail in or out of her head, and somehow or another no-one trotted along to HR and had a word that Liz maybe needed to be kept away from the forks.

But this is what, and who, you voted for. Brexit brought bats**t into the mainstream, and now the stream is nowt but sewage. They didn't put that on the bus, did they?

By giving power to the pro-Brexit loonies, the ordinary voters who just wanted things to improve handed the genetic engineering of a unicorn to people that a doctor would resignedly tell you were beyond his help. What they have created is limping and lurching around the laboratory, and the only upside is that they've smashed the Mental

Institute of Economic Affairs and proven that Britain really doesn't want a unicorn any more.

That brief period of support for Brexit evaporated within months. The latest poll shows 59% of people feel poorer as a result, including a third of those who voted Leave. Nearly 60% want a new deal, and 70% want more ties with the EU. The experiment failed, largely because it was in the hands of not-geniuses.

And so it is - or was - with Liz. Winston Churchill said there were corkscrew thinkers, and straight-line thinkers. He was wrong - there are also full-stop thinkers, who think something and then just stop.

Truss' ideas don't grow, decrease, or flex according to circumstances. They just ARE. There are no beliefs, no maths, no strategies, and when the Tories had worked their way through all the believers in decreasing levels of ability, they ended up with someone who is always capable of less.

It doesn't matter who replaces her. They'll fall too, like Frankenstein's monster after he forgot to fit any knees. There is no advantage to us in continuing with something damaging and pointless, like Liz Truss, the Conservative government, or their idea of Brexit.

It's a case of unicorn, meet wall. Brexit failed, the Right failed, the idea has failed. And do you know, this is the best thing that could have possibly happened?

Had we not voted for Brexit, there'd have been more years of Cameron, Boris would have been a liberal, Lefty PM, and Starmer would be struggling instead of soaring. The Tory Right would be there forever more, agitating for more Brexit, another vote, and telling us immigrants were the problem.

This way, the pixies have all been cleared out of the woodshed. All right, the shed's on fire, but we can rebuild that. This time, without the wingnuts, please.

Give our nuclear heroes the medal, and the recognition, that they deserve

May 28, 2018

First they watched a nuclear bomb scorch the sky, and then they were told to forget about it.

But 60 years on those once-young men who were ordered to watch the test firing of Britain's deadliest weapon are victims of a different horror: official denial.

At war pension hearings, Supreme Court appeals and over petitions and pleas, successive British governments have told our nuclear test veterans that what they did was nothing special. They were not irradiated, they cannot prove it, they have no claim.

There is evidence aplenty of what happened to those men. A University of Dundee study found a third of the veterans died before 1999, most in their 50s and from the sort of cancers that, were they at an American bomb test, would have got them a war pension.

Their wives report 3 times the normal rate of miscarriages. Their children have 10 times the normal amount of birth defects - such as missing and extra teeth, spine and skull deformities, heart and eye problems. Another study found double the rate of blood cancers that the government had admitted; another found higher rates of leukaemia, Down's syndrome and infant mortality. And we know the Grapple Y blast alone, on April 28, 1958, was 100 times more powerful than the bombs which levelled Hiroshima and Nagasaki.

Imagine how it feels to be that veteran, and told that your family's suffering is still not proof.

The British government has always insisted on a scientific link between the radiation and the veterans' claimed health issues. That sounds reasonable, until you realise that the science which could establish the truth simply hasn't been invented yet - and by the time that it is, the veterans will all be long gone. Of the 22,000 who were sent to Maralinga in Australia, Malden Island and Christmas Island in the south Pacific, and to US tests in Nevada, just 1,500 are still alive. A small and shrinking cohort who are still fighting a long-forgotten war.

But they have 155,000 descendants. You might even be one without knowing it, if there are estrangements or remarriages within your family. And scientists do agree on something - that radiation causes genetic mutation, that these mutations can last for 20 generations or 500 years, and that there is no way of knowing who will be affected.

Radiation causes random changes in the DNA. It may be pancreatic cancer, a thyroid dysfunction, or your sperm is rendered useless. It could be your children have blue eyes rather than green. A 2007 study on New Zealand veterans at British bomb tests found they had the same rate of genetic damage as survivors of the Chernobyl blast. The UK government would have you believe this is coincidence.

We need only common sense to realise that what links these men and their families to those of Chernobyl is the release of deadly, damaging material. Perhaps they were not all irradiated - perhaps they were harmed by the DDT sprayed over the island most days, or the toxic heavy metals that rain out of nuclear explosions like beryllium, or something else that was unique to the nuclear tests we conducted on two Pacific islands and two separate continents.

The British government claims the bombs were safe. If that was so, why did we build a massive military base in the middle of the South Pacific in order to explode them? If that was so, why didn't we save a lot of time and expense and test those bombs in Southampton? And if that was so, of what use could non-harmful, totally safe bombs possibly be to our military?

The answer, of course, is that it wasn't safe. We wouldn't do it today. And if we ever were to fire another nuclear weapon, you can be damned sure that we wouldn't do it with 22,000 of our own servicemen stood underneath it dressed in nothing but cotton shorts. They did not know the risks. Many were on National Service with no choice about being there. The risks they took are now perfectly clear.

On Christmas Island a few weeks ago, four of the veterans returned to dedicate a new memorial built by the impoverished islanders. They were feted by local politicians, given all respect, and invited to parade the standard of the British Nuclear Test Veterans' Association.

That is more honour than they have ever received in their own country. Here, they are told to apply for a war pension, and that to get one they'll need proof of their radiation dose, when such proof is either held by the government, never existed, or has long since been lost. So 90% of all their pension applications are rejected.

Here, £17million of taxpayer's money has been spent fighting court claims for compensation. Here, the government admits irradiating civilians but not service personnel. Here, if they want a medal they have to buy an unofficial, unrecognised one - and it's £45.

These men and their families are still living in the shadow of those bombs - in fear of their government, doubting their own experience, and needing a simple confirmation of official gratitude. Of course compensation, genetic counselling and a full apology is what they deserve - but the chances are they'll never get it. Most veterans are in their 80s and becoming resigned to the fact this is a battle their children will have to fight.

But a medal is easy. It's cheap and it's quick. The Queen signed off on one for the New Zealand survivors of our tests in 2002. If she did the same for the Brits, it would do a lot to lift the burden that they have carried for six decades. The men who have died, the widows who have grieved, the children who have struggled, and the many of whom little is left in this world but a treasured picture in a frame, deserve to be noticed rather than ignored.

They have helped us, and now it is our turn to help them. Please sign the petition, share this article, and back the Mirror's campaign to get our heroes the medal, and the recognition, they deserve.

This is how you find the proof: the determined widow waging a nuclear war with the Ministry of Defence

June 1, 2018

Shirley Denson is one of the few people who has fought the Ministry of Defence and won. And if I was the Secretary of State for Defence, I would be very worried about what this 83-year-old great-great-grandmother is capable of.

After more than 20 years of struggle she got a widow's war pension after finding proof that her late husband Eric had been irradiated while flying sampling missions during Britain's nuclear tests. Eric had piloted a converted Canberra bomber "sniff" plane through the mushroom cloud of our biggest hydrogen bomb when it was detonated over Christmas Island in the South Pacific. But when he got home he started to have crippling headaches.

Shirley told me: "One day he was holding his head with tears running down his face. He was in agony. We took him to psychiatrists but they had no idea what was wrong."

Twice Shirley found and saved her husband as he tried to commit suicide. The third time, in 1976, he succeeded, slashing his wrists in a wood near their home. Shirley was told by the MoD all of his medical records during his time at Christmas Island have disappeared. But then she discovered a radiation meter in his cockpit registered a dose of 13 Roentgen - the equivalent of 12,000 dental X-rays. Despite a series of legal hearings in which the MoD claimed Eric must have been mentally unstable because he used to wet the bed as a child, it was enough to win a war pension.

But Shirley didn't stop. After the Freedom of Information Act was passed she applied for further details of Eric's service. In December 2007 they sent her a single sheet of paper which confirmed his dose of 13R, among the records of 13 other aircrew whose names and doses were blanked out. And three months after that, they sent extra documents as "additional information". It contained a bombshell.

There, in black and white, it said: "Thus the initial experiment was carried out on personnel flying the secondary sampler."

Eric's plane, codenamed Sniff Two, was the second to enter the cloud. Eric had been subjected to an experiment.At the time veterans were trying to sue the MoD for negligence. Shirley gave their lawyers the documents, but as they had more than a million papers to read it seems to have been lost. A little while ago she came across a copy and sent it on to me, because I've been reporting on the veterans' story for the past 16 years.

Like her, I've seen a lot of these old documents. This one was about testing the film radiation badges thousands of the veterans were given during the tests, and comparing their readings to the "Charlie meter" which measured radiation in the cockpit. I read through it, and then I fell off my chair.

"Experiment"! Blimey! Three paragraphs later: "Care was taken to ensure that as little shielding effect as possible was given by the ejector seat and that no equipment of any description shielded the badges." I flicked back. For the test a badge was put behind each crew member's head, on his two arm rests, and on his seat pan. So when they maximised radiation for the badges, they were maximising exposure of the men.

His dose according to the badge in the centre of his chest was 13R, as we already knew. The dose to his head was the biggest of all - almost 19R. Could it be linked to those headaches? And the specific dose to his testicles was 8.8R. You would need to work in a modern nuclear power station for about 460 years to get the same dose.

Eric has four generations of descendants. More than a third of them have an abnormality - including skull deformities, developmental problems, and extra and missing sets of teeth. Eric knew he was flying through a mushroom cloud. He was likely aware of people testing these badges. But he wore no extra protection, and his widow is sure he was never told about a risk to his DNA.

Shirley said: "He never breathed a word about his missions to me, but if anyone had warned him about genetic damage he would never have let us have those children."

In February the chairman of the British Nuclear Test Veterans' Association, Alan Owen, told me four vets were returning to Christmas Island for the 60th anniversary of Grapple Y in April, and launching a medal campaign.

Mirror editor Alison Philips agreed to back it, and when a friend introduced me to Labour deputy leader Tom Watson I asked him to do the same. As a former defence minister he knew of the issue, and had even tried to fix it by finding the scientific missing link the MoD had always demanded. It requires scientific method that, geneticists say, has yet to be discovered.

But Tom was only in the job six months. Now, as deputy, he has some responsibility to talk about medal-giving, so said he'd throw his weight behind it. Veteran John Ward, 81, agreed to meet Tom in Parliament and talk to him about his experiences and his belief that they are to blame for his daughter Denise's extensive medical problems. And then, with the greatest of pleasure, I rang the MoD.

I've rung them for comments a lot over the years. I usually have to explain to the press officer what nuclear veterans are before I explain the story. "We've got a document from 1958 which says personnel were used in a radiation experiment," I said. "The only care taken was to ensure they weren't shielded, and the scientists knew about the possibility of genetic damage. We're running it tomorrow."

I emailed them the document. That was 9am on Tuesday morning. Over the course of the day the press office claimed the papers were just safety regulations, that it was an experiment on badges not men, and that policy documents say all kinds of stuff so it wasn't to be believed. I pointed out, repeatedly, a pilot's radiation exposure was maximised despite official awareness he might have genetic damage, and this was no blue-sky policy idea but a scientific endeavour that actually happened.

An official comment landed in my inbox at 6pm. It said veterans were welcome to apply for compensation and added: "At the time the military monitored the health of our service personnel and it is no surprise that selected quotes from historical documents refer to this."

1. The MoD has spent more than 30 years fighting every compensation and war pension claim brought by the veterans, at a cost to the public purse of more than £17million

2. Monitoring their health? Really?

The Mirror decided to hold the story until the next day, in the hope of a comment that actually addressed the story. At 9am, I rang the MoD again. I pointed out the word "monitor" did not appear in the document once, while the word "experiment" featured prominently.

Off we went again. The press officer claimed this was evidence of keeping the men safe, and I pointed out Eric had zero protection while flying through a cloud produced by a bomb 100 times more powerful than that which levelled Hiroshima. The press officer went home, another started the evening shift, and a comment finally appeared at 8.30pm.

It said: "It is not true to say that these men were subject to an experiment to look at the effects of radiation."

I didn't say it was. I said Eric was USED in an experiment involving radiation - like he was a Bunsen burner, rather than a man. I note you don't deny it.

"The British nuclear testing programme contributed towards keeping our country secure during the Cold War and regular health checks were conducted throughout."

Where are the rest of Eric's records, then? You told Shirley you don't have any.

"The National Radiological Protection Board has carried out three studies of nuclear test veterans and found no valid evidence to link participation in this programme to ill health."

There's plenty of circumstantial evidence: studies have found 1 in 3 veterans had bone cancer or leukaemia, 3 times the normal rate of miscarriage, 10 times the usual number of birth defects, and elevated rates of infant death. And in 2011 a survey by THE MOD ITSELF found 83% of veterans had up to 10 different health conditions. It's just the MoD considers this evidence invalid.

We published the story on our front page on Thursday. Tom Watson went on Sky News to demand the Defence Secretary Gavin Williamson apologise to Shirley, and reveal how many other nuclear veterans were involved in experiments. I did interviews on LBC, British Forces radio and Forces TV.

These are some of the messages I have had since from veterans and their families: "I had five sons after Christmas Island, they're all disabled"; "my nephew died aged 7 from leukaemia and my sister has an illness doctors cannot diagnose"; "my dad was at Grapple and I have extra teeth too". And these, about the Mirror's splash yesterday: "About to go and buy the Mirror, I wish my dad could have seen this." And: "The front page! I was crying as I took it out of the stand. Dad died in 1983, still a young man, never knew his grandchildren."

Best of all, though, was a phone call from Shirley.

"Thank you, darling. You've done Eric proud, and told his story so well," she said. "Now, what can I do to help you next?"

And that's the bit Gavin Williamson should worry about. What *will* we do next?

Eric's story is undeniable, which is why the MoD press office spent 35 hours coughing up a factual contortion, and he was one of dozens of aircrew. There were another 22,000 men on the ground facing different dangers. The hazards of radiation are well-known and efforts are underway at Brunel University to find that scientific DNA link the MoD has so long demanded.

The veterans might be dying, but their children and their birth defects keep coming. The fallout isn't washing away, but is instead growing more toxic the longer it is ignored. And as long as there are people like Shirley[42] - veterans, widows, children and grandchildren all determined to be an embuggerance for as long as it takes - the Defence Secretary had better keep his tin hat to hand.

[42] Shirley died, at home with her family, in 2021. She never knew the meeting she had with Williamson led to new research, which showed veterans were more likely to die, and from cancer, than other servicemen, or the result of the medal review. It was rejected several times, until 2022 when new Prime Minister Rishi Sunak finally bowed to pressure and asked the King to grant a commemorative medal for all those, at home and abroad, who served at Britain's nuclear tests. But without Shirley, and the many like her who fought so hard for so long, I doubt it would ever have happened

I marched with the only veterans at the Cenotaph who have nuked blood

November 14, 2022

They began to gather on Horse Guards Parade at 8am, as the autumn fog began to lift.

Veterans of the Falklands, the raid on St Nazaire, Afghanistan, Iraq, and the Korean wars met with friends and comrades, berets crisply placed, blazers brushed, medals clanking. There were thousands of people here, with their hair smartly cut, their shoes polished, all faces thoroughly scrubbed. There was just one group of men I could see who had no crosses, clasps, or campaign medals for the unique service they alone gave - the 12 nuclear veterans who formed up at the head of column D.

They wore instead the Missing Medal - a black and yellow pin badge, the size and shape of an empty medal ribbon. They have been refused this simple honour four times so far, on the grounds they had not proven there was enough 'risk and rigour' to the nuclear tests to justify giving them a piece of tin.

They gathered just 48 hours after the Mirror published the results of a six-month investigation which established that veterans' medical records showed they had been irradiated during the tests, and the evidence withheld from them. Parliament was told blood and urine samples were never taken, when in fact there was a Whitehall order to do so, and an archive within the Atomic Weapons Establishment held the details of the nuked blood. All veterans in our investigation who sought their records were denied access.

If I had just found out a newspaper I worked for 30 years ago had poisoned me, known about it, and not told me while I and my family suffered decades of illness and worry, I'd find it very difficult to turn up to the next staff party. And if I did, there's a strong chance I'd be spraying venom. These men were good-humoured, dignified, and deeply moved to have the chance to honour the 20,000 of their number who never made it as far as the head of column D.

The other thing which made this group stand out was that 66% were not veterans at all, but wives, daughters, sons, grandsons. In a few other columns, female veterans marched, or a wife stood in for a husband. Here, the men were outnumbered by the 21 who had never served at all.

But that's because in this group, the wives and children have experienced the effects of nuclear weapons testing for decades. They've had the miscarriages, comforted each other through loss, worried about every pregnancy scan and childhood illness. Sons have found themselves unable to father children, while daughters have decided not to risk it.

Of all the thousands of veterans who gathered yesterday, who could give you a litany of illness linked to their service, I doubt there would be one who'd tell you he had 87 different skin cancers removed, like Brian Unthank has. Many might share Terry Quinlan's memories of night terrors brought on by the pressures they faced, but none would have been asked to donate urine samples, as he was, to diagnose it. All the veterans who marched yesterday will have a greater risk of homelessness, broken marriages, and PTSD. They will all have had issues with Veterans UK accessing war pensions, and have reason to despise officers who were neither use nor ornament.

But as I walked beside these men and their families, I could not see another group of veterans who'd have any reason to think their medical records would be kept at the Atomic Weapons Establishment. Nor withheld there, consistently, for decades, as politician after politician stood at the Cenotaph year after year, to lay a poppy wreath and issue some words in a press release about the gratitude of a nation.

"I'm so proud to be here, but I'm so angry as well," said Laura Morris, who marched behind her grandad John. She and those with her were not marching for the politicians, or the cameras, or even for the public who lined Whitehall to watch. They marched for those who were not there, and to demand that they be remembered. As they laid their wreath at the Cenotaph, protected by serving troops and police snipers on the roofs of Whitehall, I remembered that just last week armed police had removed their flowers of remembrance from the steps of the MoD.

In return for their dignity yesterday, they got a brief mention by David Dimbleby on the TV commentary, but no interviews from the dozens of journalists covering the event. The Daily Telegraph carried a photo, but few words of explanation about why they wore a Missing Medal. In return for their blood, they got a higher death rate from cancer, and denials from the Ministry of Defence that it even held the blood samples until after the Mirror started showing people our evidence. In return for their service, we got a nuclear deterrent, and these men got nothing but grief.

Their blood was nuked, the evidence was gathered, and their medical records are still being withheld. While yesterday they remembered their mates, their husbands and fathers, the British Establishment would prefer if it could all be quietly forgotten. If the veterans gave up, if the Mirror stopped investigating, if the scientists turned round and said "hey, seems to us the MoD is probably right that radiation just bounces off

British skin with no ill effects at all", it would help nobody. It would not protect national security, support the case for mutually-assured destruction, or resolve the mental and physical scars of those involved.

The only thing that will fix that is an act of true remembrance - a Prime Minister who looks these men in the eye, apologises for what was done, and orders the archives opened to the men who were treated as guinea pigs.

The fog must lift, eventually.

11 good reasons why we shouldn't invite China for tea

October 22, 2015

Today Her Majesty the Queen welcomes Chinese President Xi Jinping on a state visit.

So what? She welcomes whoever she's told to and it's definitely China's turn, as they haven't officially visited for a decade. But there are a number of very good reasons why we shouldn't sit down to tea with the Chinese government – not without some serious improvements to their table manners.

1. They're at war with us

They're pretending they're not but they are. The Chinese Ministry of State Security (HI GUYS!) is undertaking espionage in half the nations of the world, including the UK. Our security agencies have warned that British businesses could be shut down at any moment by a cyberattack from Beijing. They're even thought to be spying on our capitalist Facebook profiles. Oh, and the muppets running the country want to let them run a couple of nuclear power stations too. What could possibly go wrong?

2. Ivory

Yesterday Prince William made a speech on Chinese television to point out rhino horn cannot cure cancer. The belief that it can has long been blamed for fuelling ivory poaching in Africa. Even more powerful is China's need for status symbols. As ivory becomes rarer, its price soars and its value as a commodity increases. The Chinese thirst for ivory involves funding a vast network of drug and gun running criminal gangs across Africa, including the terror networks of ISIS, Al Qaeda, Boko Haram and Al Shebaab. As a result, Middle East and Africa is aflame with well-funded forces of hate and ignorance, who when they're not chainsawing the tusks off living elephants are ruining the lives of millions of people.

3. Human rights

Tiananmen Square was the scene of pro-democracy protests by students 26 years ago. The Chinese government mobilized 300,000 troops armed with live rounds and sent in tanks to quash a peaceful request for reform. Up to 1,000 people, mostly students, died. One tank drove through the crowd leaving the square, killing 11. Afterwards 1,602 people were imprisoned. In 2012 it was reported five were unaccounted for, and two were still held. Last year Miao Deshun was named as the last known prisoner who took part in Tiananmen; he hasn't been heard from in a decade, and is said to be suffering from mental illness.

4. Steel

In the past month this country has lost one in six of its steel industry jobs. SSI shut its Redcar factory with the loss of 1,700 jobs, Tata Steel has cut 1,200 more and Midlands steel business Caparo has gone into administration threatening another 1,000 The reason? During its growth spurt the Chinese state set up and ran steel businesses, making it the biggest producer in the world. But demand fell and now China has a surplus. Subsidised by the government, it is flooding the world markets with record amounts of cheap steel. No-one else can compete without similar state backing, and our government refuses even to keep Redcar's coke ovens going or impose tariffs on Chinese imports. So after more than a century and mostly due to a short-term problem, Britain looks likely to lose an industry and all the skills that go with it. Thanks, China. Have a biscuit, why don't you?

5. The Falun Gong

This harmless bunch of hippies believe in the art of meditation, telling the truth and showing compassion. The Chinese government thinks they're dangerous in the extreme so has shut down their websites, locked them up without charge, carried out torture and put them to forced labour. Thousands are thought to have been killed after providing fresh organs for the medical industry.

6. Chinese scientists are something to behold

If you think ours are a bit keen to clone sheep, bear in mind the Chinese scientific establishment has no ethical regulation and the government we're being so friendly with is funding research into, among other things, new viruses, modifying human embryos, and isolating the "genetic traits" of people in prisons. Dr Mengele would be jealous.

7. China is missing 50 million women

Thanks to the one child policy the rich can buy their way out of, and a social stigma the government does nothing to change, parents don't want girl children. Boys earn money and look after their parents; girls are seen as a financial drain. So when pregnant with or after having had a girl baby, she's more likely to be killed or abandoned. She's less likely to get medical care, education, or justice if physically attacked. Comparing the rates at which the Chinese should have had girl babies, and the number of females currently alive, that nation is missing 11 per cent of its people or 50 million women and girls. That's the same amount as every other backward, vile misogynistic nation in the world put together.

8. Journalism

President Xi Jinping has tightened controls on journalists. Censorship has increased and foreign correspondents struggle to get visas. The BBC's China Editor Carrie Gracie was supervised by a propaganda officer even while looking at an empty cave the president once lived in. In 2013 it was reported China's journalists were being made to attend "re-education" workshops on Marxist theory and had to sit exams in Communist Party slogans. And it's not just newspapers. The president has said: "We have to make sure the front of the internet is firmly controlled by people who are loyal to Marxism, loyal to the party and loyal to the people." Journalists say they only get a story out if they can publish before the censor hears about it.

9. The Spratly Islands

You've probably never heard of them, but they're in the South China Sea and boast shipping lanes, fishing rights, and potential reserves of oil and gas. As a result they're claimed by half a dozen Asian nations, several with a military presence. Of late China has done its best to start World War Three here, firing on Vietnamese fishing vessels, bullying the US Navy and building new islands to move in as much military hardware as possible. It's in serious danger of upsetting a third of the globe, and all for the sake of some uninhabited reefs.

10. Corruption

President Xi Jinping has made a great fuss about being anti-corruption. Since he announced his latest crackdown, Chinese corruption actually got worse and the nation dropped 20 places in the international corruption index. The nepotism, bribery and embezzlement costs lives, harms health and hurts any British business that wants to invest, while lining the pockets of, guess who, Communist Party officials.

11. Africa

Maybe you've never been, and maybe you don't care. But Africa is a massively populated landmass which contains many of the world's greatest natural resources and most intractable problems. The Chinese are systematically strip-mining, logging, poaching, ripping and destroying any part of the place they can get their hands on. They're in Zimbabwe, the Congo, Uganda, Kenya, South Africa, Nigeria… oil, gold, copper, minerals for your iPhone, you name it and they've grabbed it. British colonialists did much the same, but we at least hung around and left a few schools and roads about the place. The Chinese are raping the land, leaving bare soil filled with toxic chemicals, and clearing out.

But hey, let's forget all that because George Osborne thinks we can make a buck out of them. He wants cheap steel for the HS2 rail link, government phones that can be heard in Beijing and two nuclear power stations run by Dr No.

Yes, China's a fledgling superpower but once upon a time so was the Third Reich, the Roman Empire and Genghis bloody Khan. It might mean you have to talk to them, but it doesn't mean you ought to forget yourself entirely and invite them over to have tea and a photo with the nation's granny.

Britain doesn't have much, but we do at least have principles.

Or we did, until today[43].

[43] To this list we can now add the concentration camps, forced sterilisation and systematised rape of Uighur Muslims, crushing the Honk Kong democracy protests, and failing to act like a superpower by keeping Russia in her box

All the things G7 leaders don't want you to know about their summit

June 11, 2021

Almost 2,000 years ago, in the midst of a financial crisis, the Roman emperor Caligula seized grain boats to make a temporary floating pontoon bridge two miles long in the Bay of Naples.

He dressed in gold armour, purple silk, and jewels, and rode across with his army. He lazed about for a day "as if resting from battle", then rode back in a chariot pulled by Ancient Rome's most successful racehorses. He gave a speech in praise of himself, and the bridge was dismantled.

Caligula, in the remaining years of his insane reign, demanded he be worshipped as a god, made his horse a priest, taxed weddings and prostitutes, murdered his senators on a whim, and became a sex-crazed, incestuous sadist who burned through the Roman equivalent of Jeff Bezos' bank account.

The people never did get their grain. Rome suffered a famine that was blamed on the bridge stunt, and thousands starved to death. And this weekend, as if to prove there is nothing new under the sun, seven of the most powerful people on Earth have turned up in Cornwall to see how much of our time and money they can waste in order to make themselves look good.

The summit has pledged to be carbon-neutral, plastic-free, recycling-friendly, and sustainably-fuelled. One of the main topics is the climate crisis, in which the ice caps are beginning to look like an aged mojito, prehistoric diseases are expected to emerge from the permafrost any day, and David Attenborough will soon be reduced to spluttering, incoherent, rage.

Each of those seven world leaders has flown to Newquay, even the one who didn't have to. He did at least get his picture taken on the steps of a plane with a £900,000 Union flag on the tail, and a Twitter storm. But you probably didn't know that, to bring us just one Joe Biden, the Americans require SEVEN jets - Air Force One, a decoy Air Force One, two transport planes for The Beast and its motorcade, another two 747s for the security detail - and another carrying two helicopters, currently flying sorties to no real purpose around Cornwall. Luckily for us, the US president managed to squeeze all the Secret Service agents, counter-assault team, electronic countermeasures, press officers, emergency ambulance, and nuclear codes into 30 vehicles, rather than his usual 50.

Uncle Joe's on the down-low, but Chiverton Roundabout is a no-go.

And despite the name this is not a summit of seven world leaders. Aside from the men, and one woman, who run Germany, Italy, Japan, the UK, USA, France, and Canada, there are two top bods from the EU, and the premiers of South Africa, South Korea, and Australia. India's Narendra Modhi is dialling in on Zoom, but only because his Delta variant makes him about as welcome as a cup of cold sick. They bring with them hundreds of others - security, press, spin doctors, diplomats, civil servants, negotiators, and an armful of spies. Carbis Bay is, effectively, a cocktail shaker for new types of coronavirus. You might think this many visitors means the tills go kerching in Kernow, but no.

When the last such summit was held in Northern Ireland, it cost almost £100million, but only 40% of that was spent locally. The Falmouth Packet reports that it cost the province £23million directly, with no noticeable benefit to local business. The 2005 summit at Gleneagles, meanwhile, cost Scotland £60million to host, and brought in £64.7million in trade, although local retailers reported a "significant drop" in sales beforehand. The UK government had to bung another £30million in the pot to help police the protests. Cornwall has been told the G7 might bring it £50million. The policing bill alone, so far, is thought to be £70million.

Policy briefings are coming out of the G7 every day, because many of the decisions and negotiations have taken place already. G7 health ministers met last week - more air travel, whoopee! - and their environment ministers announced fresh climate targets on May 21. Most of the leg work has been done, via email and conference call by junior ministers and civil servants. Announcements we have yet to hear were agreed by the leaders before they even left home. Others are decided but delayed, in the hope of wringing a concession from one of the others.

Yet this is not a jolly. They do work long hours, in little rooms, with the advisors shuttling between them to hammer out last-minute deals. GCHQ and its sub-contractors, who've been 'painting and decorating' Cornish hotels for the past six months, probably work round the clock, too. Amongst the bread and circuses was an agreement last week for the G7 to commit to a minimum level of 15% corporation tax, in order to stop avoidance by multinational companies who move their profits offshore. Seeing as the G7 countries already charge between 15% and 30%, it makes no difference to them and is about as ambitious a plan as Boris Johnson scratching his arse and wondering if he can fit another truckle of Cornish Yarg in before dinner.

Coupled with it was a plan to tax, and redistribute, profits of big tech to the countries in which they make sales, rather than just where they're headquartered. Last week Chancellor Rishi Sunak called it "a historic deal" and "a huge prize for the British taxpayer". This week *Private Eye,* which did the sums and is more inclined to tell the truth, reports that under this agreement both Google and Facebook would be paying less tax in the UK than under our Digital Services Tax, which we agreed to abolish in order to get this brilliant deal.

If we're terribly lucky, the G7 might agree to pay for a billion vaccines to help the rest of the world's 188 countries survive the pandemic. Which is great, but would be more useful if it was 6 billion which is how many people the rest of the world actually consists of.

The back-of-the-beermat maths, then, shows that we'll be spending millions to host a meeting about climate, covid, and taxation in which these seven people decided to burn oceans of aviation fuel, promised tax cuts to Mark Zuckerberg, allowed 70% of humanity to remain a reservoir for ever-evolving new variants of Covid-19, and produced climate targets that, we must assume, involved a bet on how many air miles they could rack up before the people who elected them all drowned, froze, or burned to a crisp.

Cornwall did not need exposure on the world stage as a tourist destination - Poldark did that for free, and it's already rammed with visitors and second home-owners. It likely won't make any money out of it, while the British taxpayer is paying 6,000 police to not do something else. What do we get in return? Images. Alpha male body language. Fashion, fanfares, and oh look! The Queen's been wheeled out.

For the past year, these egos have been working from home, like the rest of us. Diplomacy still happened, agreements and policies hammered out. They could have carried on like that. But then they would not have had the same attention. They would not get a photo with Kate. They would not be treated, by quite so many people, as being quite so special. There would be significantly less media noise about renewed special relationships, and rather more about the small print of their dodgy deals.

But with a summit, there's a shiny spectacle, and no time to think about how Joe Biden got overruled on corporation tax. No time to ask about Chinese concentration camps, or the gangster squatting in Russia, or why their only meaningful contribution to climate change was to burn half a rainforest just to get down the A30.

The G7 summit is a festival of hot air and lies we could surely have done without. Like Caligula's bridge, after the weekend the security fencing and electronic surveillance will be dismantled, and all that will remain is a fuzzy memory of someone splashing about in the sea to no useful purpose at all.

Ancient Rome was lucky - they had only one egotistical narcissist with an attention deficit. We've got seven.

Kremlin says Boris Johnson is a threat - we just don't know who's in charge of him

March 25, 2022

It's official. Boris Johnson is an absolute weapon.

Kremlin spokesman Dmitry Peskov - who, despite working for a president who's just outlawed journalism, is holding regular conference calls with any who haven't been jailed yet - labelled him the number one threat among foreign leaders. The state-run Novosti news agency quoted him saying: "As for Mr Johnson, we see him as the most active participant in the race to be anti-Russian... it will lead to a foreign policy dead end."

Brexiteers and Remainers alike always thought Boris was da bomb. But what matters most with every weapon is who's wielding it, and what it's pointed at.

In a tough-talking appearance in the House of Commons, Johnson said: "By annexing Crimea in 2014, igniting the flames of conflict in eastern Ukraine, and threatening Western democracies - including by interfering in their elections - Russia has challenged the fundamental basis of international order."

He listed the things the UK has done to punish Russia, saying: "We responded with strength and determination, expelling 4 Russian diplomats in 2007, suspending security co-operation between our respective agencies, and then by leading the EU's response to the annexation of Crimea and aggression in Ukraine, by tough sanctions co-ordinated with the US and other allies, targeting Russian state-owned banks and defence companies, restricting the energy industry that serves as the central pillar of the Russian economy, and constraining the export of oil exploration and production equipment."

The problem is that he said all that in 2018, as Foreign Secretary, following the attempted assassination of Sergei Skripal in Salisbury. And for all the tough talk, Vladimir Putin was nevertheless able to build up a £100billion stockpile of gold bullion, ramp up his military, and invade Ukraine.

In the intervening years, Johnson has given a peerage to the son of an ex-KGB colonel, ignored security service advice on just about everything up to and including his own phone, denied Russian interference in elections of exactly the sort he had previously said there was, and partied with Russian Tory donors on the same night that he knew the Z-heads were about to start bombarding Ukraine. He even managed to keep British citizens locked up in Iran, a feat beyond most Foreign Secretaries who aren't Russian.

Throw in the fact he holidayed, according to fellow travellers without family, luggage, or police protection, in the Italian villa of Evgeny Lebedev, now Baron Siberia, and it would seem that Putin has good reason to feel a little bit peeved. In a Western world that was reliably inactive, Johnson was the most publicly-vocal, yet secretly-slothful in terms of stopping Putin. But now the pet politician has turned, and bit the hand that fed him caviar at oligarch parties.

He's issued statements in Ukrainian, suggested hosting the Euros be given to Volodomyr Zelensky, and claimed Russia has all but lost the war already. In the past few days, UK sanctions have caught up with those of other countries, even to the point of freezing the assets of the London-based stepdaughter of Putin's crony Sergei Lavrov. Today it's reported Johnson will send anti-missile systems to Ukraine, and co-operate with the US in stopping Putin spending all that gold.

And all this from a man whose Brexit schemes, according to the former UK defence attache at the Moscow embassy, Carl Scott, "greatly emboldened those in Moscow". He told the FT that he now despaired "at the prospect of finding credible leadership at home in the UK among those who have compromised so long with his regime and the wealth it offered".

There is only one thing that could make Establishment diplomats and murderous tyrants both tear out their hair, and that's Boris Johnson: an agent of chaos whose principles, ethics, and next actions can neither be defined or predicted. As Zelensky has proved, a war is not politics. It is survival. And someone who can say the right things at the right time, and in the right way, can do more damage than a whole battalion of tanks.

Johnson has been unpredictable, chaotic, and inaccurate his entire life. From journalism to marriage by way of love-children and technology lessons, no-one knew what or who he would do next. He detonated his party, he blew up Brexit, he even exploded his own family. He's a man-grenade, an unstable element, and he doesn't fit in any job, category or suit. Putin may have considered Johnson a spineless dilettante with all the personal fibre of a wet jelly in a high wind, but he failed to note the one quality the man who is now Prime Minister has always reliably displayed: self-preservation.

And if the Kremlin has finally woken up to the fact that nobody is in charge of this weapon, then that is probably because he is doing something right for once, and has just taken off one of its limbs. Welcome to our world, Vlad - Britain is glad that you're finally feeling our pain.

Printed in Great Britain
by Amazon

19659510R00132